Moral Injury

Moral Injury

A Guidebook for Understanding and Engagement

Edited by Brad E. Kelle

LEXINGTON BOOKS
Lanham • Boulder • New York • London

Published by Lexington Books
An imprint of The Rowman & Littlefield Publishing Group, Inc.
4501 Forbes Boulevard, Suite 200, Lanham, Maryland 20706
www.rowman.com

6 Tinworth Street, London SE11 5AL

British Library Cataloguing in Publication Information Available

Library of Congress Cataloging-in-Publication Data Available

ISBN: 978-1-7936-0685-3 (cloth: alk. paper)
ISBN: 978-1-7936-0686-0 (electronic)

∞™ The paper used in this publication meets the minimum requirements of American National Standard for Information Sciences Permanence of Paper for Printed Library Materials, ANSI/NISO Z39.48-1992.

Contents

Part III: Engaging Moral Injury (Diverse Perspectives and Resources)

Acknowledgments

The present volume began from informal conversations leading up to and during the Annual Meeting of the American Academy of Religion and Society of Biblical Literature in November 2018. Those conversations centered on the ways that work on the emerging notion of moral injury was appearing at a rapid pace across many disciplines but had only recently begun to find a substantial place within the fields related to religion, theology, ecclesiology, and biblical studies. My conversation partners and I shared an interest in making our colleagues within our disciplines more aware of the important work being done on moral injury, as well as in helping our colleagues make creative and substantial contributions that could benefit those working on moral injury in other fields (e.g., clinical psychology, veterans care, military studies, and moral philosophy). This multiauthored collection is a step toward fulfilling those hopes. I am grateful to those friends and colleagues (some of whom have contributed to this volume) who were part of those initial conversations and have continued to be important voices in their own right on moral injury and its intersections with biblical, theological, and religious studies. These include Joseph McDonald, Rita Nakashima Brock, Shelly Rambo, Jenny Matheny, and Nancy Bowen, among others.

On a personal note, I appreciate my faculty colleagues and students in the School of Theology and Christian Ministry at Point Loma Nazarene University (PLNU), who encouraged me in the work on this volume, as well as on my own recently published monograph on moral injury (*The Bible and Moral Injury: Reading Scripture Alongside War's Unseen Wounds*). They readily engaged in beneficial conversations about my ideas, always making them better. I'm particularly thankful, as always, for the support of my dean, Mark Maddix, in both undertaking and completing this project and for valuing the pursuit of research and publication at a "teaching" university. Thanks also to the editorial team at Lexington Books, especially Michael Gibson, who accepted the proposal for this book and has seen it through to completion.

Of course my deepest gratitude goes to the contributors for their fine work and their patience during the process of bringing this large project to completion. I am especially grateful to them because of the truly interdisciplinary nature of the volume. Several contributors from various fields of study well outside of mine took a chance on someone they did not know from a field that is not their own. This is especially true for some of the clinical psychologists and military veterans who have contributed, thus making it possible for this volume to offer important insights from disparate contexts to an audience that normally seeks out primarily religious, theological, and biblical scholarship.

My gratitude and debt to the contributors is even more profound, however, because of the challenges that characterize the study of moral injury. Writing about war and the moral toll it can take on human lives is a weighty task, and each author who does so gains a renewed sense of the personal and moral ambiguity, disillusionment, and even anguish that can come from looking closely into the realities of war. Simply put, there is a cost to the study of this subject matter and there is no way to undertake it and remain unaffected by the moral uncertainty and emotional discomfort that war, violence, and moral injury create. I am deeply grateful that each of this volume's contributors have willingly taken on that task in the hopes that greater understanding and conversation may lead toward healing for those whose sense of self and the world has been wrecked by the realities of violence. Even so, I hurriedly acknowledge that the cost of studying and writing about war and moral injury pales in comparison with the cost of actually experiencing them—an experience known by many who live in my own community and throughout the world, as well as some of the contributors to this volume. Service members and veterans know directly and personally what many of the rest of us are just learning to take seriously—namely, the moral wounds inflicted by war and the moral struggles involved in trying to come home from it. So, I dedicate this volume to those who have known these realities, in the hope that it might be one more resource for the work toward a different vision of ourselves, our lives, and our world.

—Brad E. Kelle, Point Loma Nazarene University, San Diego, CA

Introduction

Brad E. Kelle

This volume offers an interdisciplinary exploration of moral injury. The eclectic collection explores the emerging notion of moral injury from a variety of perspectives and academic fields in the hopes of living up to the purpose expressed by its subtitle—namely, to provide a *Guidebook for Understanding and Engagement* of this important topic for those working in both religious and nonreligious contexts. Moral injury, loosely defined as a multidimensional, nonphysical wound that results from the violation (directly or indirectly, by oneself, others, or outside forces) of a person's core moral beliefs about themselves and the world, has found particular resonance within the study of war and the experiences of military service members and veterans, and has found its academic home primarily in fields such as clinical psychology, mental health, and ethics. Those exploring moral injury, however, have recently considered its significance for other contexts beyond those related to warfare. As the chapters in part 1 of this volume illustrate, the discussion of how to define moral injury remains ongoing. In all contexts, however, moral injury represents certain deleterious effects on moral conscience and ethical conceptions—a moral harm that can include the wrecking of a person's fundamental assumptions about "what's right" and how things should work in the world and a sense of having violated one's core moral identity and loss of any reliable, meaningful world in which to live.

The idea for this volume began from the recognition that many scholars who work within fields related to religious, theological, and biblical studies have little, if any, knowledge of the rapidly developing work on moral injury that has occurred within clinical psychology, veterans care, mental health, moral philosophy, ethics, and related areas, especially since 2009. This is the case in spite of the fact that interdisciplinary engagements with perspectives from trauma studies and other psychological approaches have been increasingly prominent within theological and biblical scholarship over the last two decades. Hence, the initial and primary goal of this volume is to bring an understanding of moral injury and the work underway on it within psychology and related fields to theologians, religious studies scholars, biblical interpreters, clergy, chaplains, and other spiritual care providers. The chapters within this volume will allow those in this target audience to hear the voices of psychologists, veterans, and military chaplains as they address key elements of moral injury. At the same time, the volume includes engagements of moral injury by theologians, biblical scholars, Christian spiritual care practitioners, and chaplains in the hopes of allowing its readers also to hear the voices of those who are already working on moral injury within those disciplines. By having these voices alongside those of psychologists, veterans, and others who work outside of religious contexts and from different assumptions and methodologies, the hope is to provide a multivoiced and multiperspectival resource for understanding moral injury and to model creative and cross-disciplinary ways of engaging moral injury's varied realities and manifestations.

The broad-ranging combination of voices makes this volume unique in today's catalogue of moral injury resources. For those new to the conversation, the multiple approaches herein offer an accurate snapshot of the nature of current work on moral injury as something that is very much in-process, unsettled, and multiperspectival. Since its beginnings, moral injury has been an intersectional and interdisciplinary term that has resisted being confined to a single discipline and has received fruitful attention within the social sciences, health care, psychology, philosophy, literature, religion, and more. There is clear benefit in my mind to reminding all who work on moral injury that this topic should be engaged from as many disciplines and perspectives as possible. In that vein, although the primary aim of the collection is to bring moral injury work from psychology and related nonreligious fields to the awareness of those working in religious contexts, I hope the volume will also be useful to those working on moral injury from nonreligious perspectives by showing ways that the study of the Bible, Christian theology, Christian ethics, and spiritual/pastoral care can make substantive contributions to all efforts to understand and engage moral injury, whatever the context of those efforts. Psychologists, mental health professionals, veterans, and moral philosophers will find in this collection concrete examples of engaging moral injury with new resources, texts, assumptions, methodologies, and insights that may further multiply the avenues by which the topic can be approached.

Toward these ends, the volume divides into three sections. In each section, however, rather than a singular viewpoint or the linear development of a single argument, the reader will find chapters that engage the topic of that section from a variety of viewpoints and methodologies. The goal in each section is to provide more than one way to address the topic under consideration and to nurture subsequent creative engagements inspired by those included here. The reader should approach each section of the volume (and indeed the volume as a whole) as something akin to a roundtable discussion offering a multivoiced dialogue that refuses to privilege one perspective over the others but emphasizes the dialogue among the various perspectives as the key to a more fully orbed understanding and engagement. The first section, "Understanding Moral Injury (Definitions, Questions, Debates)," includes three chapters that take up the unsettled and ongoing effort to define moral injury and its causes, contexts, symptoms, and responses. Not only do the chapters offer differently formulated and nuanced responses to the relevant questions, they do so from differing perspectives, with one chapter from a biblical scholar (McDonald), another from a team of psychologists led by Brett T. Litz (Coady, Carney, Frankfurt, and Litz), and a third from a theological ethicist and spiritual leader (Lettini).

The second section, "Depicting Moral Injury (Ancient and Modern Portrayals)," attempts to offer narrative, reflective, and interpretive portraits of what moral injury and its various realities look like in human life. Once again, however, the portraits draw from a variety of different contexts and perspectives and use different resources to describe the experiences. Here one finds two chapters by US veterans (Boudreau; Moon) that draw upon their own and others' military experiences in recent years to describe moral injury. The remaining two chapters use the ancient writings of the biblical literature to construct creative literary portraits of moral injury. Michael Yandell (a US veteran and theologian) rereads the New Testament story of the demon-possessed man in the Gerasenes in the Gospel of Mark as the story of one morally wounded through military experiences in the ancient Roman Empire. Likewise, Nancy Bowen (a Hebrew Bible/Old Testament scholar) reconsiders the infamous story of the city of Sodom in the book of Genesis within the context of war stories in which its characters are previously involved. This creative use of the Bible in a discussion typically dominated by clinical psychology and mental health may seem strange to some. But as Yandell explains in his chapter, the interpretation of ancient texts has always played a role in understandings of morality, and the biblical writings are as much about humanity as they are about God, exploring ancient ideas about the world and one's place in it that remain formative for contemporary life.

The third, final, and largest section, "Engaging Moral Injury (Diverse Perspectives and Resources)," constitutes the heart of the volume. Here the explorations move from elaborating the definitions and portrayals of moral injury and its experiences to providing a set of diverse, multidisciplinary engagements with moral injury, especially from approaches within religious, theological, ecclesiological, and biblical studies. The effort here is to demonstrate that these fields can make substantive and even creative contributions to the ongoing efforts to understand and address moral injury underway in nonreligious contexts. Appropriately and helpfully, the authors and their approaches are diverse, bringing to bear on moral injury a range of disciplines that include the following: psychotherapy and counseling (Currier and McCormick), spiritual formation and pastoral care (Ramsay; Larson), critical interpretation of Hebrew Bible/Old Testament and New Testament texts (Kelle; Cottrill; Carter), social analysis of American civil religion and cultural expressions of religion and war (Denton-Borhaug), Christian historical theology (Powers), and social ethics (Wiinikka-Lydon). These chapters highlight the manifold ways that religious, theological, and biblical studies can both benefit from other works on moral injury and potentially inform understandings of moral injury, personal and communal trauma, and related experiences as they are studied in diverse contexts.

Some concluding logistical notes are in order. Although I took great editorial care during the review process, the reader will note some inconsistencies—a few of which, at least, are present by design. I have not, for instance, regularized all translations (and their verse numbering differences), whether of biblical or non-biblical texts. Similarly, I have not always regularized the precise terminology and phraseology used within moral injury discourse (e.g., injury, harm, distress, treatment, healing, recovery). In these cases—and similar ones—I have deferred to the individual preferences of the contributors. On the whole, many of the inconsistencies in terminology and similar matters are often by design; at the least they are not naïve. I hope that whatever discomfort readers may experience upon encountering such discrepancies will pale in comparison to the insight afforded by the contributions contained herein. Similarly, in a large collected volume such as this one, with so many different contributors, some degree of overlap in content (or at least going over the same ground) is to be expected. In the case of this volume, such overlap is intentional and, I believe, reflects the current nature of moral injury work. To let such overlap stand is not only a matter of letting each contributor have her or his say; in an exploration of moral injury, it is also helpful, both pedagogically and interpretively. The more we examine the common ground of moral injury from multiple perspectives, the closer we move to a fuller understanding and articulation of the weighty realities represented by this term. I hope this volume will contribute to that effort.

Part I

Understanding Moral Injury (Definitions, Questions, Debates)

Chapter One

What Is Moral Injury?

Current Definitions, Perspectives, and Context

Joseph McDonald

On assignment in Fallujah in 2004, war correspondent Kevin Sites shrugged and ignored the pleas of a wounded Iraqi insurgent, leaving him among the bodies of his comrades on the floor of the mosque where they had made their final stand. Sites was not motivated by malice; he was distracted by his anger at the summary execution of another wounded Iraqi fighter that he had just witnessed. While the larger episode tugged at his conscience, it was not until several years had passed that Sites discovered that the man who had begged him for help, Taleb Salem Nidal, was himself murdered shortly after Sites left the mosque. Somehow, the journalist had failed to realize that Nidal was also in mortal danger. Instead of helping him to safety, Sites had abandoned the only other witness, and a disposable one, to an atrocity committed by the US military. When Sites later read that Nidal had been shot in the back—twenty-three times—the "shaky, stacked soapboxes" of his "belief system came tumbling down," and he sought refuge in alcohol, drugs, sex, and ceaseless activity. This self-destruction fed on and fueled Sites's growing guilt and self-hatred, which left him emotionally isolated and unable to communicate honestly about his feelings of complicity. At last, Sites contemplated killing himself in the service of what he calls "atonement" for his "crime": "simple math—a life for a life."[1]

Sites's harrowing description of his experiences in his book *The Things They Cannot Say* tracks very closely with what others have called moral injury. Moral injury is a name for the suffering that results from the violation of a human being's core moral principles. This violation may be the consequence of something a person does, or fails to do; it may stem from betrayals by what are regarded to be rightful authorities or structures, or from witnessing acts that transgress an individual's fundamental moral code. In struggling to reconcile what one thought was right with what one did, failed to do, experienced, or witnessed, a wound that is deeper than moral dissonance may grow, threatening the very possibility of continued belief in a coherent moral framework. Feelings of meaninglessness, guilt, shame, self-loathing, and despair may follow, and unchecked these can and do lead to social isolation, addiction, danger-seeking, self-harm, and suicide. Moral injuries are at once intensely personal and inherently social, and they affect not only individuals but also their families, communities, and larger social structures.

DEFINITIONS OF MORAL INJURY

The conversation about moral injury is fluid and ongoing, and involves clinicians and counselors who work with military veterans, veterans themselves, chaplains, psychologists, moral philosophers, journalists, theologians, pastors, and academics from a number of disciplines, among others. I myself am primarily a scholar of ancient texts who is interested in using the tools of the humanities to address real-world problems. Those concerned with moral injury do not always ask the same questions, and even when they do, they sometimes reach different answers. Discussions over its scope and reach, its utility and possible contexts, and whether "moral injury" is the best term for the concept all remain short of full resolution. These debates will not be settled here. Instead, I will outline the significant definitions of moral injury that have been offered so far and then consider some of the conditions and contexts that may lead to moral injury.

The Perpetration Model

The most influential definition of moral injury is that of Brett Litz and colleagues, who in a 2009 article focused closely on combat soldiers and veterans proposed that moral injury should be understood as "the lasting psychological, biological, spiritual, behavioral, and social impact of perpetrating, failing to prevent, or bearing witness to acts that transgress deeply held moral beliefs and expectations."[2]

The actions of the individual are central to this understanding of moral injury, sometimes referred to as "perpetration-based." While the definition is rooted in experiences involving killing and atrocities in wartime, the authors recognize that other contexts are also potentially morally injurious.[3] Even so, the idea that moral injury is the result of a person's own grave violation of his or her bedrock moral code, often by killing or the infliction of serious harm on others, has guided much of the subsequent conversation.

In this definition, the specific nature of the act or experience involved is less important than an individual's subjective evaluation of its meaning.

Persons may experience inner conflict or moral dissonance when they feel that something they have done, or failed to do, contradicts their moral code. This is evidence of moral health, as feeling guilt at violating one's principles is normal and points to a functioning conscience. But how one evaluates the experience strongly influences whether moral injury follows. If a soldier comes to regard his or her actions as evidence of a fundamental flaw in character, rather than something at least partly explained by the realities of a very particular and extreme situation, moral injury is much more likely.[4] This may manifest as deep and lasting anxiety, guilt, shame, and self-condemnation that can lead to a view of the self as "immoral, irredeemable, and un-reparable."[5] Unaddressed, this feeling of being "unworthy of forgiveness" can contribute to a withdrawal from loving relationships and a host of very serious problems including the following:

> *Self-harming behaviors*, such as poor self-care, alcohol and drug abuse, severe recklessness, and parasuicidal behavior, *self-handicapping behaviors*, such as retreating in the face of success or good feelings, and *demoralization*, which may entail confusion, bewilderment, futility, hopelessness, and self-loathing. Most damaging is the possibility of enduring changes in self and other beliefs that reflect regressive over-accommodation of moral violation, culpability, or expectations of injustice.[6]

As in the collapse of Kevin Sites's "shaky, stacked soapboxes" of moral meaning mentioned in the introduction above, this type of moral injury has the capacity to wreck a person's belief that life has a coherent moral structure. William Nash and Brett Litz highlight this in a subsequent study, where they argue the following:

> Central to the concept of moral injury is an event that is not only inconsistent with previous moral expectations, but which has the power to negate them. Moral injury is not merely a state of cognitive dissonance, but a state of loss of trust in previously deeply held beliefs about one's own or others' ability to keep our shared moral covenant.[7]

Michael Yandell, a US Army veteran, puts it this way: "The spiritual and emotional foundations of the world disappeared. . . . What I lost was a world that makes moral sense."[8]

Litz and colleagues maintain, however, that "forgiveness and repair is possible in all cases," at least for those who seek healing. This is hard work, demanding acknowledgment and sharing of what one has done, or failed to do, and performing good deeds that can contribute to positive moral evaluations of the self.[9] The path toward moral repair does not entail excusing or explaining away acts regarded as wrong. Well-meaning attempts to relieve guilt can stymie the process of recovery, denying agency to the injured and paradoxically underlining one of the negative outcomes of moral injury—the idea that we live in a world without a meaningful moral structure. Instead, what is needed is a way to integrate an admission of genuine wrongdoing into an understanding of the self as imperfect, but still acceptable and worthy of love. In order to facilitate this, Litz and colleagues propose a multistep therapeutic program, refined in later publications, that includes working with an unconditionally accepting therapist, dwelling with and retelling morally injurious experiences with a view toward integrating them into a positive view of the self, making amends, and reconnecting with loved ones and supportive human circles, including religious communities.[10]

The Betrayal Model

Although the perpetration model has dominated much of the recent moral injury conversation, the earliest conception of moral injury appeared in the work of psychiatrist Jonathan Shay. Developed at length in his books *Achilles in Vietnam* and *Odysseus in America*, Shay's notion of moral injury is succinctly expressed as the result of the "betrayal of 'what's right' in a high-stakes situation by someone who holds power."[11] In comparison to the perpetration model, the agent of injury is inverted here: instead of violating my own core moral values ("I did it"), my fundamental ideas of what is right and wrong are transgressed and shaken by the actions of someone with authority over me.[12] Broken trust is central to such betrayal-based moral injury. When a superior with what is regarded as legitimate power violates what was thought to be a reliable moral code, a subordinate's faith in a coherent moral universe may crumble.

Shay's creative, interdisciplinary method reads the Homeric epics of the *Iliad* and *Odyssey* alongside the stories of the Vietnam veterans that he encountered in his work at the VA's Boston Outpatient Clinic. His basic insight grows from the tale of Achilles in the *Iliad.* Agamemnon, Achilles's superior during the Greeks' siege of Troy, violates "what's right" by taking away Achilles's rightful prize of war, a captive woman named Briseis. I must firmly underline here that "what's right" is culturally formed and locally defined in a dialogue between an individual conscience and community norms. Briseis herself is a victim of outrageous trauma inflicted on her by Achilles and his men, "collateral damage" in a conflict of great brutality. But in the moral universe of the *Iliad,* Agamemnon's betrayal warps Achilles's moral foundations and damages his previously good character. Subsequently, where the old Achilles cared for his fellow soldiers, the morally wounded Achilles leaves them to die; and while once Achilles upheld humane rules of engagement, after the death of his friend Patroclus he shows no regard for any human being, even desecrating the corpse of his enemy, the Trojan

Hector. Achilles's own sense of "what's right" is ruined by his superior's violation of what had seemed to be a stable and shared moral code.[13]

Shay weaves the stories of the Vietnam veterans into his readings of the *Iliad* and the *Odyssey*, using the soldiers' voices to illustrate many parallel tragedies caused by the serious "leadership malpractice" of their commanders.[14] *Achilles in Vietnam* opens with the excruciating testimony of an infantryman who took part in a nighttime attack on boats suspected of smuggling weapons. But in the morning, he reports, "We found out we killed a lot of fishermen and kids." What compounds the soldier's torment is the cover-up engineered by his superiors: "'Don't worry about it. We'll take care of it' . . . you know in your heart it's wrong, but at the same time, here's your superiors telling you that it was okay." The whitewash was so thorough that medals were awarded up and down the chain of command, and this soldier received the Combat Infantry Badge, a coveted decoration. But a citation for the killing of unarmed civilians on faulty intelligence left him feeling "deeply dishonored."[15]

These kinds of betrayals of "what's right" destroy trust in shared perceptions and ideals and can permanently injure character, leaving only what is thought to be a "tainted, evil identity, one deserving punishment." Such "obliteration of meaning" can lead to guilt, shame, despair, substance abuse, danger-seeking, violence, incarceration, and suicide.[16] Yet Shay argues that moral injury stemming from betrayal can be addressed and, importantly, prevented. Working toward healing from moral injury requires "communalization of the trauma," a sharing of the truth of a wounded individual's story with another who can be trusted to relay it faithfully to others.[17] These injuries are "moral and social" and can only be treated by methods that are themselves moral and social.[18] The potential for morally injurious situations can be reduced, in a military context, by better training and unit cohesion. And in the armed forces and beyond, the ethical exercise of power can help prevent such moral wounds.[19]

Toward a Broad Definition of Moral Injury

Subsequent studies by Shay, Litz, and others have shown that the distinction between perpetration-based and betrayal-based definitions of moral injury is useful.[20] For example, the particular consequences of moral injury may vary between the two, with perpetration-based moral injury leading more often to guilt, shame, and feeling unforgivable, and betrayal-based moral injury leading more often to anger, mistrust, and fantasies of revenge.[21] But the contrast between these definitions can be overstated. It is clear that both definitions regard dramatic and lasting emotional reactions to the violation of core principles to be a normal, moral response, and both agree that unaddressed moral wounds can destroy faith in the possibility of a coherent moral order to the world. The grim potential outcomes of addiction and self-harm are common to both frameworks. Both also insist on giving agency to the injured, and working toward healing in community, with nonjudgmental listeners who do not deny or explain away injurious experiences. The question of "who did it" does matter, and in expanding the reach of Shay's conception of moral injury we should take care not to lose his focus on the responsibility of those in authority for the moral welfare of their subordinates. The political edge to Shay's work has the capacity to perturb the powerful, and may need regular whetting to keep it sharp.[22]

Even so, the main problem with drawing a sharp line between perpetration- and betrayal-based definitions of moral injury lies in the messy conditions that lead to and follow moral injuries. Kevin Sites blamed himself for the murder of Taleb Salem Nidal. Yet Sites never intended to get Nidal killed; indeed, he departed the scene impelled by a sense of outraged justice. And—the core of the matter—Sites did not pull the trigger and put twenty-three rounds into the back of a defenseless man. Sites's sense of complicity shook his moral foundations. But surely, too, the journalist's deepest notion of "what's right" was also violated by the criminal act of another, who betrayed a grave responsibility to behave ethically in wielding the power of life and death, and by the structures of the military and larger social and geopolitical forces that laid the ground for what happened in the mosque that day. The infantryman cited by Shay was enraged by and ashamed of his commanders' failure to acknowledge or enact the right, but the tangled roots of his feelings of dishonor grew ultimately from a war crime that he, however unwittingly, helped perpetrate. The literature on moral injury is filled with similar, if always uniquely awful, precipitating complexes of events that resist easy assignments of origin or blame.

Numerous treatments of moral injury, even if continuing to emphasize perpetration, blur the lines between the two main definitions. Nancy Sherman traces moral injury to "transgressive commissions and omissions perpetrated by oneself or others," while Larry Graham speaks of "the burden of harm and the diminishment of vitality that arises in individuals and communities when we (or others) violate our moral compasses."[23] In their book *Soul Repair*, Rita Nakashima Brock and Gabriella Lettini similarly argue that moral injury occurs "when soldiers violate their core moral beliefs" through their own actions or omissions, but also when they witness "someone else violate core moral values" or feel "betrayed by persons in authority."[24] The account of Camilo Mejía, one of the veterans profiled by Brock and Lettini, is a representative study in the complexity of moral injury. The thoroughness of his training leads Mejía, under orders, to kill a young man without hesitation—an event he cannot later even recall; he also knows about, and even watches, the torture of prisoners, but is too intimidated to denounce behavior he finds detestable. Alongside these personal acts and omissions, however, the craven acts of his commanders, more interested in the advancement of their careers than in the protection of the lives of their soldiers or local civilians, also break his trust and leave Mejía feeling profoundly betrayed.[25]

Morally injured veterans themselves raise some of the strongest voices against an either/or understanding of moral injury, at least in military contexts. Yandell argues forcefully that both models taken together "get closer to the reality of moral injury" than either could on its own: the emphases of the perpetration model show that a soldier is not an automaton, while the uncomfortable truths of the betrayal model reveal the limits of a soldier's freedom under authority.[26] US Marines veteran Tyler Boudreau captures this ambiguity: "Our moral fibers have been torn by what we were asked to do and by what we agreed to do."[27]

MORAL INJURY, PTSD, AND THE HEALING OF TRAUMA

The preceding discussion points to the need for a flexible understanding of moral injury that allows the possibility of multiple, overlapping, and interacting causes of injury. Even so, most works on moral injury identify it as a distinct phenomenon. In other words, moral injury is not a catch-all for "nonphysical" wounds, and it is not just another name for posttraumatic stress disorder (PTSD), at least as PTSD is currently defined. The relationship between moral injury and PTSD is a complex topic with few settled answers, and it is possible, at least clinically, that moral injury will eventually be accounted for under "existing mental and behavioral health diagnoses," including an expanded definition of PTSD.[28] At present, however, there are real challenges to conflating moral injury and PTSD. A diagnosis of PTSD, for example, formally "requires direct or indirect exposure to life-threat or sexual violence," but this is not a necessary condition for moral injury.[29] Moreover, PTSD is classically understood to be rooted in fear, while shame is the primary driver of moral injury. This distinction is not only theoretical, but has therapeutic ramifications, as the "most common interventions for PTSD continue to be predominantly centered on treatment of fear-based symptoms," and may thus fail entirely to address the guilt and shame felt by the morally injured.[30] Some established treatments for PTSD specifically aim at "correcting" feelings of blame toward self or others. When someone seriously harms another, however, such feelings may be not only appropriate but necessary to maintain belief in a coherent moral order.[31]

So while an individual may suffer from both moral injury and PTSD, and both conditions can generate overlapping symptoms that might contribute to the other, it is useful and could be essential to distinguish them for understanding and treatment.[32] But most who work with the morally injured are not seeking to develop a pathology or compose a fresh entry in the psychiatric diagnostic manuals. Moral injury is not a sickness or a disorder, but, as Brock has said, "a normal response to extremity" that offers proof of a working human conscience.[33]

Likewise, some have cautioned that the word "injury" may unduly medicalize the concept or imply that a morally injured individual can be "fixed," if only the right treatment can be found.[34] But injuries run on a continuum. Some heal on their own; some heal only with a certain regimen or caregiver; some heal incompletely, or leave lasting scars; some, indeed, are fatal. Moral injury, too, may be usefully considered along a continuum, both with other, less serious kinds of moral distress, and within the construct itself.[35] This variation may depend less on the circumstances than it does on the human being who experiences and reacts to them. Exposure to potentially morally injurious events does not make moral injury inevitable, or reliably predict what shape moral injury may take in an individual's life.[36] Healing, meanwhile, cannot mean a simple return to a state prior to injury. The notion of moral repair points to an integration of wounds, not to their erasure. As Graham states, "Healing in the context of moral injury . . . *reorients* persons toward the consequences of past harm perpetrated by them or upon them."[37]

One other dimension is at work in the consideration of moral injury, trauma, and healing. While it is vital to consider a morally injured person in his or her particularity, it is a mistake to focus solely on the individual. Moral codes are dialogic, evolving in negotiations between human beings and their families, communities, and cultures. In his book *Warriors between Worlds*, Zachary Moon, a practical theologian and former military chaplain, offers a valuable critique of approaches to moral injury that overlook this intricate give-and-take. Moral identity, Moon argues, is not a "static form to be altered and fixed," but a "dynamic process," and an adequate response to moral and social wounds "requires that we think in more sophisticated ways about cultural context and intersecting factors (i.e., race, gender, class, education, sexuality, etc.)."[38] These complexities also raise significant questions about the porous boundaries of the construct of moral injury. As Yandell says, "Moral injury is about human relationship," and thus personal and corporate at once: an internal scar, but also "an untended wound cut deeply into the institutions and conventions that shape social and political life."[39]

CONTEXTS FOR POTENTIAL MORAL INJURY

A final consideration in the effort to understand moral injury is to ask which contexts are most likely to lead to the experience of potentially morally injurious events. As in matters of definition, this question remains unsettled. The idea of moral injury emerged from a terrible, intense, and specific field of experience associated with military service, and above all with killing in combat. Some feel strongly that the term ought to be reserved for this particular context and its aftermath, suspecting that its application to other situations will result in a co-opted, watered-down, and ultimately meaningless concept. This concern is credible, and we should resist distorting the idea by spreading it too thin. There is broad agreement that moral injury names something that develops in true human extremity, and to trivialize it betrays the struggles, and, too often, the memory, of the morally injured.[40] But the hard work of understanding and addressing moral injury among combat veterans has suggested ways in which the construct may offer concrete aid in responding to other circumstances of serious trauma. Even as we recognize the special gravity that characterizes combat-related moral injury, we may consider how to apply the concept to other areas of human experience that reliably generate conditions that may lead to moral wounds.

First, there are military contexts beyond traditional combat scenarios that produce potentially morally injurious circumstances. Drone pilots display symptoms that are connected with moral injury, and it is possible that the peculiarities of remote warfare create conditions that are especially morally perilous. Physical remove and safety may lead to feelings of guilt at what is regarded as a less than fair fight; conversely, extended surveillance of eventual targets leads to a kind of intimacy that can amplify the trauma of killing. Drone analysts and associated personnel, meanwhile, may witness more violence, and with greater frequency, than combatants on the ground.[41] Additionally, soldiers who aid and protect combatants with intelligence and logistics are also at risk: "I didn't squeeze a trigger but I did the same thing," says a support soldier profiled in Brock and Lettini's book.[42] Other potentially injurious military contexts overlap with civilian experiences, but may display particular qualities deriving from interactions with the hierarchy and bureaucracy of the military. For example, sexual trauma is known in both civilian and military contexts. The stark asymmetries of power in the armed forces, however, may give military sexual trauma a distinctively heightened level of moral distress.[43] Medical professionals treating wounded soldiers may also struggle with guilt when they are unable to save limbs or lives, sometimes owing to institutional constraints.[44]

The potential for moral injuries is also present in contexts that are less directly related to combat. Civilians in wars of occupation may feel betrayed by occupying authorities, witness killings and atrocities, or face moral anguish over what they had to do to survive or to secure the survival of loved ones. Additionally, Nash and Litz have shown that military families are vulnerable to injury from relationship betrayals and physical and emotional violence connected to veterans' service and homecoming.[45] These veterans themselves may suffer deep shame at the secondary impacts of their own moral trauma, and the interconnections of family mean that moral injuries and their effects can ripple among members in complicated ways.[46]

The criminal justice system also displays parallels with some aspects of the military, and likewise produces potentially morally injurious circumstances. Betrayals by superiors, killing in the line of duty, and making mistakes that lead to the death of colleagues are associated with outcomes consistent with moral injury in police officers.[47] As in military contexts, policing can generate feelings of betrayal in communities, as well as events where violent abuses of power victimize civilians or witnesses. Prisons both absorb those already morally injured and offer ample grounds for new moral injuries among inmates and staff. Corrections officers who execute prisoners can suffer from deep guilt and emotional and moral damage that lead to depression, addiction, and suicide. As in warfare, the deaths of the condemned may be considered justified. Yet some who participate in executions report feeling "lower than the most despicable person," or testify to losing "a little bit of their humanity" in the process.[48]

The construct of moral injury can also be valuable in civilian contexts. Clinicians who work with morally injured veterans increasingly call for further investigations into the potential for civilian moral injury.[49] Besides the possibility of helping civilians by employing knowledge gained from the treatment of morally injured veterans, this move recognizes that military service usually involves transitions from, and back into, civilian life. Moreover, military moral injury may be worsened or triggered by trauma endured before service.[50] For example, Shay's earlier works already discussed moral injury stemming from sexual violence and abuse.[51] The ongoing crises in some Christian churches and other organizations involving institutional cover-ups of systemic abuses continue to shatter trust and create countless individual and corporate occasions for moral injury and its worst outcomes, including a loss of faith in a moral universe.

Additionally, refugees and asylum seekers, whose numbers have soared to nearly thirty million persons in recent years, face a battery of potentially morally injurious circumstances.[52] These include desperately dangerous journeys, rapacious smugglers, deaths of family members, risks of violence and sexual violation, inhumane incarceration, forcible and indefinite separation of even profoundly disabled children from their parents, all combined with the wholesale indifference of many to these realities. Even journalists covering these stories of extraordinary human suffering have reported feelings and actions that are consonant with established definitions of moral injury.[53] Civilian health care professionals have also recently found value in the concept of moral injury, as they struggle to describe the "agony of being constantly locked in double binds when every choice one makes yields a compromised outcome." Oaths sworn to privilege patient well-being are violated when doctors' best intentions meet the "deeper structural dysfunction" of a profit-driven health care system.[54] Individuals in other helping professions are also vulnerable. Joseph Currier has shown that teachers in El Salvador, who often work in contexts of poverty and violence, are exposed to a range of morally injurious experiences deriving from structural and social breakdowns. Betrayals by superiors, witnessing violence and suffering among students, and institutional obstacles to caring for students can all lead to burnout and symptoms of PTSD.[55] It is unfortunately easy to multiply examples of social contexts that could contribute to moral injuries: acts of terror such as mass shootings, so often now perpetrated with weapons developed for the battlefield; natural disasters, compounded by inept and apathetic official and social responses; parental addiction, abuse, or neglect; and many others.

There is, of course, no necessary hierarchy of suffering. Whether linked to perpetration, betrayal, or a complex alloy of traumas, moral injury is at once individual and indivisible from an array of relevant contexts and connections, circumstantial and human. Kevin Sites's moral anguish and post-traumatic stress, for example, did not come out of nowhere at the revelation of the murder of Taleb Salem Nidal. They grew from a lifetime of experiences, actions, and reflections until this discovery finally—as he puts it—took him "pro."[56] Sometimes, too, the experience of moral injury rests not on a single triggering event, but on a quiet accumulation of hurts that ends in moral injury.[57] Accordingly, much work remains to be done to refine the kinds of definitions and distinctions explored here. Efforts will require further studies with veterans, as well as new investigations into the potential for moral injury in civilian contexts. As Moon emphasizes, fresh attention needs to be paid to individuals who do not fit the demographic profile of those whose moral injuries have been studied so far, and to the meaning of moral codes or systems and how they form and evolve.[58] This work of understanding and responding to moral injury can use the help of everyone of good will, as all authorities agree that any path toward moral repair, while clearly demanding serious personal effort, must be taken in the company of others.

NOTES

1. Kevin Sites, *The Things They Cannot Say: Stories Soldiers Won't Tell You about What They've Seen, Done or Failed to Do in War* (New York: Harper Perennial, 2013), xvii–xviii, 8–20, 281–87.
2. Brett T. Litz et al., "Moral Injury and Moral Repair in War Veterans: A Preliminary Model and Intervention Strategy," *Clinical Psychology Review* 29 (2009): 697.
3. Ibid., 704–5.
4. See Brett T. Litz and Patricia K. Kerig, "Introduction to the Special Issue on Moral Injury: Conceptual Challenges, Methodological Issues, and Clinical Applications," *Journal of Traumatic Stress* 32 (June 2019): 345.
5. Litz et al., "Moral Injury and Moral Repair," 697–98, 700–701.
6. Ibid., 701 (emphasis original).
7. William P. Nash and Brett T. Litz, "Moral Injury: A Mechanism for War-Related Psychological Trauma in Military Family Members," *Clinical Child and Family Psychology Review* 16 (2013): 368; compare Litz et al., "Moral Injury and Moral Repair," 698.

8. Michael Yandell, "The War Within: A Veteran's Moral Injury," *Christian Century* 132, no. 1 (January 7, 2015): 12.
9. Litz et al., "Moral Injury and Moral Repair," 701.
10. Ibid., 702–4.
11. Jonathan Shay, *Odysseus in America: Combat Trauma and the Trials of Homecoming* (New York: Scribner, 2002), 240; see also Jonathan Shay, *Achilles in Vietnam: Combat Trauma and the Undoing of Character* (New York: Atheneum, 1994).
12. Jonathan Shay, "Moral Injury," *Psychoanalytic Psychology* 31 (2014): 182.
13. Shay, *Achilles*, 26.
14. Jonathan Shay, "Casualties," *Daedalus* 140, no. 3 (2011): 183.
15. Shay, *Achilles*, 3–4, 171.
16. Ibid., 178, 180, 186.
17. Ibid., 4, 39, 55–67.
18. Ibid., 187; Shay, *Odysseus*, 4, 162; Shay, "Moral Injury," 189.
19. Shay, *Odysseus*, 208–30, 242.
20. See Yuval Neria and Alison Pickover, "Commentary on the Special Issue on Moral Injury: Advances, Gaps in Literature, and Future Directions," *Journal of Traumatic Stress* 32 (June 2019): 459.
21. Ibid., 460; compare Joseph M. Currier, Joshua D. Foster, and Steven L. Isaak, "Moral Injury and Spiritual Struggles in Military Veterans: A Latent Profile Analysis," *Journal of Traumatic Stress* 32 (June 2019): 393, and Joseph M. Currier et al., "Development and Evaluation of the Expressions of Moral Injury Scale—Military Version," *Clinical Psychology and Psychotherapy* 25 (2018): 485–86.
22. On (some in) the military's discomfort with the construct of moral injury, see Eyal Press, "The Wounds of the Drone Warrior," *New York Times Magazine* (June 17, 2018): 35, 37.
23. Nancy Sherman, *Afterwar: Healing the Moral Wounds of Our Soldiers* (Oxford: Oxford University Press, 2015), 8; Larry Kent Graham, *Moral Injury: Restoring Wounded Souls* (Nashville: Abingdon, 2017), 13.
24. Rita Nakashima Brock and Gabriella Lettini, *Soul Repair: Recovering from Moral Injury after War* (Boston: Beacon, 2012), xv.
25. Ibid., 34–35.
26. Michael Yandell, "Moral Injury and Human Relationship: A Conversation," *Pastoral Psychology* 68 (2019): 8.
27. Tyler Boudreau, "The Morally Injured," *The Massachusetts Review* 52 (2011): 753.
28. Litz and Kerig, "Introduction," 344.
29. Ibid.
30. Sanela Dursun and Kimberley Watkins, "Moral Injury: What We Know and What We Need to Know," *Military Behavioral Health* 6 (2018): 122.
31. Neria and Pickover, "Commentary," 462; Litz and Kerig, "Introduction," 344.
32. Neria and Pickover, "Commentary," 461–62.
33. Brock as quoted in Jake Whitney, "How to Fix a Soul," *The Texas Observer* (December 2016): 14.
34. Zachary Moon, *Warriors between Worlds: Moral Injury and Identities in Crisis*, Emerging Perspectives in Pastoral Theology and Care (Lanham, MD: Lexington, 2019), 19.
35. Litz and Kerig, "Introduction," 345.
36. Brandon J. Griffin et al., "Moral Injury: An Integrative Review," *Journal of Traumatic Stress* 32 (June 2019): 351; Moon, *Warriors*, 11.
37. Graham, *Moral Injury*, 10 (emphasis mine); compare Yandell, "War Within," 13, on the chronic nature of moral injury.
38. Moon, *Warriors*, 20, 93.
39. Yandell, "Moral Injury and Human Relationship," 3.
40. See Litz and Kerig, "Introduction," 346, on the relative rarity of moral injury.
41. Press, "Wounds of the Drone Warrior"; Henry Barnes, "'The PTSD Stems from This Dirty Work': New Film Documents Regretful Drone Pilots," *The Guardian* (February 15, 2016).
42. Brock and Lettini, *Soul Repair*, 29, 58.

43. Griffin et al., "Moral Injury: An Integrative Review," 356.
44. Janice Agazio et al., "Ethical Issues Encountered by Military Nurses during Wartime," *Annual Review of Nursing Research* 34 (2016): 240–42; Carol Acton and Jane Potter, *Working in a World of Hurt: Trauma and Resilience in the Narratives of Medical Personnel in Warzones*, Cultural History of Modern War (Manchester: Manchester University Press, 2015).
45. Nash and Litz, "Moral Injury," 370–71.
46. Shay, *Odysseus*, 83; Nash and Litz, "Moral Injury," 371.
47. Konstantinos Papazoglou and Brian Chopko, "The Role of Moral Suffering (Moral Distress and Moral Injury) in Police Compassion Fatigue and PTSD: An Unexplored Topic," *Frontiers in Psychology* 8 (2017): 3.
48. Ed Pilkington, "Arkansas Executioners Will Suffer Like I Did, Warns Former Corrections Head," *The Guardian* (March 29, 2019).
49. Neria and Pickover, "Commentary," 460, 462; Griffin et al., "Moral Injury: An Integrative Review," 356.
50. A. Nazarov et al., "Role of Morality in the Experience of Guilt and Shame within the Armed Forces," *Acta Psychiatrica Scandinavica* 132 (2015): 14; Moon, *Warriors*, 93–94.
51. Shay, *Achilles*, 168, 227 n.5.
52. Angela Nickerson et al., "Moral Injury in Traumatized Refugees," *Psychotherapy and Psychosomatics* 84 (2015): 122–23.
53. Anthony Feinstein and Hannah Storm, *The Emotional Toll on Journalists Covering the Refugee Crisis* (Oxford: Reuters Institute for the Study of Journalism, 2017).
54. Wendy Dean and Simon G. Talbot, "Moral Injury and Burnout in Medicine: A Year of Lessons Learned," *STAT*, 26 July 2019. https://www.statnews.com/2019/07/26/moral-injury-burnout-medicine-lessons-learned/.
55. Joseph M. Currier et al., "Morally Injurious Experiences and Meaning in Salvadorian Teachers Exposed to Violence," *Psychological Trauma: Theory, Research, Practice, and Policy* 7 (2015): 29.
56. Sites, *The Things They Cannot Say*, 13.
57. Yandell, "Moral Injury and Human Relationship," 5.
58. Moon, *Warriors*, 18, 23–34, 93, 102–3.

BIBLIOGRAPHY

Acton, Carol and Jane Potter. *Working in a World of Hurt: Trauma and Resilience in the Narratives of Medical Personnel in Warzones*. Cultural History of Modern War. Manchester: Manchester University Press, 2015.

Agazio, Janice, Petra Goodman, Oluwakemi Opanubi, and Patricia McMullen. "Ethical Issues Encountered by Military Nurses during Wartime." *Annual Review of Nursing Research* 34 (2016): 227–46.

Barnes, Henry. "'The PTSD Stems from This Dirty Work': New Film Documents Regretful Drone Pilots." *The Guardian* (February 15, 2016).

Boudreau, Tyler. "The Morally Injured." *The Massachusetts Review* 52 (2011): 746–54.

Brock, Rita Nakashima and Gabriella Lettini. *Soul Repair: Recovering from Moral Injury after War*. Boston: Beacon, 2012.

Currier, Joseph M., Jacob K. Farnsworth, Kent D. Drescher, Ryon C. McDermott, Brook M. Sims, and David L. Albright. "Development and Evaluation of the Expressions of Moral Injury Scale—Military Version." *Clinical Psychology and Psychotherapy* 25 (2018): 474–88.

Currier, Joseph M., Joshua D. Foster, and Steven L. Isaak. "Moral Injury and Spiritual Struggles in Military Veterans: A Latent Profile Analysis." *Journal of Traumatic Stress* 32 (June 2019): 393–404.

Currier, Joseph M., Jason M. Holland, Lisseth Rojas-Flores, Sofia Herrera, and David Foy. "Morally Injurious Experiences and Meaning in Salvadorian Teachers Exposed to Violence." *Psychological Trauma: Theory, Research, Practice, and Policy* 7 (2015): 24–33.

Dean, Wendy and Simon G. Talbot. "Moral Injury and Burnout in Medicine: A Year of Lessons Learned." *STAT* (July 26, 2019). https://www.statnews.com/2019/07/26/moral-injury-burnout-medicine-lessons-learned/.

Dursun, Sanela and Kimberley Watkins. "Moral Injury: What We Know and What We Need to Know." *Military Behavioral Health* 6 (2018): 121–26.

Feinstein, Anthony and Hannah Storm. *The Emotional Toll on Journalists Covering the Refugee Crisis*. Oxford: Reuters Institute for the Study of Journalism, 2017.

Graham, Larry Kent. *Moral Injury: Restoring Wounded Souls*. Nashville: Abingdon, 2017.

Griffin, Brandon J., Natalie Purcell, Kristine Burkman, Brett T. Litz, Craig J. Bryan, Martha Schmitz, Claudia Villierme, Jessica Walsh, and Shira Maguen. "Moral Injury: An Integrative Review." *Journal of Traumatic Stress* 32 (June 2019): 350–62.

Litz, Brett T. and Patricia K. Kerig. "Introduction to the Special Issue on Moral Injury: Conceptual Challenges, Methodological Issues, and Clinical Applications." *Journal of Traumatic Stress* 32 (June 2019): 341–49.

Litz, Brett T., Nathan Stein, Eileen Delaney, Leslie Lebowitz, William P. Nash, Caroline Silva, and Shira Maguen. "Moral Injury and Moral Repair in War Veterans: A Preliminary Model and Intervention Strategy." *Clinical Psychology Review* 29 (2009): 695–706.

Moon, Zachary. *Warriors between Worlds: Moral Injury and Identities in Crisis*. Emerging Perspectives in Pastoral Theology and Care. Lanham, MD: Lexington, 2019.

Nash, William P. and Brett T. Litz. "Moral Injury: A Mechanism for War-Related Psychological Trauma in Military Family Members." *Clinical Child and Family Psychology Review* 16 (2013): 365–75.

Nazarov, A., R. Jetly, H. McNeely, M. Kiang, R. Lanius, and M. C. McKinnon. "Role of Morality in the Experience of Guilt and Shame within the Armed Forces." *Acta Psychiatrica Scandinavica* 132 (2015): 4–19.

Neria, Yuval and Alison Pickover. "Commentary on the Special Issue on Moral Injury: Advances, Gaps in Literature, and Future Directions." *Journal of Traumatic Stress* 32 (June 2019): 459–64.

Nickerson, Angela, Ulrich Schnyder, Richard A. Bryant, Matthis Schick, Julia Mueller, and Naser Morina. "Moral Injury in Traumatized Refugees." *Psychotherapy and Psychosomatics* 84 (2015): 122–23.

Papazoglou, Konstantinos and Brian Chopko. "The Role of Moral Suffering (Moral Distress and Moral Injury) in Police Compassion Fatigue and PTSD: An Unexplored Topic." *Frontiers in Psychology* 8 (2017): 1–5.

Pilkington, Ed. "Arkansas Executioners Will Suffer Like I Did, Warns Former Corrections Head." *The Guardian* (March 29, 2019).

Press, Eyal. "The Wounds of the Drone Warrior." *The New York Times Magazine* (June 17, 2018): 30–37, 47, 49.

Shay, Jonathan. *Achilles in Vietnam: Combat Trauma and the Undoing of Character*. New York: Atheneum, 1994.

—. "Casualties." *Daedalus* 140, no. 3 (2011): 179–88.

—. Jonathan. "Moral Injury." *Psychoanalytic Psychology* 31 (2014): 182–91.

—. *Odysseus in America: Combat Trauma and the Trials of Homecoming*. New York: Scribner, 2002.

Sherman, Nancy. *Afterwar: Healing the Moral Wounds of Our Soldiers*. Oxford: Oxford University Press, 2015.

Sites, Kevin. *The Things They Cannot Say: Stories Soldiers Won't Tell You about What They've Seen, Done or Failed to Do in War*. New York: Harper Perennial, 2013.

Whitney, Jake. "How to Fix a Soul." *The Texas Observer* (December 2016): 12–15.

Yandell, Michael. "Moral Injury and Human Relationship: A Conversation." *Pastoral Psychology* 68 (2019): 3–14.

Yandell, Michael. "The War Within: A Veteran's Moral Injury." *Christian Century* 132, no. 1 (7 January 2015): 12–13.

Chapter Two

The Emergence and Development of the Concept of Moral Injury

Alanna Coady, Jessica R. Carney, Sheila Frankfurt, and Brett T. Litz

Moral injury is a hypothetical construct that is commonly accepted to entail multidimensional impairment and suffering experienced after severe transgressions, committed either by oneself or others, of one's moral values.[1] Acts that involve violations of one's moral beliefs and expectations are called Potentially Morally Injurious Events (PMIEs) because events, no matter how egregious, are only potentially damaging. Moral transgressions and suffering as a result of those transgressions are part of the human condition; it is only recently that mental and behavioral health care communities have begun to regard perceived transgressions as potential traumas causing lasting harm. Moral injury is proposed by some to lead to a complex set of outcomes, such as unbidden memories and intrusive emotional reminders of the PMIE, avoidance and emotional numbing, embitterment and rage, guilt and shame, and maladaptive attempts to cope, such as substance misuse, social withdrawal and isolation, or, in extreme cases, suicide.

The idea of moral injury as a clinical syndrome was developed by US psychologists, working with combat veterans, who recognized the inadequacy of models of trauma that emphasize fear and victimization experiences. Unfortunately, there is no field-wide consensus about which events should qualify as PMIEs, the clinical picture of moral injury, or how exactly moral injury develops after PMIEs. Because of these open questions, it is not clear whether and to what extent moral injury is distinct from posttraumatic stress disorder (PTSD). This chapter will review the development of the moral injury syndrome to explore how and why moral injury emerged as a concept and where the moral injury field stands today, ten years after its introduction to psychological clinical literature. The goal of this chapter is to provide readers with an understanding of the history of moral injury and how it may or may not differ from PTSD.

PREHISTORY OF MORAL INJURY

Early Models of Trauma

The dominant model of combat trauma has changed from a primarily physiological pathology to a primarily psychological pathology over the course of the twentieth century. Different early models of combat trauma attributed traumatic stress to physiological health, precombat personality structure, intrapsychic conflict, or exhaustion and fatigue. Service members in World War I, for example, suffered from "combat exhaustion" (gradual onset) or "shell shock" (sudden onset), which included symptoms of severe anxiety, fatigue, and a general inability to function. These conditions were thought to result from physical deprivation and proximity to explosions and therefore applied only to those who had experienced combat in war.

Service members in World War II, however, were recognized to suffer from traumatic psychological conditions that were not solely due to combat-related physical experiences.[2] Case studies of war-related trauma also began to recognize that so-called moral emotions such as guilt, shame, and resentment could be prominent aspects of the psychological and emotional aftermath of war trauma for both civilians and combatants. For example, clinical work with World War II-era concentration camp survivors inspired a more comprehensive account of traumatic stress that went beyond physiologic impact by recognizing symptoms of survivor's guilt and grief, referred to as "survivor syndrome."[3] In 1974, Sarah Haley, a US Department of Veterans Affairs social worker who worked with heavily combat-exposed Vietnam veterans provided an account of the psychological distress of veterans who had committed atrocities and the unique therapeutic challenges of treating traumas that involved harming others.[4] In these ways, mental health providers recognized that existential conflict and moral struggles of conscience were often part of the clinical picture, even if people's sense of guilt, shame, responsibility, and accountability did not always correspond to their actual responsibility or accountability for traumatic events.

Development of the Notion of Traumatic Stress as a Psychiatric Disorder

The creation of PTSD as a diagnostic category initiated the formal medical recognition that psychological injury could result from catastrophic life events. The official establishment of PTSD as a diagnostic category was due, in large part, to the combined advocacy of two disparate groups of trauma survivors—namely, rape victims and US Vietnam War veterans, as well as the psychiatrists and mental health providers who worked with them. PTSD could encapsulate the suffering of survivors of these very different types of traumatic experiences by prioritizing life-threat and fear-conditioning models of traumatic life events and traumatic responses, since life-threat and fear are presumably experienced as part of both combat and sexual assault.

The notion that it is right for a person to feel responsible for his or her suffering or to feel guilt or shame over his or her actions fits more appropriately with combat trauma. By contrast, it would be victim-blaming in the context of sexual assault to suggest that survivors could be responsible for sexual violence against them. In the development of the notion of trauma, psychologists deemphasized some aspects specifically related to combat trauma in order to accommodate the very different experiences of warfare and sexual assault under the same label. The notion of moral injury retrieves these dropped aspects of combat trauma, especially those that trouble the notion of a purely victim-based trauma experience—namely, agency, accountability, and perpetration.

The PTSD Diagnosis over Time

Some attention to moral distress was present in the first appearance of PTSD as a formal diagnosis in the third edition of the American Psychiatric Association's *Diagnostic and Statistical Manual of Mental Disorders* (DSM-III) in 1980.[5] From its inception, the PTSD diagnosis has required that an individual report a traumatic event, termed a Criterion A event. A DSM-III Criterion A event was defined as a markedly distressing experience "outside the range of usual human experience" (e.g., severe physical or sexual assault, military combat, or unusually severe auto accidents), thus distinguishing traumatic events as distressing above and beyond normal life stressors that would be tolerated well by most others. It is possible to construe potential traumatic experiences (PTEs) listed as Criterion A events in the DSM-III as morally injurious; rape, for example, has been described in recent moral injury literature as a moral violation. Further, the presence of guilt about one's actions (in the DSM-III's Criterion D) indicated an attention to the moral elements of perpetration-based traumatic experiences and their subsequent conditions in this initial version of PTSD diagnostic criteria.

The PTSD diagnosis was soon modified, however, in the revised version of the DSM-III (DSM-III-R),[6] which omitted symptoms related to perceived moral responsibility. The DSM-III-R provided a list of potentially traumatic Criterion A events, such as injury or serious threat of injury to oneself or loved ones, the destruction of one's community or home, and witnessing or learning about extreme injury or violence inflicted upon others. DSM-III-R's

Criterion A shifted the definition to life-threatening events that people experienced or survived, and not those in which people took part. The traumatic stressors included in the DSM-III-R's Criterion A arguably included moral dimensions, as elements of any of these experiences could certainly violate one's sense of right and wrong; however, none of the included Criterion A stressors recognized elements of culpability or accountability.

The publication of the DSM-IV in 1994 presented a more pronounced erasure of the possibility of trauma resulting from participation in combat or having an active role in perpetrating a traumatic event.[7] DSM-IV and the subsequent text revision (DSM-IV-TR) defined traumas as "events that involved actual or threatened death or serious injury, or a threat to the physical integrity of self or others" (Criterion A.1) that elicited reactions of "intense fear, helplessness, or horror" (Criterion A.2). The A.2 criterion foregrounded a primarily fear-based and victimization-based model of PTSD. The inclusion of "horror" in the A.2 criterion could be considered a type of moral revulsion during trauma; however, within the context of life-threat-based traumas, horror may be understood primarily as a response to others' actions, and not one's own.

It is possible to construe potential PTEs listed as Criterion A events more generally as involving violations of deeply held moral standards. Typically, though, PTEs emphasize the effects of experiencing such violations, rather than perpetrating them. As a result, the psychological harm of committing moral transgressions is largely ignored in PTEs. In sum, the progression of PTSD diagnostic criteria in versions of the DSM saw a gradual removal of suffering related to perpetrating moral harms in accordance with dominant trauma theories at the time, which increasingly emphasized fear as the driving force of subsequent traumatic stress responses.

THE EMERGENCE OF THE MORAL INJURY CONSTRUCT

The DSM-IV fear-based model of PTSD in the 1990s was the background against which the construct of moral injury emerged. The term "moral injury" was first introduced in 1994 when Jonathan Shay detailed the concept in his seminal book on the subject, *Achilles in Vietnam*.[8] Shay's work identified similarities in accounts of betrayal and consequent suffering between the famed warrior Achilles in Homer's epic poem, *The Iliad,* and the Vietnam veterans with whom Shay worked as a psychiatrist at VA Boston. *Achilles in Vietnam* focused on events experienced by warriors in which a trusted military leader committed a high-stakes betrayal of what is morally right in a combat context. Using the case study of the wrath of Achilles compared with numerous case studies from Vietnam veterans, Shay proposed that such a betrayal can result in all-consuming anger, social withdrawal, self-condemnation, and bitterness, which he termed "moral injury" and aptly described as "the undoing of character." The parallels in these case studies indicated the ways in which, across times and cultural contexts, warriors frequently experience and are exposed to betrayals that transgress their morals and result in lasting psychological harm. In this way, Shay foregrounded the potential moral complexity and pain of combat trauma.

It was not until 2009, however, that the notion of moral injury was introduced to psychological research by Brett Litz and colleagues.[9] In contrast to Shay's focus on betrayal, this work foregrounded potential suffering for perpetrators of moral transgressions in war, often connected to incapacitating shame and guilt. In so doing, important aspects of trauma, which were otherwise absent from both Shay's conceptualization of moral injury and the DSM-IV PTSD construct, were addressed by recognizing the potential harms of acting in ways that are traumatizing, both to oneself and to others.

DEFINING MORAL INJURY AND ITS RELATED EXPERIENCES

Moral injury literature often creates confusion because some discussions use "moral injury" to refer to the events that potentially cause moral stress, while others use the same label to refer to the outcomes produced by those events. This multiple usage results in confusion as to what moral injury is, what causes it, and how cause and effect are related.[10] We may, however, distinguish between moral injury syndrome and potentially morally injurious events (PMIEs).

Moral Injury Syndrome

The most commonly cited definition of moral injury is the "lasting psychological, biological, spiritual, behavioral and social impact"[11] of moral transgressions. Definitional issues remain, however, as researchers have attempted to fill in the gaps in multiple ways in accordance with varying theoretical views of moral injury. Currently, more than seventeen definitions of moral injury are in circulation, with each emphasizing different aspects or understandings of the construct.[12] Although there is informal consensus around key propositions of moral injury as an outcome (i.e., individuals can be traumatized by their own—or others'—immoral acts, and that varying combinations of guilt, shame, and rage are characteristic of this trauma type), it is not currently possible to demarcate clearly the symptoms of moral injury and no diagnostic boundaries have been firmly established.

Potentially Morally Injurious Events

PMIEs are most commonly defined according to two complimentary definitions. Litz and colleagues state that PMIEs involve "perpetrating, failing to prevent, bearing witness to, or learning about acts that transgress deeply held moral beliefs and expectations,"[13] while Shay defines PMIEs as "a betrayal of what's right, by someone who holds legitimate authority, in a high-stakes situation."[14] The latter definition emphasizes betrayal and the role of authority figures in morally transgressive events, while the former recognizes perpetration of moral violations as a potential source of moral distress.

The causes of moral injury are typically organized into two categories: (1) PMIE-Self, in which the morally injured person perpetrated the transgressive act; and (2) PMIE-Other, in which the morally injured person witnessed or experienced a transgression perpetrated by another person. Examples of PMIE-Self include killing or participating in atrocities or excessive violence. Notably, this can include killing of any kind, whether within or outside the rules of engagement. PMIE-Others might involve witnessing comrades or others commit atrocities, harm civilians, or torture or degrade prisoners of war, or personally experiencing a transgression by someone else. An act experienced as a betrayal can also be a type of PMIE-Other. PMIE categories may occur simultaneously or overlap, as a service member who witnesses others commit unconscionable harm may also perceive the event as a PMIE-Self for failing to prevent the transgression. Betrayal-based PMIEs often involve experiences of betrayal by one's commanding authorities who may, for example, prioritize political optics at the expense of service members' well-being or safety. Further, military sexual trauma may also constitute a betrayal at both the personal and the institutional level.[15]

HOW MORAL INJURY DEVELOPS IN PERSONS

Questions remain concerning how moral injury develops following PMIE exposure, and proposals of causal models have outpaced empirical research on this point. One idea of how moral injury develops or unfolds is in terms of changes in character born out of betrayal-based grief, rage, and embitterment.[16] Another prominent idea is that severe psychological conflict borne of the struggle of veterans to reconcile their actions and experiences in war with their deeply held moral beliefs may result in a negative shift in their sense of who they are, accompanied by severe self-blame and debilitating anxiety, guilt, or shame, which then cause social withdrawal and isolation.[17] Other models view moral injury primarily through a spiritual lens, claiming that it stems from the loss of spiritual beliefs or a ruptured relationship with God,[18] or difficulty in making meaning out of morally transgressive experiences.[19]

PMIEs may exist on a spectrum distinguishable by increasing levels of severity. For instance, generalized, ongoing experiences that have no immediate self-relevance could be *moral challenges* that elicit a proportional response of *moral frustration* (e.g., concerns about the environment in response to climate change).[20] More severe and directly self-referential events, however, may be characterized as *moral stressors* that are more likely to result in *moral distress* (e.g., pains after being cheated or robbed). In these terms, moral injury is distinguished by the severity of suffering and impairment and the event's impact on someone's identity. This continuum model of PMIEs lands where Shay suggested, that moral injury involves suffering so intense that it affects people's longstanding and habitual character or personality.

At this point, very little empirical research has tested specific aspects of these different understandings of PMIEs or how they may relate to one another. Clinicians and laypersons working from different perspectives and backgrounds may gravitate to different understandings.

DIFFERENTIATING PTSD AND MORAL INJURY

In light of the understandings surveyed above, determining the difference between PTSD and moral injury is challenging. Several factors complicate the effort. First, both syndromes could result from the same event in that the Criterion A trauma category and PMIE category are not mutually exclusive. In the case of combat traumas, it is difficult to disentangle the respective impacts of danger versus action. One might experience moral transgressions because some threat of harm is presumed to be constantly present in a warzone. Second, there is no consensus on how or why PTEs lead to PTSD or PMIEs lead to moral injury. PTSD symptoms were previously believed to develop because of trauma-related fear conditioning, and the diagnosis was housed in the Fear and Anxiety Disorders chapter in the DSM-IV. The field of psychiatry is now largely agnostic about how or why PTSD develops; reflecting this, PTSD is in a newly created Trauma and Other Stressor-related Disorders chapter, indicating a shift toward a category that does not explicitly attach itself to any one model of trauma in the DSM-5. That moral injury and PTSD share similar origins makes it difficult to differentiate them as two separate syndromes stemming from the same causes.

PTSD and moral injury as syndromes also share features. The 2013 publication of the DSM-5 (the version of the DSM currently in use) reintroduced moral emotions, including guilt, shame, and anger, to PTSD Criterion D,[21] resulting in significant overlap between PTSD symptoms and those proposed as core characteristics of moral injury. Early moral injury research had attempted to supplement the PTSD field's overemphasis on fear-based traumas and incomplete attention to perpetration-based traumas in the DSM-IV by highlighting the debilitating effects of posttraumatic guilt and shame. The inclusion of moral emotions in the DSM-5 PTSD diagnosis, however, has challenged efforts to cleanly delineate moral injury from PTSD based on the presence of these emotions. Additional symptoms proposed for a formal codification of moral injury are also core symptoms of the PTSD diagnosis, further obscuring the relationship between the two. For example, Litz and colleagues[22] proposed that moral injury is characterized by reexperiencing symptoms related to the traumatic event, as well as avoidance and emotional numbing, all of which fall under PTSD diagnostic Criterion B (reexperiencing symptoms) or C (avoidance symptoms). In sum, there are insufficient symptom-level differences between the DSM-5 PTSD diagnosis and the purported moral injury syndrome to distinguish the two on this basis.

Even so, the categories of PTSD and moral injury remain distinct because they serve different functions. PTSD is a descriptive psychiatric diagnosis that captures specific symptoms tied to an event; beyond the original Criterion A event, diagnostic criteria are not meant to offer an explanation for why these symptoms develop after a traumatic experience. Moral injury, in contrast, is not currently a formal diagnosis, but can help conceptualize a patient's presenting issue and to plan appropriate treatment. The notion of moral injury offers an explanation for why combat traumas that involve unequivocal moral violations so severely haunt the lives of service members and veterans.[23]

Moral injury may thus offer a novel conceptualization of symptoms of guilt and shame, owing largely to its attention to perpetration-based traumas. Personal culpability and responsibility-taking, as well as the moral emotions that result (guilt and shame), appear in DSM-5 as an irrational reaction to trauma that can be modified through treatment. The attention to victimization experiences over those of perpetration in the origins of the PTSD diagnosis shaped this pathological framing, as self-blame leading to feelings of guilt and shame following victimization-based traumatic experiences is considered inappropriate. By contrast, moral injury does not pathologize guilt and shame but recognizes these as possible indicators of a clear understanding and acknowledgment of personal responsibility for harms done. The development of moral injury redresses the lack of attention to the ways that combat veterans can be traumatized by what they did to prosecute war, as well as what they did to survive.

THE FUTURE OF MORAL INJURY

Up to this point, the field of psychology has dominated the study of moral injury. Interdisciplinary perspectives, however, could enrich the notion. In particular, development of the moral injury concept would be greatly enhanced by an increased attention to historical dialogues on the ethics of war, the role of veterans' broader communities in addressing moral injury, specific cultural and moral values that shape the development and presentation of moral injury, and the possibility of moral injury occurring outside of military contexts.

Practitioners who work with individuals suffering from moral injury may also benefit from greater knowledge of military ethical doctrine, as this may fundamentally shape service members' moral expectations of themselves and of wartime behavior. Practitioners may seek to understand the broader cultural and military ethical expectations placed on service members and how these intersect or conflict with each individual's set of values. Recognizing the forces that shape service members' sense of moral responsibility for their actions in war more directly attends to previously neglected concerns about personal culpability in traumatic events.

Researchers should also familiarize themselves with the Just War Doctrine, a significant historical development in the ethical conduct of war. The Just War Doctrine originated in the works of Augustine in the fifth century and was later developed by Thomas Aquinas as a means of reconciling Christian values of nonviolence with political imperialist goals.[24] Detailing the criteria by which a war may be judged morally just and therefore justified, the Just War Doctrine remains the guiding standard for military undertakings today. This doctrine serves as the background against which some psychological reactions to the moral transgressions of war are formed, placing the onus on individuals for experiencing psychological distress in response to their immoral actions in an otherwise collectively morally sanctioned war. Service members and veterans individually bear the burdens of a society that valorizes war and its warriors while neglecting to acknowledge or take responsibility for the implicit expectation that warriors be subjected to trauma as a result.

Both care providers and researchers would benefit from understanding social pressures inside and outside the military, and how these may foster conditions of PMIEs and thereby moral injury. Overall, moral injury work within clinical psychology has eschewed any political critique of war. It is a common concern that critiquing war may be considered an act of disrespect to veterans' service and sacrifice. Critique, however, may also serve veterans by recognizing the suffering they are asked to endure and the wisdom and perspective they gain concerning the moral challenges of war.

Religious leaders and ministers may be better prepared than mental and behavioral health providers to discuss the responsibility of communities and society as a whole both in inflicting harm and facilitating healing for veterans and others who suffer from moral injury. Morality is necessarily entwined with society and social norms, yet current theoretical and empirical investigations of moral injury have focused most centrally on the individual, his or her moral emotions, cognitions, and impaired behavior or functioning. In a study on how PMIEs occur, service members and veterans cited extremely complex situations in which a confluence of psychological, environmental, cultural, and organizational factors contributed to instances of individuals violating their own values or morals.[25] Research has focused on psychological and some environmental or contextual factors, but significantly less attention has been paid to cultural, organizational, and political factors contributing to PMIEs.

Detailed research on morality and individual and cultural moral values would be especially helpful in elucidating how and why moral injury occurs. Although there has been some suggestion that the value system emphasizing personal responsibility specific to military culture may exacerbate service members' vulnerability to moral injury, there has been no systematic inquiry into which moral values are pertinent to moral injury or the myriad ways in which military culture itself may serve to deepen or even instigate moral distress.[26] Because morality is intricately connected to sociocultural morals, pressures, and expectations, and because moral injury is so deeply interpersonal in nature, the role of communities, social relationships, and pressures cannot be ignored in understanding what causes moral injury, as well as how it is sustained or healed.

Finally, the notion of moral injury in nonmilitary contexts remains relatively unexplored. The moral injury concept emerged among US Department of Veterans Affairs psychologists and psychiatrists primarily because of soldiers' heightened risk of exposure to severe moral challenges or violations. As a result, most of the development on the topic has occurred with veterans or service members and is therefore specific to military contexts. Moral injury research has emphasized the ways in which sociopolitical forces, power structures, and institutional factors may contribute to the conditions of PMIEs, particularly those involving betrayal. Researchers could further clarify the construct of moral injury by examining such factors in nonmilitary institutions and contexts.

NOTES

1. Brett T. Litz, Nathan Stein, Eileen Delaney, Leslie Lebowitz, William P. Nash, Caroline Silva, and Shira Maguen, "Moral Injury and Moral Repair in War Veterans: A Preliminary Model and Intervention Strategy," *Clinical Psychology Review* 29 (2009): 695–706. Author's note: Sheila Frankfurt's work related to this article was supported by the US Department of Veterans Affairs (VA) Career Development Award—1 (IK1RX002427-01A2) from the Rehabilitation Research and Development Service of the VA Office of Research and Development. The views expressed in this article are those of the authors and do not necessarily reflect the position or policy of the VA.

2. Abram Kardiner, *The Traumatic Neuroses of War* (Washington, DC: US National Research Council, 1941).

3. William Niederland, "The Problem of the Survivor: Part I, Some Remarks on the Psychiatric Evaluation of Emotional Disorders in Survivors of Nazi Persecution," *Journal of the Hillside Hospital* (1961): 233–47.

4. Sarah A. Haley, "When the Patient Reports Atrocities: Specific Treatment Considerations of the Vietnam Veteran," *Archives of General Psychiatry* 30 (1974): 191–96.

5. American Psychiatric Association, *Diagnostic and Statistical Manual of Mental Disorders*, 3rd ed. (Washington, DC: APA, 1980).

6. American Psychiatric Association, *Diagnostic and Statistical Manual of Mental Disorders*, 3rd revised ed. (Washington, DC: APA, 1987).

7. American Psychiatric Association, *Diagnostic and Statistical Manual of Mental Disorders*, 4th ed. (Washington, DC: APA, 1994).

8. Jonathan Shay, *Achilles in Vietnam: Combat Trauma and the Undoing of Character* (New York: Simon and Schuster, 1994).

9. Litz et al., "Moral Injury and Moral Repair in War Veterans."

10. Sheila Frankfurt and Patricia Frazier, "A Review of Research on Moral Injury in Combat Veterans," *Military Psychology* 28 (2016): 318–30.

11. Litz et al., "Moral Injury and Moral Repair in War Veterans," 695.

12. See Timothy Hodgson and Lindsay Carey, "Moral Injury and Definitional Clarity: Betrayal, Spirituality and the Role of Chaplains," *Journal of Religion and Health* 56 (2017): 1212–228, for a table of circulating definitions of moral injury. This is not a comprehensive list.

13. Litz et al., "Moral Injury and Moral Repair in War Veterans," 695.

14. Jonathan Shay, "Moral injury," *Intertexts* 16 (2012): 59.

15. Sheila Frankfurt, Bryann DeBeer, Sandra Morissette, Nathan Kimbrel, Heidi La Bash, and Eric Meyer, "Mechanisms of Moral Injury Following Military Sexual Trauma and Combat in Post-9/11 U.S. War Veterans," *Frontiers in Psychiatry* (2018). doi: 10.3389/fpsyt.2018.00520.

16. See Shay, *Achilles in Vietnam.*

17. See Litz et al., "Moral Injury and Moral Repair in War Veterans."

18. J. Irene Harris, Timothy Usset, Cory Voecks, Paul Thuras, Joseph Currier, and Christopher Erbes, "Spiritually Integrated Care for PTSD: A Randomized Controlled Trial of 'Building Spiritual Strength,'" *Psychiatry Research* 267 (2018): 420–28.

19. Joseph Currier, Jason Holland, and Jesse Malott, "Moral Injury, Meaning Making, and Mental Health in Returning Veterans," *Journal of Clinical Psychology* 71 (2015): 229–40.

20. Brett Litz and Patricia Kerig, "Introduction to the Special Issue on Moral Injury: Conceptual Challenges, Methodological Issues, and Clinical Applications," *Journal of Traumatic Stress* 32 (2019): 341–49.

21. American Psychiatric Association, *Diagnostic and Statistical Manual of Mental Disorders*, 5th ed. (Washington, DC: APA, 2013).

22. Brett T. Litz, Nathan Stein, Eileen Delaney, Leslie Lebowitz, William P. Nash, Caroline Silva, and Shira Maguen, "Moral Injury and Moral Repair in War Veterans: A Preliminary Model and Intervention Strategy," *Clinical Psychology Review* 29 (2009): 695–706.

23. Sheila Frankfurt, Alanna Coady, Breanna Grunthal, Stephanie Larew-Ellickson, and Brett Litz, "Moral Injury in Service Members and Veterans," in *Routledge International Handbook of Military Psychology and Mental Health,* ed. U. Kumar (Oxford: Taylor and Francis, in press).

24. For more on this, see Robert Meagher, *Killing From the Inside Out: Moral Injury and Just War* (Eugene: Cascade, 2014).

25. Joseph M. Currier, Wesley McCormick, and Kent D. Drescher, "How Do Morally Injurious Events Occur? A Qualitative Analysis of Perspectives of Veterans with PTSD," *Traumatology* 21 (2015): 106–16.

26. See Zachary Moon, *Warriors Between Worlds: Moral Injuries and Identities in Crisis*, Emerging Perspectives in Pastoral Theology and Care (Lanham, MD: Lexington Books, 2019).

BIBLIOGRAPHY

American Psychiatric Association. *Diagnostic and Statistical Manual of Mental Disorders*, 3rd ed. Washington, DC: APA, 1980.

—. *Diagnostic and Statistical Manual of Mental Disorders*, 3rd revised ed. Washington, DC: APA, 1987.

—. *Diagnostic and Statistical Manual of Mental Disorders*, 4th ed. Washington, DC: APA, 1994.

—. *Diagnostic and Statistical Manual of Mental Disorders*, 5th ed. Washington, DC: APA, 2013.

Currier, Joseph, Jason Holland, and Jesse Malott. "Moral Injury, Meaning Making, and Mental Health in Returning Veterans." *Journal of Clinical Psychology* 71 (2015): 229–40.

Currier, Joseph M., Wesley McCormick, and Kent D. Drescher. "How Do Morally Injurious Events Occur? A Qualitative Analysis of Perspectives of Veterans with PTSD." *Traumatology* 21 (2015): 106–16.

Frankfurt, Sheila and Patricia Frazier. "A Review of Research on Moral Injury in Combat Veterans." *Military Psychology* 28 (2016): 318–30.

Frankfurt, Sheila, Alanna Coady, Breanna Grunthal, Stephanie Ellickson-Larew, and Brett Litz. "Moral Injury in Service Members and Veterans." In *Routledge International Handbook of Military Psychology and Mental Health.* Edited by U. Kumar. Oxford: Taylor and Francis, in press.

Frankfurt, Sheila, Bryann DeBeer, Sandra Morissette, Nathan Kimbrel, Heidi La Bash, and Eric Meyer. "Mechanisms of Moral Injury Following Military Sexual Trauma and Combat in Post-9/11 U.S. War Veterans." *Frontiers in Psychiatry* (2018). doi: 10.3389/fpsyt.2018.00520 .

Haley, Sarah A. "When the Patient Reports Atrocities: Specific Treatment Considerations of the Vietnam Veteran." *Archives of General Psychiatry* 30 (1974): 191–96.

Harris, J. Irene, Timothy Usset, Cory Voecks, Paul Thuras, Joseph Currier, Christopher Erbes. "Spiritually Integrated Care for PTSD: A Randomized Controlled Trial of 'Building Spiritual Strength.'" *Psychiatry Research* 267 (2018): 420–28.

Hodgson, Timothy J. and Lindsay B. Carey. "Moral Injury and Definitional Clarity: Betrayal, Spirituality and the Role of Chaplains." *Journal of Religion and Health* 56 (2017): 1212–228.

Kardiner, Abram. *The Traumatic Neuroses of War.* Washington, DC: US National Research Council, 1941.

Litz, Brett and Patricia Kerig. "Introduction to the Special Issue on Moral Injury: Conceptual Challenges, Methodological Issues, and Clinical Applications." *Journal of Traumatic Stress* 32 (2019): 341–49.

Litz, Brett, Nathan Stein, Eileen Delaney, Leslie Lebowitz, William Nash, Caroline Silva, and Shira Maguen. "Moral Injury and Moral Repair in War Veterans: A Preliminary Model and Intervention Strategy." *Clinical Psychology Review* 29 (2009): 695–706.

Meagher, Robert. *Killing From the Inside Out: Moral Injury and Just War.* Eugene: Cascade, 2014.

Moon, Zachary. *Warriors Between Worlds: Moral Injuries and Identities in Crisis.* Emerging Perspectives in Pastoral Theology and Care. Lanham, MD: Lexington Books, 2019.

Niederland, William. "The Problem of the Survivor: Part I, Some Remarks on the Psychiatric Evaluation of Emotional Disorders in Survivors of Nazi Persecution." *Journal of the Hillside Hospital* (1961): 233–47.

Shay, Jonathan. *Achilles in Vietnam: Combat Trauma and the Undoing of Character.* New York: Simon and Schuster, 1994.

Shay, Jonathan. "Moral injury." *Intertexts* 16 (2012): 59.

Chapter Three

Moral Injury and Its Causes, Symptoms, and Responses

Gabriella Lettini

Before theories and definitions, there are lives, people, and the stories people tell to make sense of their lives. Scholars try to organize these stories to better study and understand them. Sometimes they help us see connections and patterns where we saw only chaos, offering new glimpses of understanding and meaning, enabling the telling of other stories and the expression of more truths. Sometimes scholars limit or distort truth-telling, oversimplify and misrepresent narratives, overimpose their cultural assumptions, scientific biases, and points of view, and silence some voices. Writers, poets, musicians, and visual artists are often better equipped to paint the complexity of life and to respect the uniqueness and ambiguity of personal experiences that can be lost in statistics and quantitative studies. Yet, when interpretative processes have integrity, new fragments of truth are revealed.

Addressing moral injury needs to be located in this complex context, lest we believe simplistic narratives about what it is, who "discovered" it, who suffers from it, and how it can be engaged or even cured. Moral injury is a way to describe a complex human condition. As such, it cannot and should not be encompassed only by one definition, as the very way we frame a lived reality is always socially located, partial, and related to our agendas and exercise of power in the world. This means that any study of moral injury needs to be interdisciplinary, intersectional, contextualized, and polyvocal, and that no particular discipline, organization, or cultural context can claim an exclusionary stake to it.

These multiple and sometimes cacophonous perspectives should not be seen as de facto detrimental or a scientific failure. On the contrary, in my view, they respect the multiple ways in which people experience, frame, and address moral injury. From this multiplicity, we can learn more complex truths. We can also learn to respect the specific lenses of individual fields of inquiry and honor the located knowledge of different communities. At the same time, it is essential to continue to dialogue across fields of inquiry and different contexts to promote greater complexity of thought and nurture new learning.

Since 2010, in the United States we have witnessed a flourishing of studies on moral injury concerning the devastating effects of the wars in Iraq and Afghanistan on many US service members. Veterans have shared feelings of profound transgression of their sense of morality, even in situations when they were following orders or were fighting for survival. After witnessing the horrors of war and occupation, obeying orders they did not believe in, understanding the political fallacies that led to the suffering of countless soldiers and civilians, some soldiers felt deeply betrayed, could not forgive themselves, and could no longer make sense of the world. Veteran suicide rates kept rising. This is the context that led me to co-organize the Truth Commission on Conscience in War in 2010 and to coauthor *Soul Repair: Recovering from Moral Injury after War* as an urgent public call to understand and address the impact of the spiritual wounds of war in a moment when many in the United States kept forgetting the country was even at war. While there had been a lot of progress in understanding the physical and psychological effects of post- and ongoing traumatic stress, little had been written about the spiritual effects, often without reaching the general public and faith communities.

Recent US studies on moral injury have, at times, led some academics and parts of the general public to understand this phenomenon as primarily or uniquely related to war and soldiers. Although members of the military do not have exclusive rights to the experience of moral injury, they certainly have unique experiences of moral injury which still need to be addressed in dialogue concerning the experiences of the people they fought against. Even so, US studies on moral injury in relation to veterans suffer from some significant limitations, especially for those interested in a more complex understanding of moral injury. For example, such studies are obviously culturally located, and most often they do not engage their cultural assumptions and limitations, and even less admit their complex loyalties to the military machine of one of the most powerful imperial powers of the world. They have mostly been unilaterally focused on the effects of war on one side of the people involved in conflict, without dialogical engagement with scholars, veterans, and surviving civilians from other sides of the conflict and occupation. Another limitation of much US literature on moral injury is that it has given priority recognition and credibility to studies within the discipline of psychology while regarding other disciplines such as theology, ethics, and philosophy as secondary. Yet, while clinical studies about moral injury have gathered important data and have been useful in addressing veterans' challenges, they are often limited both by their relationship to the US military and Veterans Administration (VA) and by their understanding of moral injury as a sort of mental disorder or maladaptive adjustment that needs to engaged therapeutically and fixed.

As a theo-ethicist and spiritual leader, I believe that any human being can experience moral injury, as a victim, perpetrator, or very often victim/perpetrator. In a historical moment in which hundreds of migrants die each month crossing the Mediterranean Sea, children are separated from their parents and put in cages on the US borders, economic resources are created on the blood of the poor and hoarded by the wealthy, the effects of climate change and environmental racism are obvious, and violence against women, transgender, and nonbinary people is a daily reality, we need to acknowledge that structural violence takes many forms and its victims and perpetrators are everywhere. People develop moral injury not because they are soldiers, but because they are human beings with a moral conscience.

UNDERSTANDING MORAL INJURY THROUGH ITS CAUSES, SYMPTOMS, AND RESPONSES

Some of the pathologizing of moral injury in psychological and therapeutic terms within US clinical studies may be due to the fact that the definition emerged in relation to the study of PTSD.[1] Clinicians identified a condition that appeared in many veterans suffering from PTSD, but that escaped the symptoms of and treatments for it. There is now growing consensus that moral injury is not to be situated under the PTSD umbrella as they are different phenomena, even if they can coexist in the same person. PTSD is a trauma response with symptoms including: flashbacks, nightmares, dissociative episodes, fear, and hypervigilance. One can develop PTSD after any accident and traumatic experience. Moral injury is instead a valued-based injury, a negative self-judgment based on having transgressed core moral beliefs and values or of feeling betrayed by authorities, communities, and institutions. It is reflected in the destruction of a moral identity and loss of meaning. Symptoms include: shame, survivor guilt, depression, despair, addiction, distrust, anger, a need to make amends, and the loss of a desire to live. Moral injury is not a threat-based injury. One may experience it right after a specific incident or may come to the realization after years of struggle and reflection. Additionally, while PTSD is a reaction to some kind of trauma, one does not need to be directly involved in a violent or oppressive situation to develop moral injury; some people will develop it by feeling responsible or somehow morally tainted by actions taken by others.

Moral injury is also not just a synonym for guilt, burnout, or moral fatigue. People can carry guilt about particular actions they have taken or not taken without such guilt affecting their whole sense of moral self or leading them to doubt the existence of any moral universe. Moral injury can be developed by people in untenable service situations that lead to burnout (e.g., doctors, social workers, and journalists covering refugee crises), yet it is not one and the same with burnout. The former is a moral judgment; the latter is a reaction to the depletion of one's emotional and spiritual resources.

Within the US context, psychiatrist Jonathan Shay, author of *Achilles in Vietnam* and *Odysseus in America*, is often said to have coined the term "moral injury" in the 1990s.[2] Yet his pivotal work used ideas and terminology that were not new, as he acknowledged when he referred to moral injury's occurrence in ancient Greek literature. Ancient sacred texts from different traditions also tell stories of moral injury, as illustrated in the edited volume *Exploring Moral Injury in Sacred Texts*.[3] *Iniuria* (injury) was already an important concept in ancient Roman law, and it included injury to one's sense of honor, moral integrity, and human value. The concept of *ingiuria morale* has a long history, and it is still in use in contemporary Italian law. Bishop Joseph Butler wrote about "moral injury" in his sermons as early as the 1700s.[4] In 1981, Peter Marin wrote about "moral pain" in relation to the war in Vietnam, already foreshadowing some of the discussion on moral injury related to the conflicts/occupations in Iraq and Afghanistan:

> We seem as a society to have few useful ways to approach moral pain or guilt; it remains for us a form of neurosis or a pathological symptom, something to escape rather than something to learn from, a disease rather than, as it may well be for the vets—an appropriate if painful response to the past.[5]

It is possible to distinguish three major ways of understanding moral injury, while also noticing the points of connections among them:

1. The experience of being betrayed by a person in a position of authority in a significant situation. In this case, the one suffering from moral injury is the victim of a person, institution, or community by which they feel betrayed.
2. Self-betrayal of one's own moral universe and values, which generates deep internal suffering. On the one hand, this kind of moral suffering can be a healthy, necessary reaction, and a sign of moral strength. Conversely, such moral injury could be an extreme form of moral dissonance based on an initial false assumption—namely, that subjects learn from their actions that they are not who they thought they were, and thus develop maladaptive reactions to this new awareness. In this second case, we may rightly consider moral injury something to be

cured. I add to this category the complex suffering caused by understanding that a situation of systemic injustice has pushed one into a position where actions and ways of life cause extreme, often irreparable harm to other human beings. In this case, the subject is a victimizer yet also a victim of a larger system. Thus, moral injury is not merely individual, but also communal and inherently political.

3. The deep spiritual pain experienced by those who suffer under systems of injustice that harm their sense of self, human dignity, and integrity.

Shay addressed the first understanding of moral injury, articulating it as a "betrayal of what's right by someone who holds legitimate authority."[6] His use of "injury" was intentional, as his goal was to convince the military to treat this experience as a wound on par with bodily trauma. The language of injury and wounds, Shay argued, would be a significant step in treating psychological harm, as it would change our value hierarchies that praise physical injuries as sacrifice and heroism but consider psychological illness with suspicion and as a sign of weakness or lack of courage and moral fiber. Shay approached moral injury as an issue caused by the betrayal of the moral order by someone in a position of authority, specifically within the military. That person may have caused (or forced) others to betray their values. For Shay, when people in authority act in conflict with the stated values of their organization, they create a ripple effect that can be experienced with the force of a physical attack. Their betrayal of what is right is not just disappointing but destructive of the integrity of the group and individuals around them, putting people at odds with the ethical codes of their culture. A sense of lack of meaning can ensue.

Shay's definition is consistent with experiences of betrayal by people in positions of nonmilitary authority, including spiritual and moral authority (e.g., the experiences of victims of sexual violence within families, religious organizations, and educational institutions). Moral injury can be generated by the abuse itself, shattering the victim's faith in their supervisors and mentors and even in their previously held religious beliefs, or by the experiences that follow the exposure of the abuse. When institutions refuse to take abuse seriously and cover for the abuser, the victim can lose faith in the whole system and the moral order that it represented. All systems and moral universes may become meaningless or suspicious.

The second understanding of moral injury mentioned above can be helpful in addressing other kinds of suffering not encompassed by Shay's definition. Many of the witnesses I encountered while working on the Truth Commission on Conscience in War addressed the sense of betrayal by superiors and the military machine in general, but the focus of the veterans' anguish was the injury they had inflicted upon themselves by the choices or reflexive actions they took in war. It is important to reference both conscious choices and reflexive actions, since after World War II, US soldiers have been trained to shoot reflexively, bypassing, any moment of moral decision-making.

As the number of veterans' suicides reached an alarming high of at least twenty-two per day, much higher than for the civilian population, in December 2009 a group of VA clinical psychologists published a study that identified moral injury as a wound of war that is related but also different from PTSD. This study used the terminology of moral injury, but in a broader way than Shay's initial work. According to this study by Brett Litz and his colleagues, moral injury is not a pathology, but a spiritual wound caused by "perpetrating, failing to prevent, or bearing witness to acts that transgress deeply held moral beliefs and expectations." This study claimed that long-term impact can be "emotionally, psychologically, behaviorally, spiritually, and socially" devastating, sometimes lasting an entire lifetime, and it can foster internal conflict and self-condemnation so severe that their burdens become intolerable and lead to suicide.[7] This understanding of moral injury integrates betrayal from superiors in a high-stakes situation with the recognition of self-betrayal of one's conscience or sense of right and wrong.

Seen in this way, moral injury may also manifest itself as an irreversible challenge to one's assumed moral goodness. Duane Larson and Jeff Zust define moral injury as "the complex 'soul' wound that results from a person's inability to resolve the difference between the idealized values and their perceived experiences. This wound produces a chain of emotions and maladaptive behaviors that corrode character and damage an individual's capacity for living."[8] Michael Yandell, a veteran and theologian, described his moral injury as a "ripping away of the veil, a permanent showing, a continuous truth-telling"—a discovery that he was not who he thought he was, but something he never wanted to be.[9] When he saw the fear in the eyes of Iraqi civilians, he realized that the moral self he had thought he cultivated throughout his life was actually not there. In that absence or void, Yandell could not feel the presence of God. The unveiling Yandell described is not only an unveiling of whom he had become but of the fact that he was never who he thought he was. He did not think he could heal from such recognition or return to some lost wholeness. Rather, he had to come to terms with it and then look for transformation, not restoration.

Many veterans share a sense that moral injury is not reversible. When Rita Nakashima Brock and I decided to title our book on moral injury *Soul Repair*, it was with a sense that the repairing does not bring one back to a previous state of innocence, goodness, or well-being. It is not an undoing but the intentional engagement with one's sense of fractured moral self, an engagement that requires truth-telling and self-confession, ongoing reparation that can never be an erasure of what happened, and a different way of being in the world.

The second understanding of moral injury noted above can also refer to the spiritual effects of recognizing one's role in systemic oppression. One of the many discussions I had with veteran and author Camilo Mejía exemplifies this understanding.[10] I confessed that I deeply resonated with moral injury as I, a white European, had been struggling since a young age with a deep sense of inner laceration, borne of the awareness that my very life depended on the exploitation, suffering, and death of so many around the world and that Christian Europeans carried the burden of the gravest systematic atrocities in the history of the world. At the same time, I also had a sense of the many ways in which I, a woman from a poor working-class family and from a historically persecuted religious minority,[11] was also a victim of the same system of exploitation. I was both a victim and a perpetrator of heteropatriarchal white supremacist capitalism. I was also a powerless and desperate bystander. I asked Mejía if he thought I also could use the framework of moral injury to describe my inner struggle. He responded affirmatively but asked me to exercise caution. I could because moral injury is a way to describe a set of human reactions, a spiritual struggle, which clearly do not occur only in relation to war. I could because even in relation to war, the whole society that sends people to war should bear the moral burden for the pain and destruction caused by war. I should exercise caution, however, because taking the life of another human being is a uniquely harrowing experience that cannot be understood by someone who has not had the experience. He also told me that he thought a generalized sense of moral injury might much more easily be set aside when convenient. This was not the case for him. He felt that moral injury was like a backpack that he could not take on and off as he wanted, but something he had to carry constantly and forever. I respected this answer. Yet, for me today, the difference may not be in the nature of the action that generated moral injury but in the subject's moral reactions to the "backpack" of moral injury. Some veterans never develop moral injury after killing an enemy, even as some civilians spiritually struggle their whole life because of their complex relationship with the systemic violence of racism, economic exploitation, and climate change. The realization of one's culpability in the world's greatest crimes can be devastating. I have encountered that deep level of spiritual suffering in myself, my students, and communities. Perhaps we should consider moral injury's suffering on a spectrum, which allows us to acknowledge different experience without denying the particularity of any person's suffering.

Mejía's image of moral injury as a backpack he could not take on and off but had to carry forever resonates with another image that I have engaged as a white educator since I first came to the United States. Peggy MacIntosh uses the image of a "knapsack" to discuss white privilege.[12] This knapsack is where white people carry their privileges without being aware of it. This knapsack can indeed contain other privileges in relation to gender, class, ethnicity, sexual orientation, abilities, and speciesism. Perhaps moral injury is a healthy response to seeing and taking responsibility for the knapsack of one's systemic privileges.

The third understanding of moral injury noted above is one that has been less thoroughly articulated and addressed in recent literature on the subject, yet seems to be an ever-present thread in memoirs and fiction. Jewish Italian writer Primo Levi puzzled over why people like him, who in Nazi concentration camps had been subjected to such cruelty and powerlessness, often feel shame and guilt over what they witnessed:

> It was the same shame which we knew so well, which submerged us after the selections, and every time we had to witness or undergo an outrage: the shame that the Germans never knew, the shame which the just man experiences when confronted by a crime committed by another, and he feels remorse because of its existence, because of its having been irrevocably introduced into the world of existing things, and because his will has proven nonexistent or feeble and was incapable of putting up a good defense. [13]

The shame comes from a removal of the veil, which shows human nature in all of its brutality. And yet Levi was also concerned to stress that in some contexts the difference between victim and victimizer was not ambiguous:

> I know that I was a guiltless victim, and I was not a murderer. I know that the murderers existed, and not only in Germany, and still exist retired or on active duty, and that to confuse them with their victim is a moral disease or an aesthetic affectation or a sinister sign of complicity: above all, it is precious service rendered (intentionally or not) to the negators of truth . . . confusing the two roles means wanting to becloud our need for justice at its foundation. [14]

These words suggest that it is essential to keep exploring moral injury as a spiritual suffering that accompanies physical and psychological trauma without equating moral injury with that trauma.

Reflecting further on moral suffering under systems of injustice, Jessica Vazquez Torres, a self-defined 1.5 generation, English-as-a-second-language, queer, Latinx of Puerto Rican descent, addressed her experiences of moral injury in relation to white supremacy and racism in the United States. She asserts that one should never speak of racism without also speaking about white supremacy, an example of "structural arrangements that misuse power in ways that benefit whites and destroy all non-whites."[15] Vazquez Torres experienced moral injury at the hands of white supremacy in the invisibilization of her identity as Latinx and in the discovery of her own internalized oppressions in relation to race, gender, and sexual orientation.

Vazquez Torres articulates how white supremacy pushes different oppressed groups to silence and to compete with each other instead of fighting white supremacy. This is one of the many moral injuries inflicted by white supremacy. The moral injury that white supremacy causes in people of color is a questioning of the very foundation of their reality and identity. To suffer moral injury is to know that one is a worthy human being, and yet not to be treated like one; to know that one is a citizen and has human rights, and yet not to experience such rights on a daily basis; and to know that one's people have a history or histories, and yet never read about them in history books. Both egregious acts of racism and racist microaggressions continue to fertilize the soil of white supremacy and deepen the wounds of moral injury.

CONCLUSION

The way one addresses moral injury is related to the way one understands it within their particular spiritual and moral universe. There is no universal approach to engaging moral injury, as there is no universal definition of it. Multiple approaches are needed to account for the specificity of different contexts and lived experiences, as well as people's different spiritual, religious, and philosophical belief systems.

If one understands moral injury as a problem of the individual, then one will look only at individual approaches and focus on ways to correct it or make it more bearable. Some situations may warrant this approach (e.g., the case of responsibility in death caused by a car accident). Unfortunately, within the context of the US military, the burden for the moral injury caused by war is still predominantly placed on the soldiers themselves. The understanding of moral injury currently embraced by many programs for veterans focuses too narrowly on their need to forgive themselves and reframe reality so that they can move on and be reintegrated in civilian life. The emphasis is on normalization. This is the case with the model known as "Adaptive Disclosure," a type of cognitive behavior therapy with the treatment goal of helping veterans examine their self-narratives to reclaim their goodness and self-worth.[16]

I find it useful, however, to differentiate between curing moral injury and finding ways to name, address, engage, and live with it. This means that a range of techniques that have been used with veterans of war, such as storytelling, journaling, art-making, rituals of purification, nature immersions and somatic therapies, and theological reflection, should be seen as tools to engage with moral injury, not as cures for it. Such approaches can help people to face their inner struggles and create meaningful narratives, so they can engage the causes of their injury. People may find it helpful to engage critically with their own belief systems in order to reframe themselves and their actions within a belief narrative. Such a narrative may involve the need for penance, as well as forgiveness by a transcendent God or by transformative community of love. If one understands moral injury as also inherently relational and collective, however, this personal approach is necessary but inadequate, as it eases personal pain but does not address the broader harm done and does not engage in transformative actions to change the conditions that created systemic violence and injustice. One could get trapped in easy self-absolution or in a perpetual loop of easing and intensifying the suffering of more injury.

For veterans such as Camilo Mejía to be able to live with moral injury without causing more suffering and destruction to themselves or others, they must become aware of their injury, name it, and carry its burden at all times. Even the morally injured need to perceive, and bear witness to, the damage they have inflicted on others, focusing on the others' pain and not only on their personal suffering. Such a process would be unbearable and fruitless if not carried out collectively and politically, with the whole communities and societies that created the conditions for moral injury. Honestly addressing in community the pain caused to others, and being engaged in repairing the damage caused on a systemic level, can make one's moral injury more bearable, and even transformative.

The most effective responses to moral injury may involve assuming responsibility—responsibility as both the admission of culpability and the ability to respond to violence and injustice, while refusing to be defined by them. To understand the depth of moral injury means to know that there is no shortcut to forgiveness of self and others, as premature forgiveness requires amnesia or anesthesia to the full extent of the harm inflicted.

Even with the lack of easy solutions, moral injury may provide an inherent critique of all that is oppressive and thus may be necessary for the regeneration of the fractured social fibers of humanity. Moral injury can lead us to reimagine who we are and who we could be as human beings and in relation to all beings. This engagement may be the only pathway to justice, healing, and even human survival. And spiritual communities must keep creating, nurturing, and protecting spaces where these tasks can be accomplished.

NOTES

1. I use PTSD as it is widely used in the literature related to veterans of war, yet the terminology of posttraumatic Stress (PTS) seems more appropriate in order to avoid pathologizing reactions to trauma. Additionally, even PTS is a reductive definition, as in many contexts, trauma is ongoing, like for people living under occupation or systemic racism.

2. Jonathan Shay, *Achilles in Vietnam: Combat Trauma and the Undoing of Character* (New York: Touchstone, 1994); Jonathan Shay, *Odysseus in America: Combat Trauma and the Trials of Homecoming* (New York: Scribner, 2002).

3. Joseph McDonald, ed., *Exploring Moral Injury in Sacred Texts*, Studies in Religion and Theology (London: Jessica Kingsley, 2017).
4. Joseph Butler, "Forgiveness of Injuries," in *Fifteen Sermons and Other Writings on Ethics*, ed. David McNaughton (Oxford: Oxford University Press, 2017), 75–83.
5. Peter Marin, "Living in Moral Pain," in *The Vietnam Reader*, ed. Walter Capps (New York: Routledge, 1991), 43.
6. Jonathan Shay, "Casualties," *Daedalus* 140, no. 3 (Summer 2011): 183.
7. Brett T. Litz, Nathan Stein, Eileen Delaney, Leslie Lebowitz, William P. Nash, C. Silva, and S. Maguen, "Moral Injury and Moral Repair in War Veterans: A Preliminary Model and Intervention Strategy," *Clinical Psychology Review* 29, no. 8 (2009): 700, 695.
8. Duane Larson and Jeff Zust, *Care for the Sorrowing Soul: Healing Moral Injuries from Military Service and Implications for the Rest of Us* (Eugene, OR: Cascade, 2017), 93.
9. Michael Yandell, "Hope in the Void: How Veterans with Moral Injury Can Help Us Face Reality," *Plough Quarterly Magazine* 8 (Spring 2017). https://www.plough.com/en/topics/justice/nonviolence/hope-in-the-void.
10. See Brock and Lettini, *Soul Repair*, 113.
11. The Waldensian Church in Italy, heir of the "heretical" movement borne in the twelfth century and persecuted through the nineteenth century. Italian Waldensians were granted civil rights only in 1848. For a historical overview of the Waldensian movement, see Giorgio Tourn, *You Are My Witnesses: The Waldensians across 800 Years* (Torino: Claudiana, 1989).
12. Peggy MacIntosh, "White Privilege: Unpacking the Invisible Knapsack," in *On Privilege, Fraudulence, and Teaching as Learning: Selected Essays 1981–2019* (New York: Routledge, 2019), 29–34.
13. Primo Levi, *The Drowned and the Saved*, trans. Raymond Rosenthal (New York: Vintage, 1989), 48–49.
14. Levi, *The Drowned and Saved*, 49.
15. Jessica Vazquez Torres, "Does Moral Injury Have a Color? On Moral Injury and Race in the United States," paper presented at the American Academy of Religion Annual Meeting, Moral Injury Group (San Diego: CA, 2014).
16. Brett T. Litz, Leslie Lebowitz, Matt J. Gray, and William P. Nash, *Adaptive Disclosure: A New Treatment for Military Trauma, Loss and Moral Injury* (New York: Guilford, 2015).

BIBLIOGRAPHY

Brock, Rita Nakashima and Gabriella Lettini. *Soul Repair: Recovering from Moral Injury after War*. Boston: Beacon, 2012.

Butler, Joseph. "Forgiveness of Injuries." In *Fifteen Sermons and Other Writings on Ethics*, ed. David McNaughton. Oxford: Oxford University Press, 2017.

Larson, Duane and Jeff Zust. *Care for the Sorrowing Soul: Healing Moral Injuries from Military Service and Implications for the Rest of Us*. Eugene, OR: Cascade, 2017.

Levi, Primo. *The Drowned and the Saved.* Translated by Raymond Rosenthal. New York: Vintage, 1989.

Litz, Brett T., Leslie Lebowitz, Matt J. Gray, and William P. Nash. *Adaptive Disclosure: A New Treatment for Military Trauma, Loss and Moral Injury*. New York: Guilford, 2015.

Litz, Brett T., N. Stein, E. Delaney, L. Lebowitz, W. P. Nash, C. Silva, and S. Maguen. "Moral Injury and Moral Repair in War Veterans: A Preliminary Model and Intervention Strategy." *Clinical Psychology Review* 29, no. 8 (2009): 695–706.

MacIntosh, Peggy. "White Privilege: Unpacking the Invisible Knapsack." Pages 29–34 in *On Privilege, Fraudulence, and Teaching as Learning: Selected Essays 1981–2019*. New York: Routledge, 2019.

Marin, Peter. "Living in Moral Pain." Pages 40–53 in *The Vietnam Reader*. Edited by Walter Capps. New York: Routledge, 1991.

McDonald, Joseph, ed. *Exploring Moral Injury in Sacred Texts.* Studies in Religion and Theology. London: Jessica Kingsley, 2017.

Shay, Jonathan. *Achilles in Vietnam: Combat Trauma and the Undoing of Character.* New York: Scribner, 1984.

—. "Casualties." *Daedalus* 140, no. 3 (Summer 2011): 179–88.

—. *Odysseus in America. Combat Trauma and the Trials of Homecoming*. New York: Scribner, 2002.

Tourn, Giorgio. *You Are My Witnesses: The Waldensians across 800 Years*. Torino: Claudiana, 1989.

Vazquez Torres, Jessica. "Does Moral Injury Have a Color? On Moral Injury and Race in the United States." Paper presented at the American Academy of Religion Annual Meeting, Moral Injury Group, San Diego, CA, 2014.

Yandell, Michael. "Hope in the Void: How Veterans with Moral Injury Can Help Us Face Reality." *Plough Quarterly Magazine* (Spring 2017). https://www.plough.com/en/topics/justice/nonviolence/hope-in-the-void.

Part II

Depicting Moral Injury (Ancient and Modern Portrayals)

Chapter Four

Feast or Famine

A Veteran's Reflection on Moral Injury and Recovery

Tyler Boudreau

In Iraq, as an officer working in the operations section of an infantry battalion, the bulk of my deployment in 2004 was spent in a space called the Command Operations Center (COC). This was a space through which all information flowed and missions were orchestrated, a space from which units and patrols were dispatched, directed, overseen, reinforced, resupplied, and so forth, and when combat ensued, the COC was the place where commanders would often position themselves to assess tactical situations, make decisions, and issue orders. In short, the COC lay at the heart of all our operations. The people who filled this space around the clock on a daily basis (i.e., operations and intelligence personnel, radio operators, medics, guards, clerks, etc.) would always find themselves in one of two dramatically different states of being—acute boredom, when our Area of Operations (AO) was quiet, or heart-racing fervor, when the AO was teeming with violence.

There was a phrase thrown around the COC to describe this perpetual swinging between extremes of high and low activity, a phrase spoken frequently and in a tone falling somewhere between jocular and peevish: "feast or famine." These were the words used over and over by troops and officers alike. *Feast or famine*. At the time, I didn't give a great deal of thought to the expression or our casual use of it. I accepted it as I believe it was intended—a way of articulating an evident pattern of oscillation between long stretches of waiting with nothing much to do, decide, or think about, and sudden frenzies of urgent events, calls for support, intense exchanges, frantic reports, frustration, panic, and so on, always thrown upon us all at once. However, looking back on those days, on the actions we took and the attitudes we carried, I must admit I've come to question the innocence of this phrase. Can I be sure which of these extremes was the *feast* and which was the *famine*?

After all, feasts are generally associated with positive social events with an abundance of food, drink, and mirth. A feast suggests a gathering of happy and healthy people. On the other hand, famines are rarely thought of as anything but terrible episodes of scarcity and death. So why then did we flip the connotations of these words in Iraq? Why did we so consistently set the range of violence along this particular continuum? Why did we characterize the fighting days as bountiful and, conversely, peaceful days as dearth? The phrase, *feast or famine*, may have been spoken with intentional irony or maybe it was just a poorly applied metaphor that needn't be overly scrutinized. Either way, I believe it would be rash to dismiss this paradox as irrelevant because, regardless of one's intention, the words *feast* and *famine* had to settle themselves in the consciousness aligned either with combat or quietude. So which was which? It may be impossible to declare each individual's own interpretation; however, given the frequency of the utterance combined with the military's assiduous cultivation of enthusiasm for battle, I suspect, for all of us in the COC, that the "feast" could quite reasonably be assumed to be the fight. Now while this minor incongruity cannot, in itself, be the key to recovery from some form of moral disturbance, it may offer a glimpse into the obstacles one will face along the way.

MORAL DISTURBANCE

I understand a moral disturbance as the result of a harmful act perpetrated by an individual at the behest of a larger societal institution. The institutional origin of an operation and the orders it comprises tends to give individual acts of violence a sense of legitimacy while simultaneously creating a degree of moral and legal ambiguity. It seems clear enough from historical examples that official orders, by themselves, cannot exculpate those who commit clear crimes against humanity; however, in occupation operations there are far more examples of acts committed that are harmful in some way—and morally problematic—but not technically illegal. This makes the occupation environment extremely difficult to navigate morally. One of the profound difficulties of a felt moral disturbance lies in the fact that the disturbance itself must be expressed and mediated through shared language and shared moral frameworks, and so any strategy of recovery will necessarily bear an epistemological component.[1] This difficulty is profound precisely because there is no understanding of either language or morality that is shared universally.

What, for instance, do the words "recovery" or "healing" mean to people from different social, cultural, political, or economic backgrounds? What do these words actually look like, or sound like, or even feel like "on the ground" in real life? How might we describe the goal of these therapeutic processes in more tangible terms? How many different ways might a person imagine the ideals of morality and, therefore, the ideals of moral repair? Whatever strategies are employed, I believe it's imperative to confront the epistemological assumptions that lie beneath such strategies, in order to reconcile one's sense of the problem with the methods one applies.

This chapter bears two important characteristics that I'd like to announce from the outset. The first is that both my understanding of moral disturbances and the processes of recovery are derived through a social constructionist epistemology.[2] The second is that my exploration into these issues does not come by way of clinical experience with others; rather, this is a description of my own journey, understandings, and approaches to recovery accumulated over the years since coming home from Iraq. It was only when I went to address my own moral angst that I began to notice the absence of any established framework that I could readily apply. This forced me to contend with some uncomfortable questions. For example, why do I experience moral consternation now, after the fact, after the acts have been committed, after the damage has been done and the blood has been spilled? Why do I now regard these same deeds as harmful where I once thought them honorable? Why do I now question the very combat scenarios I trained for as though I had no way of anticipating their flaws prior to my deployment?

Clearly the interpretive framework that put me into this moral distress in the first place could not be reapplied to deliver me back out. I needed a new way of understanding. This was, in fact, the actuating notion that pushed me toward the ideas presented below, which will proceed along two parallel arcs. First, I will offer a general discussion of the epistemological and discursive aspects of recovery, and second, a personal narrative, a description of sorts, of how I've compiled and stitched together a bricolage of strategies that have helped me to hold (not purge) this moral disturbance with care (not contempt) and take on the necessary life-long work that transforms theoretical strategies into daily life practices directed toward moral repair. The tension here is between self-care and social responsibility, a tension that is, in my view, the most crucial piece in any recovery project intended to address a moral disturbance. Genuine moral repair cannot be imagined and certainly not accomplished without an urgent commitment to both.

THE PURSUIT OF MEANING

After I resigned my commission and left the military in 2005, I began scouring my memories of Iraq obsessively, doggedly, for years, as though I needed to account for every tactical decision ever made, every order issued, every political speech and policy shift, every roadside bomb, every shot fired, every body felled, every detail from the beginning to the end of the occupation, as though a static compilation of facts and figures could ever aid in my recovery, or that this fanatical pursuit of "meaning" could ever lead to salvation. I'd cloaked myself in contemplation very similarly to how we'd layered ourselves with steel in Iraq. From the fences on the Forward Operating Bases to the armor on our backs, we were entirely masked from our environment, and our environment, in turn, was masked from us. Now it's certainly likely I will be taking inventory of my memories of Iraq for the rest of my days, but I've come to suspect that memories lose their meaning or meaning loses its value when separated from the backdrop of new experiences. So in order to remember meaningfully, one must push that contemplating body into motion, especially into unfamiliar social contexts, so as to give one's memories and contemplations the opportunity to produce continuously new applications rather than allowing them to fester uselessly in an isolated mind, serving only to perpetuate one's anguish or nostalgia.

On the other hand, the pursuit of new understandings of an event, new vantage points, and new information can be unsettling because even a single event in one's life experience cannot be too rigorously redefined or distorted without altering the dimensions of one's entire social universe, including one's own identity. The instant one's perspective is altered, the order of everything, as well as one's moral standing, are suddenly thrown into disarray, and the distress is only compounded when one is unexpectedly accosted by a creeping sense of culpability. It was far easier to avoid critique when my world felt stable and comprehensible and more congruous with my beliefs. And it was certainly more appealing to be thought of as a protector, warrior, hero, or at the very least a man in the service of his country. The problem, however, was that the world I'd been regarding from that single vantage point bore neither dimension nor humanity. And the beliefs I'd been holding as a young man were not really beliefs at all, not substantial ones at any rate—more so ideological adornments for my presentation of self. Suddenly, in the act of undoing my world, I perceived in the mirror the face of a perpetrator rather than a protector, a man who'd been feasting on violence and calling it sacrifice. Here lies the difficulty in applying new meanings to an event in the aftermath. In whatever way I choose to define a given event and the words employed to understand it, I must apply those same definitions to my identity; otherwise, I force myself into unproductive and unhealthy cognitive dissonance. The question, "What is the meaning of this event?" cannot be separated from "Who am I?" as a participant of the event. These are not two questions, after all, but one. So my search for meaning and a process of recovery required an epistemological inquiry into the very ways I'd narrated my experiences and my sense of self.

One problem with such an inquiry, often unanticipated, is that questions that are strictly theoretical, answered or not, don't alter the material or social conditions of one's existence. The array of new definitions and understandings that I'd compiled over the years after Iraq and figured for "truth" had no way of manifesting themselves in my daily life. Consequently, these understandings of my time in the military amounted to nothing more meaningful than a highly detailed mythology whose only application could ever only be the production of more mythology. I refer to these historical moments as "mythology" even though they occurred in real life because they'd become untethered from all present and ongoing social interactions and so rendered any critique of the experience essentially valueless in terms of producing tangible change for the world and, in turn, for myself.

If, however, knowledge is understood as coconstructed through interacting bodies that are situated in particular places and times with specific worldviews and experiences, then logically the pursuit of knowledge must be understood as situated, as well, requiring collective retrieval and sense-making. What is significant about this point is that there is reciprocal constitution occurring between the individuals constructing narratives and the narratives themselves. In other words, as historians of our own identities, we cannot produce any sort of personal or historical account of our lives without, in the process, altering the very identities of which we are seeking more stable understandings. So the analysis of my self in Iraq was tainted from the start without my even noticing, since the interpretive frameworks I'd been implementing were also narratively produced and internalized at some earlier period in my life and had never, themselves, been interrogated. I wasn't noticing the moral migration of my sense of self in the process of creating a new story of my time in Iraq because I took for granted the stability of identity in a changing environment. This was a problem that would eventually come home to roost.

I want to emphasize the mediation that must take place between people, groups, organizations, communities, and society as a whole. For people to convey their internal experiences of external events to other people in understandable terms, their stories must be conveyed across the foundations of that which has already been shared. There must already be in place shared narratives, shared interpretive frameworks and values, shared language, and other shared mediating acts; otherwise, the story will make no sense to the audience and the teller will become unrecognizable as a member of that society, consequently placing one's identity in jeopardy. This recognizability and acceptance of one's narrative as legitimate is crucial, both to one's social existence in general and to the recovery process in particular. Moral repair cannot even begin if one isn't seen, if one's story is not believed and legitimized, and if one is utterly cut off from society. Whatever recovery strategy one chooses, it will inevitably involve some dramatic changes in perception. A static epistemological orientation will prove a formidable opponent to such change. But if one allows knowledge, narrative, and identity to be understood as inseparable, mutually constitutive, embodied, and so always evolving, then the possibilities for innovating worldviews and daily life practices become much more accessible.

For me, experiencing this moral disturbance from Iraq created two apparently contradictory needs: a need to be understood, believed, and recognized by others, pulling me in one direction, and pulling me in the other direction, a need to change, to grow, and to become a different person who is far more circumspect about such morally contentious events in the future. The years I spent analyzing in solitude were eventually fruitful, but the fruit didn't bear until after I extended my process beyond this paper-thin critique based on an incoherent interpretive framework and unsupported by any action whatsoever in my daily life (since my daily life had been reduced to little more than obsessive analysis). I began to feel the centripetal force of a mind moving in circles, covering the same ground over and over, with time ticking by, stripping that very ground of any sound, smell, taste, or anything else tangibly felt in my body. Iraq was slipping away from a freshly lived experience, to flickering memories, to the flotsam of ideas and arguments about Iraq adrift in my consciousness, growing more scattered and hazy by the day, and more detached from my contemporaneous reality.

THE BECOMING OF TRUTH

A new question was needed to disrupt this cycle of inquiry and break myself out from the captivity of endless contemplation. The question I fell upon was this: What am I to do? This turns out to be another version of the same questions I'd been posing from the start; however, the vital distinction is that this question demanded a response that would supplement my static thoughts with action, thereby transforming being into becoming, and enabling change. For me, the most immediate obstacle to this question—What am I to do?—turned out to be my own identity. I'd certainly become more concerned about social justice over time, and yet, in isolation, my analytical exercises were not so very different from the training exercises I'd done for so many years in the military. Both were essentially exercises of the imagination in that they were always conducted in a vacuum of hypotheticals. Neither my critiques nor my training had any real-world consequences for me or anyone else. In training, the interactions were always staged (and so imaginary), and after Iraq, inside my house, inside my head, endlessly analyzing, there were very few interactions to speak of at all. But it is within the perpetual unfolding of consequences and interactions all over the world where we find true meaning, the kind of meaning that moves and morphs in daily life and produces new social landscapes and moral dynamics, not the meanings found in data and texts that hold their poses indefinitely, irrespective of context.

My entire belief system was essentially fantasy. And so again the question arose: What am I to do? What could I do? And with whom? I'd turned away from my community in the military and those who supported my role as a soldier. My sense of what was important, or humorous, or sad, or beautiful, or ethical had changed so radically, and my deconstruction of self had been so extreme, I'd unwittingly torn myself down to the point of being virtually unrecognizable to the people who once made up my social universe, and that included me. I struggled to recognize and understand the person peering back at me in the mirror. The loss of my community meant the loss of an audience for my narrative. And since I was inherently a member of my own lost audience, I'd lost myself, as well. It was at this juncture that I realized the most difficult task in this process of recovery was not going to be the deconstruction of self; rather, it would be the reconstruction of self in some recognizable way. Power structures and one's connection to them are relatively easy to dismantle intellectually. But what mantle, I asked, might I wrap myself in now so as to be seen and accepted in a new social sphere or community which, at that point, was not yet known to me?

I have found that one's sense of identity and agency suffers the greatest disruption in the moral disturbances under discussion in this volume. One's moral framework is so integral to one's identity, a collapse of one necessarily implies a collapse of the other. That is why I view a moral disturbance as a loss of self and why moral repair is, for me, a remaking rather than merely a rethinking. But this task in life is not as simple as it appears in print. And so I ask again: What am I to do? The question rears its head incessantly as we are all in perpetual states of becoming. It's crucial to remember, however, that not all people are becoming under the same material and social conditions, and so reforming one's worldview is not enough to ameliorate the moral distress. One's identity includes a body that cannot be changed, a body that may or may not have access to resources and support. Recovery itself will often be impeded by the politicized physical categories one inhabits. What is significant about this point, for me, is that in the process of dismantling and reformulating my narrative and ethical viewpoints, I realized that my own moral disturbance could not be exclusively a product of my participation in the occupation of Iraq; it had to include my participation in the systems of oppression at home as well.

I would say, further, that the latter is exactly what primed me for the former. Quietly present in one's "truth" and in the personal narration of one's history are the interpretive frameworks that shape that story and surreptitiously install a range of narrative constraints that prevent the story from straying outside particular ideological lines. Meanwhile, personal narratives are still thought of and described as truths, sometimes even sacred truths. But how can I be certain this "truth" is my own? How do I know this "truth" doesn't belong to an institution, system, or society in which I've been participating and conditioned? The occupation of Iraq could only make sense to me if I'd already come to understand myself, others, and the world in a very specific and inflexible way. The value of knowledge as doing is, in part, the rejection of static ideals and identity paragons, making room for more diverse (always imperfect and incomplete) understandings of self. It was the rigidity in my narrative identity that enabled a willful naïveté that led me into a morally dubious situation. What was needed most to contend with that moral disturbance and to become a more socially aware and productive person was what I would call narrative agility.

NARRATIVE AGILITY AND SOCIAL RESPONSIBILITY

While it's clearly impossible to narrate every detail of a lived experience, there is a persistent and popular notion that personal narratives generally capture and relay the most salient aspects of an experience, and so are accepted as essentially factual summaries of past events. This is a problematic notion in that it creates resistance to change, a resistance that is activated by the very same ideological constraints responsible for shaping the narrative from the beginning. Underlying that resistance is the epistemological and narrative rigidity that brought on the moral disturbance, and it is that same rigidity that prevents moral growth. Narrative agility does not imply a steering around a moral disturbance—that is actually the function of rigidity—rather, narrative agility enables an envelopment of the disturbance into one's identity so that it may serve as a platform from which new perspectives and new ways of being can be developed. Given the vastness and complexity of any experience and the limited time one has to describe it, a narrative must, by necessity, conceal far more than it could ever reveal. This is the natural relationship between time and narrative, not a condition to be overcome, but an opportunity to dig deep into one's consciousness, to mine one's memories in search of alternative details that can and will alter the narrative itself, its meanings, its moral implications, and the possibilities for change that all of these afford.

The expression "feast or famine"—as it was employed so consistently in the COC—relied on the rigid narratives of both the occupation of Iraq and the identities of its participants. There was no opportunity for any customized interpretations of those words or any option to question the expression itself. In that context and culture, circumscribed within those ponderous ideological walls, the "feast" could only be imagined as the fight. To tamper with that metaphor, insignificant though it may appear in writing, would be to risk irreparable damage to a soldier's understanding of self and his or her role in the occupation. Under such violent circumstances, this is a forceful constraint on a personal narrative. Any claim to be a "warrior" within a culture of warriors will certainly prove less convincing when accompanied by the further claim that days of fighting and violence should only be thought of as moral famine. I imagine such a sentiment would not land well in the military community, effectively leaving that community two choices: accept the claim, which would force them to question their own morality, or, reject both the claim and the claimant altogether, leaving their own narrative identities intact.

Removing myself from the military environment indeed increased my opportunities for narrative reform. But again, in the process of deconstructing my narrative, I found my identity still deeply entrenched in a vast regime of oppressive social systems at home that not only correlate with wars and occupations but create the necessity for them. This makes it virtually impossible to isolate and swear off any one aspect of a society's constitution, its collective narratives, or its structures of power, without creating multiple ruptures in one's consciousness and identity. If, for example, I choose to understand America's presence in Iraq as a morally bankrupt operation then I must also accept the social dynamics that precipitated that operation as morally bankrupt. The same social dynamics that produced the conflict with Iraq also produced my willingness to take part in it. The problem is that I cannot resign my way out of society as I'd resigned from the military. So any recovery strategy I might adopt now will have to address directly and concretely not only my actions and attitudes in Iraq, but also my actions and attitudes at home. In short, the work of moral repair is foremost about social responsibility.

From my perspective, what remains most important in the conversation about recovery from a moral disturbance is the pursuit of responsibility—not a passive acceptance of responsibility for one's past actions, but a committed, impassioned, active responsibility for one's past and future roles in society. Morality is an inherent component of social coexistence. A moral disturbance is not an inner conflict; it is a conflict produced within the vast array of mutually constitutive relationships between individuals, social structures, and the various discourses and power dynamics within them. One cannot progress from a moral disturbance without understanding the social conditions that contributed to its occurrence in the first place and the meanings that people have applied to those conditions.

For me, this emphasis on social responsibility prompts some reluctance about the word "injury" in a conversation about moral transgressions. There is no question that many of the morally troubling acts committed by soldiers were encouraged or directly ordered by higher authorities, and so in that sense, I acknowledge and agree that these acts call for collective responsibility, not strictly individual responsibility. I would, however, caution against a disproportionate focus on the "injury" over responsibility within any process of recovery to avoid the potential fetishization of a veteran's moral distress or a faulty conflation of it with experiences of "survivors guilt," which produces a very different form of anxiety and doesn't demand the same kind of simultaneous engagement with harm felt and harm done. My hunch is that the overwhelming rates of veteran suicides after Iraq and Afghanistan prompted a discourse that heavily (and appropriately) prioritized self-forgiveness. While it is absolutely necessary to direct care inward in order to progress emotionally and function in daily life, there is significant risk that the term "moral *injury*" will begin to sound and function very much like the public discourse on posttraumatic stress—a discourse of sympathy for veterans, but seldom, if ever, a sympathy for the people of Iraq or Afghanistan who were harmed by those veterans.

There's no question that communal support and sympathy is necessary for recovery from a moral disturbance or a traumatic experience. But this is a discussion about moral *transgressions* (first and foremost), and neither the perpetrators nor the public can or should expect to see any genuine recovery take place without putting those harmed at the center of the conversation. If a moral transgression has been committed, then one's moral compass must be realigned with one's new path through an attitude of responsibility. Feelings of contrition are not enough to reconcile fully oneself with one's deeds. Contrition and apologies do not mark the end of this conversation, but the beginning, and together function as the foundation for continual reparative actions. The most important idea to hold inviolate in one's mind is that whatever harm was perpetrated, the pain, loss, and grief caused by these perpetrations will remain felt by those harmed forever, no matter how long they live or how well they've managed to cope over time; therefore, the perpetrator's commitment to moral reform must also go on forever.

CONCLUSION

Grappling with a moral disturbance isn't primarily about personal atonement, coming to terms with one's own wrongdoings, or finding peace within oneself. These are all desirable outcomes, certainly, and may even inspire and initiate a process of recovery, but in my view these cannot be the objective of that process. If one's involvement in a publicly sanctioned but morally problematic social system has produced a moral disturbance, I believe that disturbance represents a far more searing commentary on society than it does on the individual. Ultimately, the true objective of one's grappling and processing must be to alter the moral conditions of the society that created such vast amounts of moral disturbance across its own citizenry.

Over the years, throughout my own process, I've noticed a great deal of emphasis placed on the idea of communal healing, with which I agree absolutely, but I've also noticed that the stress on "communal" is generally directed toward community members in terms of the support they can offer individual veterans, but seldom toward the veterans themselves in terms of the support they can offer in return. The moral burden of society must be carried by all of its citizens, for all of its activities and operations, and it is not unsympathetic to suggest that the participants of military occupations need to be included in that number. One cannot claim a moral disturbance without conceding the harmful acts that have been committed, and further, accepting one's share in the work of genuine community healing.

In Iraq, we spoke of feasts and famines. One feast meant a man's decapitation, the next feast, an incineration. In another feast, bodies were burned and blown to bits. And all of the feasts to follow were similarly tragic—limbs lost, organs ruptured, children orphaned, families displaced, and so on. These were the "feasts" of Iraq. And what did we call those times when we were sitting in the COC, staring numbly at the walls, waiting for our next feast? We called them famines. We called them famines because that was the culture from which we came, and that culture was created at home in America, not in Iraq. If we're going to have a conversation about the moral disturbances felt by veterans, if we're going to dig into the transgressions committed against the people of Iraq and Afghanistan, and finally, if we're going to explore various approaches to recovery for veterans, then we'll need to begin by understanding both the transgressions and the recovery processes as equally communal. If we truly believe and are committed to the moral repair of veterans, then we must also commit ourselves to the moral repair of society and maintain that work indefinitely until no feast, foreign or domestic, is ever again imagined as a bounty of desolation.

NOTES

1. For the purposes of this chapter, I'll use the term "epistemology" as shorthand to reference the means by which knowledge is produced and sense-making occurs in society.

2. Social constructionism is, in essence, an epistemological orientation that describes knowledge production as an accumulation of social interactions, discourses, and narratives that have been reproduced and sedimented in the popular consciousness over time.

Chapter Five

Moral Injury and the Role of Chaplains

Zachary Moon

MORAL EMOTIONS, MORAL DISTRESS, AND MORAL INJURY

The work on moral injury is an ongoing project still refining its definitions, theoretical frameworks, and cultivating its best practices of care. Thus far the bulk of this work has centered on the human suffering borne of military service, driven largely by the disturbing headlines concerning veteran suicide. Confounded by glimpsing the severity of many veterans' suffering through a morally maladapted lens, American society has sought answers. Moral injury has been presented as an answer.

Chaplains and other care providers have been and will continue to be on the frontlines of moral injury. What do chaplains need to know about moral injury, and what do they need to integrate into their care approaches and practices to provide effective care? This chapter will provide definition and vision for moral-injury-informed care and consider key challenges and opportunities for chaplains.

Moral injury looks a lot like PTSD in as much as their symptomology and related behaviors are similar. Posttraumatic stress symptoms, whether generated by life threat, traumatic loss and grief, or moral injury, may include some combination of the following:

- Re-experiencing/intrusive memories during flashbacks, dreams, nightmares
- Hypervigilant avoidance of perceived dangers
- Irritability, trouble concentrating, difficulty maintaining calm disposition due to persistent and unmanageable alertness of the mind and body

To understand the difference between PTSD and moral injury, track the emotional experience of the trauma: PTSD will be rooted primarily in a fear experience; moral injury will be rooted primarily in one or more moral emotions: guilt, shame, contempt, and/or disgust. Guilt and shame are inwardly/self-directed moral appraisals. "Guilt" and "shame" are sometimes used interchangeably but for our purposes, we should use guilt as remorse for one's actions or inactions, in other words, "I did something wrong," whereas shame totalizes the judgment beyond specific actions to encompass the whole self, in other words, "I am wrong." Contempt and disgust are outwardly/other-directed moral appraisals.

Moral emotions are rooted in one's assessment of responsibility. If one is experiencing guilt or shame, it's because one feels responsible. If one is experiencing contempt or disgust, it's because one feels another is responsible. All of us navigate moral worlds, with constructed orders of powers and responsibility, with expectations for ourselves and for others. Sometimes when that moral order is violated, there are clear pathways to reparation. However, in situations without clear pathways or with hostile agents who allude justice, in situations that overwhelm our expectations or confound our need for assimilation of changes to the moral order, it is natural to experience moral traumatic stress. When that moral traumatic stress renders our moral identity and moral agency powerless, and we become ensconced in the chaos left in the aftermath, we are contending with moral injury.

While moral emotions are core to moral injuries, the emotion that may be most visible is anger. Anger appears as an alarm signal that something in one's life is not as it should be, something important is being threatened. While we can think of any number of life-limiting and/or harmful expressions of anger, at its root anger calls us to attention. It is when we fail to pay attention that anger becomes problematic in our lives. In the case of moral injury, anger fuels the negative appraisals of those deemed morally responsible. If you see someone raging at another or despairing their image, or see someone "beating themselves up" with harsh and condemning evaluations, you should read deeper into the moral dimensions of that interpersonal or intrapersonal experience because you may find moral distress just below the surface.

It should be noted that nothing in that description of moral injury is fundamental to military service or the human experience of war-making. Moral injury can be found in many other professional contexts in which institutional powers are at odds with the moral identities of those involved. Consider how many professional contexts suffer from frequent "burnout": teachers, medical professionals, activists, ministry professionals, and so on. Where you find "burnout" attributed to low pay or long hours, it is worth exploring the moral suffering that this context creates. For example, many public school teachers (who are underpaid and overworked) experience moral distress. Their deep vocational sense of responsibility to children's learning and well-being is compromised on a daily basis by systems that criminalize children's behavior (such as zero tolerance policies) and that dehumanize children in the process of learning (such as an overemphasis on standardized testing). In this case, the current moral world of public school education is systemically at odds with many teachers' sense of core moral responsibility, leading to moral distress.

This example of public school education generating moral distress reveals a simple and significant, yet often overlooked, function of moral injury: moral emotions, including those present in moral injury, have a positive social-relational purpose. In as much as a person feels responsibility for an action that breaches the moral covenant or circumstances that are morally corrupt, their moral distress is alerting them to a problem in need of reconciliation, brokenness in need of reparation. To view moral injury as merely a mental health crisis, or a pathology of symptoms in need of treatment, is to diminish, if not utterly betray, the function of moral responsibility and moral agency in our society and world. It is crucial that care professionals, those in ministry roles like chaplains most of all, recognize the clarion call of moral injuries.

A CONVERSATION

There are some conversations that never leave you. This one took place at Camp Wilson, which is miles deep in Twentynine Palms Marine Corps Base, and no more than a series of rudimentary structures for hygiene, eating, sleeping, and church services. We sat on metal benches in the only air-conditioned building available, sipping on ice cold sodas. We wore the same uniform, the same rank, and that day we wore the same dusty desert grime. A real shower was still three days away.

We had known each other for more than two years, which is an eternity in the ever-rotating military. He was a junior officer with multiple deployments, but different than other officers I knew: he had a calm demeanor and was quick to smile; he was ready to risk his own neck for every Marine in his charge; and he always wanted to collaborate and learn from others. I was his chaplain, born and raised a pacifist in Berkeley, California, ever wondering at the turn in my life that had brought me to this work.

His multiple deployments had been marked by combat, and all the dangers and losses therein. He had seen a lot in Afghanistan, and some of it still haunted him. But that day, his anguish spanned disparate worlds because of an experience off base and out of uniform.

"I was driving and there was a crash up ahead. I got out and ran up to the vehicle. I got the driver out and cleared his airway. He was making this gurgling sound from his throat. The blood was in there and . . . just this gurgling. The smell of the wrecked vehicles, burned metal, and melted tires. His blood was on me. Some of it got into my mouth. I can still taste it. That taste and the smells. I was right back in the shit of battle. Dammit—why did his blood get in my mouth?"

His military training had saved the driver's life, but his military experience, replete with manifold traumas, was also a part of this experience. The sensory experiences of his trauma were inscribed in his memory, evoked again by the sights, smells, and even tastes of violent assaults on human flesh. But military training doesn't only teach what to do when facing casualities; it teaches you to run toward the suffering. He didn't leave the safety of his own vehicle because he knew he could be of help; he went because someone in need was his responsibility.

Understanding his sense of responsibility, surrounded by peril, whether there or here, undergirds his traumatic experience. Recognizing the moral dimensions of these experiences clarifies how these experiences remain in his memory and in his body. We didn't talk about God that day, about church or faith, or why bad things happen to good people, but good chaplain work often invites us beyond the dogmas and creeds of our religious identities. By virtue of our shared experience and the relationship that had been forged, he entrusted me with these hauntings, asking only what any of us would ask in the aftermath: "What the hell am I supposed to do with this?"

MORAL-INJURY-INFORMED CARE

If chaplains and other ministry professionals are going to respond to moral injury effectively, it is crucial to understand why care providers may not engage moral injury when it's staring right at us. Moral injury has a social-relational dimension, and in this sense is not "your moral injury" but "our moral injury." While care providers may seek some clinical boundary maintenance from this ours-ness, such denial of broader responsibility leads to a number of problems: limited or compromised trust-building, pursuit of therapeutic practices and modalities that remain individual-focused and lack communal engagement, and so on. And while care providers may wish to close themselves off from feelings of responsibility, being opened by those feelings can be dangerous: overidentification with the care seeker, compassion fatigue, guilt, and so on.

The moral complexity of responding to moral injury can animate other internal messages that may compromise provision of care. When hearing a care seeker ventilate their moral anguish, we may become occupied thinking, "This person has done something morally wrong—they should suffer." As harsh as this may seem, in a way it holds an important social truth. Herman

Keizer said, "Moral injury is a reaction of the conscience."[1] If we turn this message into a prosocial statement that normalizes moral anguish, rather than a condemnation, the truth of Keizer's wisdom can serve the recovery process instead of impede it.

Another kind of message can occupy our minds when we hear the horrors of moral injury: "Helping this person makes me an accomplice to their moral transgressions." This idea is triggered when our care-provision links in co-occurring responsibility-taking. It is necessary for care providers to reflect on their professional boundaries adequate to the task of compartmentalizing our responsibilities with others' responsibilities. Effective care providers experience their own sense of responsibility in anchored and life-giving ways, and recognize transference and counter-transference when it's taking place in a care encounter.

Civilian care providers may hesitate offering care to military care seekers given the pervasive adherence to the idea that "veterans would rather talk to other veterans." This may be true, yet even if true, it does not alleviate the need for helping relationships within the civilian world. Military veterans have endured some unique and powerful experiences, and there may be experiences which are difficult to entrust to those perceived as unknowledgeable. This is a reality created by profound trauma-bonding and entrenched by the insensitivity of a civilian populace raised on Hollywood war drama; in other words, veterans may well seek to protect themselves and their experiences from the prying gaze of the uninitiated. Whether due to the care seekers' defensive posture, or the care providers' hesitancy, or some combination of the two, this relational gap is death-dealing, particularly today. The war-fighting since 2001, the longest wars in American history, has been performed by less than 1 percent of the nation's citizens. There is much that must be interrogated concerning this reality but for our purposes here, we must understand that the returning veteran today does not return to a community inundated by other veterans or marked by the impact of military experience, as was the case following World War II, and to a lesser extent the war in Vietnam. Today's military veteran often finds it hard to secure civilian employment, attend college, or participate in religious communities in which they find other veterans of their generation. If the collective civilian response to veterans boils down to "talk to someone else," we are condemning today's veterans to a severely contracted social-relational world. A world that leaves their suffering unheard and unengaged, and their moral injury left to fester without regard.

Working with those who have served in the military may also surface other internalized messages including, "All veterans are morally injured because war is morally wrong." The issue arises around the collision course of moral appraisements of war-making (an always satisfying arm-chair debate) and the self-identification process for those who suffer. More space would be needed to address adequately either of these phenomena, so for our purposes let it be stated that war-making and violence of any kind exact a moral toll on those involved, joining the company of the physical, psychological, material, and environmental costs. The question of who bears the responsibility has been argued for millennia. Moral injury is not a clinical diagnosis, and therefore the process of identification with the experience should be entirely within the agency of the one in anguish. If someone suffering, or showing no signs of suffering, differently identifies or locates themselves in other ways, it is not our role to judge or label. Following the line of reasoning demonstrated in "all veterans are morally injured" leads to viewing all who don't self-identify as morally deficient, if not sociopathic.

Because the United States has not exercised a military draft system to populate its Armed Forces, the military is instead recruited and enlisted by those who volunteer. A myriad of factors motivate volunteerism in military service, but the process of volunteering, or signing one's own name to a contract, elevates one's sense of reasonability and accountability to the experience and its outcomes. This internalized message for military service members is reciprocated by others who may project, "They volunteered; they should have known what they were signing up for." Such messaging, whether internalized by or projected onto the care seeker, can create significant barriers to seeking and receiving necessary care and support. The onus is put entirely on the one suffering. Much like asking a sexual assault survivor why they wore that outfit to the party, the statement is clear: you have brought this on yourself and bear its responsibility. When this happens in the aftermath of moral trauma, the effects can be debilitating. One's already intensified sense of responsibility is compounded by the social-relational world, and exacerbates feelings of alienation and isolation.

Care providers may see a care seeker suffering with moral injury and perceive that given the circumstances there is not time or space to deal with it. This is often the case with military chaplains. The terms of operational conditions render both time and space unattainable, and so instead the chaplain becomes a coconspirator in repressing the moral injury and getting the sufferer back to functioning. As harsh as this may sound, it is often the only available response. In such circumstances, however, it is crucial that the chaplain acknowledges the limitations of the environment that influence their response, so as not to convey that such repression is the ideal path for survival. Chaplains work with those in the worst of circumstances, and we often wield immeasurable pastoral authority in the eyes of the care seeker. Therefore, even in the face of death-dealing, we must resolve to be persistent harbingers of life.

Because a sense of responsibility is core to experience of moral injury, a care provider may with good intention seek to alleviate the suffering by alleviating the sense of responsibility. Many of us have fallen into this trap of wishing to help another person feel better about a situation, and so we respond: "That's not your fault." Unfortunately, with moral injury such an approach can be deeply counterproductive because our response shames their shame, and "guilts" their guilt. The care seeker has already identified their sense of responsibility; to take that away from them may drive them further out of the social-relational network they dearly need.

Many care providers (especially chaplains) and some care seekers come from religious backgrounds in which reassurance, absolution, and forgiveness of sins represent the core of religious identity. Moral injuries, and the moral emotions that fuel them, have a prosocial function. As devastating as the moral anguish may be, within the suffering is a call to reparation. What that reparation may look like will vary with each person and each moral injury. What happens when that demand for reparation is met with a quickly offered appeasement? The care seeker may wish it, and the care provider may offer it, but the effects of a cheap absolution can be a betrayal as intense as the moral injury itself. A moral-injury-informed approach to care must take seriously the nature of the moral injury and the power created by the sense of responsibility. In other words, to offer reconciliation before truth has been spoken and heard with integrity will be calamity.

There are a number of helpful engagements of moral injury, and chaplains should be equipped to draw as widely from these resources as possible while realizing that each care seeker will need their own balance of recovery opportunities. All responses to moral injuries should constructively engage the matrix of moral emotions and the sense of responsibility experienced by the care seeker. Rather than seeking to alleviate moral emotions and/or a sense of responsibility, the care provider must elevate the prosocial and pro-reparative functions within the moral injury. While guilt, shame, disgust, and contempt may have life-limiting consequences and lead to unhealthy expressions, even these moral emotions serve our functional and just life together.

Guilt, shame, disgust, and contempt are not the only moral emotions, however, and our care provision directly benefits from engaging the full spectrum of moral emotions including compassion, trust, accountability, loyalty, and honor. Mapping this full spectrum of moral emotions will benefit our consideration and understanding of the moral agency and sense of reasonability that has been violated in the moral injury.

Many spiritual practices and religious rituals can serve the response and recovery process. Each chaplain or religious leader who is providing care with those suffering with moral injury should consider the resources of their respective traditions. Some Christian traditions will be able to mobilize communion/Eucharist, confession, and baptism as resources that can be liturgized in moral-injury-informed ways. Further, practices that engage the moral value of service-oriented community improvement work can reconnect those suffering with moral injury to their social-relational world and repair past damage to their agency in the moral covenant.

Similarly, care approaches that include other kinds of embodied practice, such as pet-based or horse-based therapies, yoga, and meditation, can work in support of recovery. In all of these cases, the care seeker experiences reconnection to the goodness of life and their particular worth located in that life.

REBUILDING ONE'S HOUSE

In my work as a chaplain with combat veterans diagnosed with PTSD, I started using the following house metaphor to visualize and explore moral identity, moral injury, and the process of recovery.[2] The metaphor envisions one's moral identity as a house, built over many years and established before one can even remember, constructed by and with members of one's family, close friends, mentors, teachers, and other moral leaders (ministers, coaches, etc.). This house is defined by these relationships and imbued with our values and beliefs. This house is built to protect us from all kinds of existential catastrophes. Occasional inflictions of doubt, stress, and crisis may befall us, but our house weathers these temporary storms.

There are situations, circumstances, and events, however, which cannot be repelled by our houses. In clinical terms, we call these traumas, and they may include traumatic moral injuries. Our normal, baseline system of accommodations and assimilations, of responding and coping, is overwhelmed beyond resilience. Our house's foundations crumble, the walls topple, the roof caves in, and we are left with something uninhabitable.

It is instructive to imagine the emotions that such a collapse would generate. Standing outside, looking over the rubble of what once was your home, your sanctuary, your safety, your sense of meaning. I ask care seekers what emotions they would feel looking at this aftermath of destruction: grief, loss, anger, guilt, fear, shame, betrayal, alienation, isolation, helplessness, despair. What if you looked around and everybody else's house looked just fine? What if you saw your neighbors shutter their windows when they saw you and your calamity, muttering under their breaths, "But for the grace of God. . ."? What would you do next? Expecting another storm to befall you at any moment, would you try hastily to rebuild some shelter? Would you walk away believing this is punishment, having been marked like the biblical character Cain to wander without a home (see Gen 4:15)?

This visualization has been helpful not only in naming and acknowledging the devastation of moral injury but also in considering the process of recovery. If and when a person who has suffered this extremity of ruin is ready, a rebuilding process is possible. While it may look as though the house has been torn asunder, there are materials present in the midst of the rubble that are worth retaining, that can be part of constructing a new house. So we should ask: What here is worth keeping, and what can still provide something necessary to my moral identity? Likewise there are materials present in the midst of the rubble that should be cast aside and left behind. So we should ask: What here must be lost in order for a new, stronger house to be built? Discerning what needs to retained and what needs to be relinquished is a necessary part of the recovery (rebuilding) process. Without this discernment, we are likely to reconstruct a house no better than the one that has recently collapsed. Overall, this house metaphor is meant to acknowledge our moral identity—the materials noted here are values and beliefs. As with good materials and weak materials, values and beliefs can provide structural integrity or compromise it. When good theological education or Clinical Pastoral Education invite students to understand better their lived experience, or their embedded theology, the task is to comprehend the strengths and weaknesses of one's moral identity, just as a building might undergo an assessment.

The recovery process also has a social-relation dimension. Moral identity is socially and relationally constructed; our house is built by many hands. Hence, moral injury devastates our social-relational web of support for this very reason. Therefore, the rebuilding process needs support from trustworthy others. The trap here for both care seeker and care provider (chaplain) is to oversubscribe the architectural prowess of the care provider. The care seeker comes in crisis, their house destroyed, while the care provider is presumed to have a better house and to be better at making houses overall. Whether a projection of the care seeker or an overindulgence of a savior complex on the part of the care provider, this is a recipe for disaster. Even the most capable moral leader cannot adequately build another person's house. We must be our own architects, and one's recovery process must be empowered as such. All this being acknowledged, we do not need to labor alone. Someone reeling from the desolation of their home should seek (to the best of their ability) help, and helpers must come ready to work. Care providers (chaplains) would do well to remember that they are helpers, not master builders, and their care practice should resemble this condition. Sometimes the greatest gift a care provider can offer is a good referral. The only lasting solution in the aftermath of moral injury is a community of engaged mutual thriving.

WHAT ABOUT MY HOUSE?

I shared this visualization at a moral injury conference and was approached by a chaplain in uniform after the presentation. He looked me square in the eyes and said, "You were talking about me and my house. Because I was the chaplain, I thought I needed to have it together all the time so that when others would look at me they'd see stability. So I kept repainting the outside of my house to keep up appearances, while inside my life was falling apart."

There is a significant amount of literature on compassion fatigue and secondary trauma, and all of us who work with those who are suffering know the personal toll. Understanding moral injury can offer new dimensions to the compassion fatigue and secondary trauma formulations. While proximity to suffering and the expending of empathy and compassion exact a cost, chaplaincy is a responsibility-thick vocation. Most of us theologize a sense of call (responsibility to God) in getting into this work, as well as a responsibility to others. Most of us have experienced failures and other shortcomings that trouble us still, a sense of "What could I have done differently to render a different outcome?" These regrets and reflections are borne of a sense of responsibility, and we must recognize how moral dimensions influence our work and our pastoral professional identities.

Whether we are painting the exterior or deferring necessary maintenance, we are risking the kind of burnout that will negatively impact not only ourselves, but our families, our communities, and the care seekers we wish to serve. "Self-care" has been trotted out so many times that it's become a cliché, so let's talk about the care provider's house instead. The water is only in the attic from that leak in the roof, but how long will that last? Maybe consider replacing your old windows with more energy-efficient ones. Which rooms need to be decluttered? What renovations would make this a better house in which to live? As you consider the work that is needed, remember you don't need to do this work alone in the secrecy of night. Who is ready and available to join your work team—mentors, colleagues, trusted friends, or family?

Moral injury is best understood as a severe, debilitating moral anguish comparable to PTSD in seriousness and symptomology. But moral distress is best recognized as a spectrum of suffering, with moral injury at the pole of most radical suffering. Our engagement of moral injury, therefore, doesn't need to remain exclusively with the most critical cases of moral anguish. We can better understand moral suffering in its many permutations by tracking a sense of responsibility and the activation of moral emotions. As mentioned above, many professions are inflicted with burnout and those include care providers like chaplains. A moral-injury-informed approach to care is not only in service to care seekers, but just as crucially to their care providers.

NOTES

1. https://blogs.hope.edu/thebigread/uncategorized/moral-injury-after-war-colonel-herman-keizer-jr/. Accessed December 23, 2019.

2. Zachary Moon, *Coming Home: Ministry That Matters with Veterans and Military Families* (St. Louis, MO: Chalice, 2015); Zachary Moon, *Warriors Between Worlds: Moral Injury and Identities in Crisis* (Lanham, MD: Lexington, 2019).

BIBLIOGRAPHY

Brock, Rita Nakashima and Gabriella Lettini. *Soul Repair: Recovering from Moral Injury after War*. Boston: Beacon, 2012.

Doehring, C. "Intercultural Spiritual Care in the Aftermath of Trauma." Pages 148–65 in *Transforming Wisdom: The Practice of Psychotherapy in Theological Perspective*. Edited by F. Kelcourse and K. B. Lyon. Eugene, OR: Wipf and Stock, 2015.

—. "Military Moral Injury: An Evidence-Based and Intercultural Approach to Spiritual Care." *Pastoral Psychology* 68 (2019): 15–30. doi: 10.1007/s11089-018-0813-5.

—. "Resilience as the Relational Ability to Spiritually Integrate Moral Stress." *Pastoral Psychology* 64 (2015): 635–49. https://doi.org/10.1007/s11089-015-0643-7.

Drescher, Kent D. and D. W. Foy. "When Horror and Loss Intersect: Traumatic Experiences and Traumatic Bereavement." *Pastoral Psychology 59* (2010): 147–58. https://doi.org/10.1007/s11089-009-0262-2.

Drescher, Kent D., D. W. Foy, C. Kelly, A. Leshner, K. Schutz, and B. T. Litz. "An Exploration of the Usefulness of the Construct of Moral Injury in War Veterans." *Traumatology* 17 (2011): 8–13. https://doi.org/10.1177/1534765610395615.

Haidt, J. "The Moral Emotions." Pages 852–70 in *Handbook of Affective Sciences*. Edited by R. J. Davidson, K. R. Scherer, and H. H. Goldsmith. New York: Oxford University Press, 2003.

Hutcherson, C. A. and J. J. Gross. "The Moral Emotions: A Social–Functionalist Account of Anger, Disgust, and Contempt." *Journal of Personality and Social Psychology* 100 (2011): 719–37.

Jordan, A. H., E. Eisen, E. Bolton, W. P. Nash, and B. T. Litz. "Distinguishing War-Related PTSD Resulting from Perpetration- and Betrayal-Based Morally Injurious Events." *Psychological Trauma: Theory, Research, Practice, and Policy* 9 (2017): 627–34.

Kinghorn, Warren. "Combat Trauma and Moral Fragmentation: A Theological Account of Moral Injury." *Journal of the Society of Christian Ethics* 32 (2012): 57–74.

Litz, Brett T., L. Lebowitz, M. Gray, and W. P. Nash. *Adaptive Disclosure: A New Treatment for Military Trauma, Loss, and Moral Injury*. New York: Guilford, 2016.

Moon, Zachary. *Coming Home: Ministry That Matters with Veterans and Military Families*. St. Louis, MO: Chalice, 2015.

—. "Pastoral Care and Counseling with Military Families." *Journal of Pastoral Care and Counseling* 70 (2016): 128–35.

—. *Warriors Between Worlds: Moral Injury and Identities in Crisis*. Lanham, MD: Lexington, 2019.

Ramsay, Nancy and Carrie Doehring, eds. *Military Moral Injury and Spiritual Care*. St. Louis, MO: Chalice, 2019.

Stallinga, B. "What Spills Blood Wounds Spirit: Chaplains, Spiritual Care, and Operational Stress Injury." *Reflective Practice: Formation and Supervision in Ministry 33* (2013): 13–31.

Tangney, J. P. and R. Dearing. *Shame and Guilt*. New York: Guilford, 2002.

Tangney, J. P., J. Stuewig, and D. J. Mashek. "Moral Emotions and Moral Behavior." *Annual Review of Psychology* 58 (2007): 345–72.

Chapter Six

"Do Not Torment Me"

The Morally Injured Gerasene Demoniac (Mark 5:1–20)

Michael Yandell

"My name is Legion, for we are many" (Mark 5:9).[1] In keeping with this most familiar line in the story, valuable interpretations of Jesus's healing of the Gerasene demoniac are likewise many. This chapter is a reading of Mark 5:1–20 through the lens of moral injury, from the perspective of a US Army veteran. In this reading, the "demoniac" is a person who suffers moral injury. I turn to this ancient story of the demoniac for two reasons. First, ancient texts and their interpretations are always, at the very least, in the background of the way morality is understood today. Second, ancient texts like this one found in the New Testament are about divinity as well as humanity; or, put another way, these texts are about the world and one's place in it. My approach to this ancient text is twofold: I offer a reading of the story of the Gerasene demoniac as a depiction of moral injury in order to take a second step—to make a theological claim about moral injury today. I argue that this ancient story is one of despair and of hope, and so is the story of moral injury today.

Like the ancient story, there are many definitions and nuanced interpretations of the term "moral injury," a survey of which can be found in the first section of this book. Taken together, two strands of moral injury definitions come closer to naming accurately moral injury than either definition does on its own. The work of Jonathan Shay focuses on moral injury in the form of betrayal by a superior or authority figure in a military context. The work of Brett Litz, alongside a host of other scholars and clinicians, focuses on moral injury in the form of an individual transgressing her or his own morals and values.[2] Moral injury, in my view, comprises both definitional strands and more. In a previous reflection on the topic, I tried to combine the definitions in my own experience: “Moral injury is about human relationship. I have never waged a war, but I have fought in one.”[3] The truth is, military moral injury involves betrayals, transgressions, and violations that occur in war and occupation. When individuals become aware of their direct or indirect responsibility for those betrayals, transgressions, and violations, they experience moral injury. Part of that awareness, however, includes the context of the war itself, for which the individual is not responsible. When individuals become aware of the war itself as betrayal, transgression, and violation, they experience moral injury. Military personnel who experience moral injury often stand at this intersection—as war fighters, they become the violator for those whose countries are invaded and occupied; they also feel betrayed by their own country—the war wager—that sent them to violate others.

Moral injury arises out of the experience of betraying and being betrayed, of transgressing and being transgressed, of violating and being violated. That is the fount from which moral injury springs, but what is moral injury itself? I offer my own distillation of the literature for the purposes of this chapter: moral injury is despair of the world, and of oneself.

I read the Gerasene demoniac as a story about one who despairs of the world and oneself. The story does not end in despair, but it also does not end with any easy answers. Hope is a word that sometimes appears suspicious, especially to those who have reason to despair of the world and themselves. False hope abounds. What is needed is a hope that does not erase the past and its consequences but that allows for a future in which the past is fully acknowledged and reckoned with.

“A MAN OUT OF THE TOMBS”

Who is the person that “immediately” meets Jesus on the shore of the sea? The author of Mark does not give him a name, neither before nor after the man’s confrontation with Jesus. He is simply the one who comes “out of the tombs,” one who has “lived among the tombs” (Mark 5:2–3). Jesus, however, demands a name from the man; when asked directly, the man from the tombs provides the notoriously puzzling answer—“My name is Legion; for we are many” (5:9). Ched Myers describes the exchange in this way: “Jesus wrests from this powerful demonic horde its name: Legion. A Latinism, this term had only one meaning in Mark’s social world: a division of Roman soldiers.”[4] Joel Marcus agrees, asserting that “the demon employs a Roman military term.”[5] Thus, the name provided in response to Jesus becomes a signifier of Roman military force. The plurality in the word establishes that there is a plurality of demonic forces residing in the man from the tombs. Assuming that it is the demonic that speaks to Jesus in providing the name “Legion,” one can arrive at a valuable reading of this text in which “this unlikely story offers a symbolic portrait of how Roman imperialism was destroying the hearts and minds of a colonized people."[6] The reader need not take for granted, however, that it is the unclean spirit(s) residing in the man that speaks here.

Consider for a moment that the man out of the tombs is speaking for himself. Note the confusion between the one and the many in the giving of his name: "My name is Legion, for we are many."[7] It is difficult to distinguish who exactly is speaking. Marcus suggests an identity crisis, in which "the man's identity has been swallowed up by the demon's so that he speaks with the demon's voice, tries to protect the demon from eviction from his own body, and becomes the demon's instrument for his own torture."[8] It is clear that the man is in crisis. But the issue regarding whose voice is speaking needs further nuance. The image of the man's identity or voice being "swallowed up" by that of the demons misses the singular/plural ambiguity in the naming. I suggest that there is no clear distinction between the demonic voice and the man's voice. Both are speaking in response to Jesus, or perhaps both are one and the same. Rather than a "swallowing" of identity, there is a conflation of identity in this man out of the tombs. The one and the many are collapsed, blurred, and paradoxically the same when he says, "My name is Legion, for we are many." It is not a matter of the man's voice at odds with the demonic; there is simply no longer a separation of voices. The problem confronting Jesus when this man out of the tombs rushes to meet him is not merely a problem of demon possession; it is an unsustainable conflation of identity in which the many and the one are simultaneous.

What bearing does this have on interpreting the text? While it is certainly valuable when read as an analogy of Roman military occupation, I suggest a reading that hears the man out of the tombs speaking with more than analogy. Rather than a symbol of military occupation, the man himself can be seen as one who was once a member of the Roman military—that is, part of a legion. Reading the man as a veteran is speculative in the sense that the text does not provide explicit details with which to describe the man's background with certainty. Even so, reading the man as a veteran is not culturally implausible. Indeed, the term "Legion" itself—as mentioned above—sets a military tone. Moreover, Myers describes the "country of the Gerasenes" (5:1) where the man is encountered as an area "settled by many veterans of the Imperial army who had been given conquered lands as payment for their service."[9] Suppose one of these veterans could not rest with the fruits of his past labors. Perhaps, even though he had left the legion, the legion would not leave him.

From my own personal experience as a soldier in the US Army, I recall the feeling of putting on the uniform and lacing up the boots. Each morning, my identity became one with the uniformity of the Army as a whole. Having clothed myself with the Army, representationally I became the Army for those with whom I interacted. My actions and the actions of the US military were one and the same. Individuating myself from the Army was more difficult than signing paperwork and putting away the uniform when I was discharged. The name "veteran" forever establishes a link between my own self and the plurality that is the US military. When I fuse the elements of this text from Mark with elements of my own experience, "My name is Legion, for we are many" is much more than an analogy. It puts into words a reality that defies definition. Who bears the burden of guilt, the burden of self-reflection, and the burden of memory for a military institution? Who bears the burden of despair? It is not the institution itself; it is the one, and it is the many. It is the many individuals who put on a uniform and become identified, in their own eyes and the eyes of others, with the institution the uniform represents. Perhaps they have acted in ways contrary to their own conscience, or perhaps they see themselves as implicit and complicit agents in a project larger than themselves, which they find unconscionable. I posit that this man in the country of the Gerasenes, through experiences and memories of transgressions and violations, despaired of the world and himself. This ancient man in an ancient story, like so many morally injured military women and men today, could not stand the comforts of the city and took to the tombs.

To remember betrayal, transgression, and violation is to remember trauma. Serene Jones suggests that there is an "assault-like character of a trauma; it involves an attack by an external agent upon a vulnerable human body in such a way that a wounding occurs."[10] The man from the tombs has, however, taken to "howling and bruising *himself* with stones" (5:5). There is not an external agent at work assaulting the man. Simone Weil observes that "violence overwhelms those it touches. In the end, it seems as external to the one who wields it as to the one who endures it."[11] Reading the man from the tombs as a Roman veteran, he likely inflicted violence on others. As he inflicted violence, he was also part of a vast project of Roman military conquest. Put another way, he inflicted violence *on* others *on behalf of* others. Tyler Boudreau, a former Marine officer writing about the US military in Iraq, describes the contemporary version of this dilemma: "A man might wring his hands and say in anguish, 'I killed!' But it's not as though he thought it up and did it on his own. There were other factors and other agents involved."[12] That there are other factors and other agents involved is not a free pass from the consequences of violence and moral wrongdoing; rather, it makes one feel damned from all directions. Trauma, in contemporary studies, has been extended "to the mind and the emotions, focusing on the effects of violence on our vast interior worlds."[13] If one cannot distinguish one's identity from the military as a whole, the violence of an entire empire becomes part of one's "vast interior world." One sees the world and oneself drenched in betrayal, transgression, and violation, and one despairs. "He was always howling and bruising himself with stones" (Mark 5:5).

Jones suggests that "violence can leave you with a wounded soul—a life marked by obsessive thoughts, acute anxiety, depression . . . and low-grade forms of misery lingering so long that they become normalized and cease to appear woundlike at all."[14] Hence, the man in the tombs becomes part of the landscape; his choice to live in the tombs becomes normalized: "no one could restrain him anymore, even with a chain; for he had often been restrained with shackles and chains, but the chains he wrenched apart, and the shackles he broke in pieces; and no one had the strength to subdue him" (5:4). Who bears the burden of despair? This one does, this one whose wounded soul cannot help but reflect on the many, this one who resists being taken back into society. Camillo C. "Mac" Bica, a philosopher of war, former US Marines Captain, and Vietnam veteran, frames this well in contemporary terms as he reflects on his own experience:

> What I failed to realize at the time was that, at least in spirit, we were all dead already. . . . [Soldiers] are the victims of politicians' hypocrisy, the scapegoats for the inevitable affront to the national conscience, and the sacrificial lambs sent to slaughter in retribution for our collective guilt and inadequacies. In fact, no one knows the sacrilege of war better than we who must fight it and then have to live with the memories of what we have done and what we have become.[15]

The collective guilt Bica refers to best gets at the identity conflation that traumatizes this man in the tombs, that which sends him to the tombs in the first place. The man wrestles not only with his own guilt, with the violence he himself has embodied, but he wrestles with the guilt of the many. Shelly Rambo suggests that after trauma "death remains in the experience of survival and life is reshaped in light of death—not in light of its finality but its persistence. Persons who experience trauma live in the suspended middle territory, between death and life."[16] This is exactly the sort of person who rushes to meet Jesus on the shore: one who lives in the tombs, whose moral identity has been lost between the one and many—stuck between life and death, and damned from all sides.

AVOIDANCE AND ATTRACTION

"When he saw Jesus from a distance, he ran and bowed down before him; and he shouted at the top of his voice, 'What have you to do with me, Jesus, Son of the Most High God? I adjure you by God, do not torment me'" (Mark 5:6–7). There is another paradox in this story beyond the simultaneous one and many in the name "Legion." There is a preunderstanding, a kind of supernatural recognition and foreknowledge of who Jesus is. Upon seeing Jesus and recognizing who he is, the man at once rushes to him while immediately begging Jesus not to torment him. Why rush to meet the very source of one's torment? Marcus describes the scene aptly as a "somewhat eerie mixture of avoidance and attraction."[17] Marcus provides three questions with which to consider the action:

> Is the demoniac's approach and obeisance an indication that, at some level, the lost human being trapped inside the destructive forces is still aware of his plight and wants to be liberated? Or do the demons experience a "fatal attraction" for their eschatological destroyer? Or are they, with the cunning servility of a Uriah Heep, prudently acknowledging the superior force of their opponent while casting about for a way to outwit and defraud him?[18]

Regarding the first question, I have suggested that the man is not lost somewhere inside the identity of "Legion," but rather that the man's identity and the identity of the military arm of the empire have been conflated and collapsed into one and the same thing. A question remains however: given this collapse of identity, what does liberation look like? I suggest that it is not liberation from a hostile and controlling entity that is desired here, but rather a release from the weight of collective guilt—the perception of uniformity with a lethally violent empire.

Regarding the question of fatal attraction, I argue that the man has no idea what will happen to him when he meets Jesus. He is already one resigned to life in the tombs, hanging between death and life, screaming night and day while cutting and bruising himself. In this case, a fatal confrontation may be appealing. According to Rita Nakashima Brock and Gabriella Lettini, "Moral injury destroys meaning and forsakes noble cause. It sinks warriors into states of silent, solitary suffering, where bonds of intimacy and care seem impossible. Its torments to the soul can make death a mercy."[19] In this light, the scenario can be read as one in which the outcome is unknown, but in which death would be acceptable. The third question of attempting to outwit and defraud Jesus can be ruled out in the framework I am using here; I am considering the man's plight to be one of identity crisis, not one in which there are conniving forces living inside the man.

Why does the man beg Jesus not to torment him? What is worse than the living death the man is already living/dying, especially if the finality of death itself would be welcomed as liberation? The key here is the man's immediate recognition of Jesus, whom he names "son of the Most High God," which, according to Myers, is a Hellenistic title found elsewhere only sparingly in the New Testament.[20] The title of "Most High God" in the Hebrew Bible and Jewish texts is associated with the way Gentiles referred to the God of Israel, as well as the sovereignty of that God over the entire world.[21] The use of this Gentile name for Israel's God is in keeping with my proposal that the man is a veteran of the Roman military. This understanding of Jesus as "son of the Most High God" suggests, however, that the man knows more about the identity of Jesus in Mark's gospel than we should expect anyone to know at this point in the text. Rather than attribute this knowledge to a demonic presence within the man, I suggest at this point that we must read this knowledge in light of the entire gospel. The man from the tombs knows what the reader or the hearer of this text already knows—that Jesus is/will be the one crucified by the empire—the empire with which the man's individual identity is conflated. Jesus, the crucified individual, also represents a collective—the many put to death by imperial conquest. The man, burdened by the guilt of his own violent actions and the violent actions of the empire, recognizes in Jesus the recipient(s) of those violent actions. He sees Jesus at once as the potential source of his redemption as well as the source of his condemnation.

"GO HOME . . . AND TELL THEM . . ."

> *"This world is all we have," says Joseph. "It's all you have to work with. It is not too much for you. You will not be rescued."*[22]

At this point, my interpretation of the story of the Gerasene demoniac becomes less biblical exegesis and more an application of the story to moral injury today to make a theological and ethical claim. Something has shifted in the life of the demoniac. Joseph's words, "You will not be rescued," in Margaret Atwood's compelling short story, "The Sin Eater," are similar to the manner in which Jesus sends the Gerasene man away after dispatching the "unclean spirits" into a herd of swine:

> As [Jesus] was getting into the boat, the man who had been possessed by demons begged him that he might be with him. But Jesus refused, and said to him, "Go home to your friends, and tell them how much the Lord has done for you, and what mercy he has shown you." (5:18–19)

The confrontation with Jesus did not end in death, nor did it end in a return to the tombs. The man is given work to do. This is the point at which the text leaves the man who had lived in the tombs, but it is also the point where his life becomes even more complex. His wish is to leave the region and to be with Jesus; he wishes to be rescued, to depart the place where he once lived in the tombs and where the people sought to restrain him rather than understand him. But he is told to go back to the people and explain what has happened. The people themselves wanted no part in it: "They came to Jesus and saw the demoniac sitting there, clothed and in his right mind, the very man who had had the legion; and they were afraid. . . . Then they began to beg Jesus to leave their neighborhood" (5:15, 17). They are afraid, I argue, because they must reckon with who the man really is, and who they are in relation to him.

Moral injury involves much more than an individual clashing violently with another individual. Boudreau states it clearly for us today:

> Nobody wants to talk about the Iraqis. It's always about *the troops*. But "moral injury" by definition includes the memories of those who have been harmed. Without the Iraqi people, the troops can have no moral injuries to speak of. And the only way Americans can fathom the meaning of this term, "moral injury," is to acknowledge the humanity of the Iraqis.[23]

Boudreau names three groups of people: the troops, the Iraqis, and the Americans. If Americans can reduce troops to caricatures and stereotypes of mental illness and brokenness, then Americans can talk about what a shame that is for our troops without having to think about Iraqis (and all others who have suffered in twenty-first-century global war). If the demoniac's "friends" can shackle him and leave him to his cave, then they can forget about all whom the empire has crucified. If moral injury is taken seriously, none of these people can be ignored any longer. Moral injury flows from the memory of people being treated as less than human. From that memory comes despair of the world and oneself. There is no rescue from the memory; there is no erasing what happened. The only way forward from despair is to acknowledge humanity—especially the humanity of those who have been harmed.

One question remains: What exactly happened to the man out of the tombs? What was done for him? The man that had been in the tombs is now in his right mind. Jesus restored the man's humanity—the humanity that was obscured by treating others as less than human. His identity is no longer conflated with the Roman legion. Living in the tombs, the man had been stuck in the "suspended middle territory, between death and life."[24] What Jesus gives the man is movement out of that place. He is given this imperative: "Go home to your friends, and tell them how much the Lord has done for you, and what *mercy* he has shown you" (5:19, emphasis mine). Rambo describes reading with a "traumatic lens" as "reading from the middle, [where] any interpretation of redemption must acknowledge that death and life are inextricably bound, in such a way that theologians must account for death's remainder, death's haunting, so to speak."[25] Mercy and redemption rest in the act of telling. What the man has done is not erased or forgotten; indeed, it must be remembered for the telling to happen. Memories had trapped him in despair—of the world and of himself. The way out of the place of despair is to speak from it.

In my reading and application of the Gerasene demoniac, the man from the tombs had been stuck in the middle territory—in the middle between the empire and Jesus. Today, the morally injured are in the middle—between the United States and all with whom the United States wages war. They present the part of the equation—the part of death's remainder—from which theologians shy away. The morally injured carry more than their own guilt and responsibility. They carry the guilt and shame of all their "friends" at home who cannot bear to speak of or wrestle with the moral questions of war. The community that does not acknowledge its own guilt and complicity in war forges the shackles and digs the tomb where the morally injured imprison themselves. It is much easier to leave the few of them there in the tombs and wash our hands of war and responsibility. Sometimes, though, people will come out of the tomb and tell the truth about their own experiences. This truth-telling is what Joseph Wiinikka-Lydon calls the "prophetic potential of moral injury," where "moral injury is a visceral experience of policy, as well as cultural assumptions, that are put into effect corporately on the ground through the bodies of soldiers and others." Through the experience of embodying policy and cultural assumptions that dehumanize others, there is potential for "prophetic insight, understanding prophetic as seeing deeply and radically into the truth of the present and how one's country is actually affecting others throughout the world."[26]

The community surrounding the man from the tombs is left, at the end of the story, to hear what he has to say. If we apply this point to the context of a contemporary combat veteran and her or his community, there are a number of comparisons we can make. We might see the parades and celebrations, the tributes and ceremonies, and the media frenzies and political scandals surrounding the US military as shackles and chains—strategies to avoid confronting the trauma of war as a collective community while placing the burden of guilt regarding war on a few individuals. Mercy and hope can be found only when these strategies are abandoned, when the one abandoned to the tombs is compelled to speak the truth of experience and the community is compelled to listen.

This is what mercy looks like in my own life: it is bearing witness to all that was lost in violence and in war while somehow declaring mercy—the mercy that comes from the declaration. Moral injury is not something wrong with an individual from which an individual should expect to fully recover; it is a recognition of something gone wrong with the world. Moral injury is despair of the world and oneself—an internalized scream: "This should not have happened! I should not have been a part of this!" When moral injury is given voice—when it is declared—there is movement once again. Responsibility and accountability are restored; and, most importantly, the humanity of others is acknowledged. There is pain involved in taking responsibility for betrayal, transgression, and violation, but there is mercy there as well. Jürgen Moltmann provides a theological litmus test that always comes to bear in my reflection on my involvement in war: "Whatever can stand before the face of the crucified Christ is true Christian theology. What cannot stand there must disappear."[27] I think this is also true of human beings. The man out of the tombs, who called himself Legion, could not remain in the presence of

Christ—not as he was. Nor could he continue the journey with Jesus to Jerusalem. There was work that needed to be done for the man to be with Jesus. At first, he could only ask, "What have you to do with me?" (5:7). This question is on the lips of all morally injured combat veterans who recognize the humanity of those upon whom they once unleashed violence, or upon whom the empire they served unleashed violence. We recognize that we cannot stand before the crucified one—not as we are. Yet, when we ask "What have you to do with me?" we are not destroyed. We are given the task of telling the truth, of bearing witness. That is all we have. It is not too much. We will not be rescued.

NOTES

1. For an earlier version of this article, see Michael Yandell, "'Do Not Torment Me': The Morally Injured Gerasene Demoniac," in *Exploring Moral Injury in Sacred Texts*, ed. Joseph McDonald, Studies in Religion and Theology (London: Jessica Kingsley, 2017), 135–50 (used here with permission). All Bible translations taken from the NRSV.

2. The literature on moral injury is constantly expanding. The works I have in mind specifically in these introductory remarks include the following: Rita Nakashima Brock and Gabriella Lettini, *Soul Repair: Recovering from Moral Injury after War* (Boston: Beacon Press, 2012); Kent D. Drescher et al., "An Exploration of the Viability and Usefulness of the Construct of Moral Injury in War Veterans," *Traumatology* 17, no. 1 (March 1, 2011): 8–13, https://doi.org/10.1177/1534765610395615; Brett T. Litz et al., "Moral Injury and Moral Repair in War Veterans: A Preliminary Model and Intervention Strategy," *Clinical Psychology Review* 29 (2009): 695–706; Jonathan Shay, *Achilles in Vietnam: Combat Trauma and the Undoing of Character* (New York: Scribner, 1994); and Jonathan Shay, *Odysseus in America: Combat Trauma and the Trials of Homecoming* (New York: Scribner, 2002).

3. Michael Yandell, "Moral Injury and Human Relationship: A Conversation," *Pastoral Psychology* 68, no. 1 (February 2019), 4.

4. Ched Myers, *Binding the Strong Man: A Political Reading of Mark's Story of Jesus* (Ossining, NY: Orbis, 1988), 191.

5. Joel Marcus, *Mark 1–8: A New Translation with Introduction and Commentary*, AB 27 (New York: Doubleday, 2000), 344.

6. Ched Myers and Karen Lattea, *Say To This Mountain: Mark's Story of Discipleship* (Ossining, NY: Orbis, 1996), 59.

7. Myers and Lattea, *Say to This Mountain*, 59.

8. Marcus, *Mark: A New Translation with Introduction and Commentary*, 348–49.

9. Myers and Lattea, *Say To This Mountain: Mark's Story of Discipleship*, 58.

10. Serene Jones, *Trauma and Grace: Theology in a Ruptured World* (Louisville, KY: Westminster John Knox, 2009), 12.

11. Simone Weil, *Simone Weil's The Iliad, or, The Poem of Force: A Critical Edition*, ed. James P. Holoka (New York: Peter Lang, 2003), 57.

12. Tyler Boudreau, "The Morally Injured," *The Massachusetts Review* 53, no. 3 (2011), 748–49.

13. Jones, *Trauma and Grace*, 12.

14. Jones, *Trauma and Grace*, 13.

15. Brock and Lettini, *Soul Repair*, 21.

16. Shelly Rambo, *Spirit and Trauma: A Theology of Remaining* (Louisville, KY: Westminster John Knox, 2010), 25.

17. Marcus, *Mark: A New Translation with Introduction and Commentary*, 350.

18. Marcus, *Mark: A New Translation with Introduction and Commentary*, 350.

19. Brock and Lettini, *Soul Repair*, xvi.

20. Myers, *Binding the Strong Man: A Political Reading of Mark's Story of Jesus*, 191.
21. Marcus, *Mark: A New Translation with Introduction and Commentary*, 344.
22. Margaret Atwood, "The Sin Eater," in *Dancing Girls and Other Stories* (New York: Simon and Schuster, 1977), 222.
23. Boudreau, "The Morally Injured," 751 (italics original).
24. Rambo, *Spirit and Trauma*, 25.
25. Rambo, *Spirit and Trauma*, 156.
26. Joseph Wiinikka-Lydon, "Moral Injury as Inherent Political Critique: The Prophetic Possibilities of a New Term," *Political Theology* 18, no. 3 (April 2016): 228, https://doi.org/10.1080/1462317X.2015.1104205.
27. Jürgen Moltmann, *The Crucified God: The Cross of Christ as the Foundation and Criticism of Christian Theology* (Minneapolis: Fortress, 1993), x.

BIBLIOGRAPHY

Boudreau, Tyler. "The Morally Injured." *The Massachusetts Review* 53, no. 3 (2011): 746–54.
Brock, Rita Nakashima and Gabriella Lettini. *Soul Repair: Recovering from Moral Injury after War*. Boston: Beacon, 2012.
Drescher, Kent D. et al. "An Exploration of the Viability and Usefulness of the Construct of Moral Injury in War Veterans." *Traumatology* 17, no. 1 (March 1, 2011): 8–13. https://doi.org/10.1177/1534765610395615.
Jones, Serene. *Trauma and Grace: Theology in a Ruptured World*. Louisville, KY: Westminster John Knox, 2009.
Litz, Brett T. et al., "Moral Injury and Moral Repair in War Veterans: A Preliminary Model and Intervention Strategy." *Clinical Psychology Review* 29 (2009): 695–706.
Marcus, Joel. *Mark 1–8: A New Translation with Introduction and Commentary*. Anchor Bible 27. New York: Doubleday, 2000.
Moltmann, Jürgen. *The Crucified God: The Cross of Christ as the Foundation and Criticism of Christian Theology*. Minneapolis: Fortress, 1993.
Myers, Ched. *Binding the Strong Man: A Political Reading of Mark's Story of Jesus*. Ossining, NY: Orbis, 1988.
Myers, Ched and Karen Lattea. *Say To This Mountain: Mark's Story of Discipleship*. Ossining, NY: Orbis, 1996.
Rambo, Shelly. *Spirit and Trauma: A Theology of Remaining*. Louisville, KY: Westminster John Knox, 2010.
Shay, Jonathan. *Achilles in Vietnam: Combat Trauma and the Undoing of Character*. New York: Scribner, 1994.
—. *Odysseus in America: Combat Trauma and the Trials of Homecoming*. New York: Scribner, 2002.
Weil, Simone. *Simone Weil's The Iliad, or, The Poem of Force: A Critical Edition*. Edited by James P. Holoka. New York: Peter Lang, 2003.
Wiinikka-Lydon, Joseph. "Moral Injury as Inherent Political Critique: The Prophetic Possibilities of a New Term," *Political Theology* 18, no. 3 (2016): 219–32, https://doi.org/10.1080/1462317X.2015.1104205.
Yandell, Michael. "Moral Injury and Human Relationship: A Conversation," *Pastoral Psychology* 68, no. 1 (2019).
Yandell, Michael. "'Do Not Torment Me': The Morally Injured Gerasene Demoniac." Pages 135–50 in *Exploring Moral Injury in Sacred Texts*. Edited by Joseph McDonald. Studies in Religion and Theology. London: Jessica Kingsley, 2017.

Chapter Seven

Moral Injury in Genesis 19 and Moral Repair in the Book of Ruth

Nancy R. Bowen

The purpose of this analysis is to consider how concepts of moral injury may illuminate the story of the city of Sodom and the family of Lot in Genesis 19. Reading this story through the lens of moral injury is an exercise in imagination.[1] Biblical narrative rarely describes a character's inner thoughts or feelings, which are key to understanding moral injury. Therefore, moral injury must be inferred from the events, what is known of ancient moral codes, and what we know today of moral injury.

GENESIS 14:1–16

The story of Genesis 19 actually begins in Genesis 14. This chapter contains a story that involves a war, the city of Sodom, and Lot and his family. There is a war between a coalition of eastern nations and the cities around the Dead Sea, including Sodom and Gomorrah (vv. 1–2). The cities had existed as enslaved territories for twelve years. That they rebelled in the thirteenth year (v. 4) suggests oppressive conditions. The eastern kings come to suppress the rebellion with lethal force.

As the kings of Sodom and Gomorrah and their armies run for their lives, some of their soldiers die while fleeing and others make it to safety (v. 10). The eastern kings then loot the cities for plunder, taking goods, provisions, and captives, one of whom is Lot (vv. 11–12). We learn a few verses later that his wife and daughters were probably also captured (v. 16). Upon receiving news of Lot's fate from one of the survivors, Abram (later to be known as Abraham) mounts his own expedition (v. 14). Abram successfully defeats the eastern kings and returns with Lot, along with all the looted goods and other captives (vv. 15–16).

Now, let's imagine where moral injury might have occurred. Under oppressive conditions, perhaps the kings of the Dead Sea cities and their subjects violated morals in order to survive. In the rebellion and subsequent battle, we might assume some of them committed acts of perpetration that commonly occur in war. When the armies fled, some had to leave behind comrades to die in the tar pits to save themselves, an act of failure to save others. The account always lists the kings of Sodom and Gomorrah first, and it is their cities that were plundered, suggesting they were the instigators of the rebellion. Perhaps their fighting men, as they fled to the hills, felt betrayed by their leaders for involving them in an unnecessary war, an act of disillusionment. Since v. 10 explicitly states that the kings of Sodom and Gomorrah fled, perhaps the kings would be ashamed of their loss in battle and afraid their subjects, and the larger world, would condemn them as cowards for running away.

What of Lot, the women, and others who were taken as captives? One question is why Lot was in the city to begin with. Perhaps as a "resident alien,"[2] he was not permitted by the king of Sodom to participate in the battle. Would he have been ashamed that he was not trusted to fight for his adopted home of Sodom? In addition, he experienced an act of failure insofar as he was unable to prevent his family being taken captive. I assume that his wife and daughters were among the "women" that Abram brought back. What would they have done to survive? Although in Gen 19 Lot will claim his daughters "have not known a man," perhaps he lied. Captors always had access to the bodies of captives.[3]

If we infer these possible occasions of moral injury, we could also infer the emotional and psychological consequences. In the timeline of the narrative, somewhere between fourteen and twenty-five years elapse between Gen 14 and Gen 19, which is less than a generation. In the real world, we would be considering the ongoing and lingering effects of moral injuries. I want to suggest that even in the narrative world, the ongoing and lingering effects are evident in the events that follow in Gen 19.

GENESIS 19:1–3

The subsequent story involving Lot and his family begins with two men arriving at the gates of Sodom, where Lot greets them and invites them to his house. The sociological categories of group- and individual-orientation as a lens for reading Gen 19 give a better sense of possible moral parameters at work in the story.[4] In group-orientation, an individual's dominant identity arises from their bonds to the household and society to which they belong.

The welfare of the group is considered synonymous with the welfare of the individual.

In group-oriented societies, the boundaries and limits of the group must be clearly defined. The boundaries function positively to protect the group. Insiders are viewed as good and contributing to the life of the group through protection, cooperation, and mutual assistance. Negatively, boundary violations are dangerous because they can threaten the existence of the group. Thus, outsiders are generally viewed as threatening and endangering to the group.

The two messengers (NRSV "angels") who arrive at the boundary of Sodom are by their nature outsiders to the group. In the Hebrew Bible, there are both divine and human messengers. Human messengers are sent by those of high standing, especially kings. From the perspective of the residents of Sodom, the war with the eastern kings makes these messengers more ambiguous and threatening. Are they from hostile kings, possibly coming as spies for the next attack? From the perspective of group-orientation, the moral imperative is to keep the city safe. Failure to do so could theoretically result in moral injury.

Lot's position in the community is also precarious. He is not related to the group by birth or marriage, so he is not an insider. But he is also not an outsider. He resides there as a resident alien. His marginal position in the community was already evident in his exclusion from battle described in Gen 14.

Lot encounters these two messengers at the gate. At this point, not even Lot knows whether God or human kings sent these messengers. Their presence presents him with a number of moral dilemmas. Perhaps he would normally be inclined to extend hospitality, a moral value that he perhaps shared with his uncle Abraham as evidenced by how his greeting and offer of lodging mirrors that of Abraham in Gen 18:1–8. If these men were spies, however, the offer of hospitality may inadvertently threaten the safety of Sodom, thereby threatening his own safety and that of his family. Extending hospitality may benefit Lot as it allows him to act within his moral code, but will that benefit accrue at the expense of the larger community? In the end, Lot urges the messengers to spend the night at his house. Can this be viewed as an attempt at moral repair from the events of the war in Gen 14? Instead of isolating himself, as he will later, here Lot is shown as able to offer and extend care to others.

GENESIS 19:4–5, 9–11

One of the ways war can be morally disruptive is that it leads to the dehumanization of the enemy. This may be experienced not only by those directly engaged in war, but by the culture that sends them to war. In the United States, we need look only to the internment of Japanese Americans during World War II and the current social hostility toward Muslims in the aftermath of 9/11 to illustrate this point. This view of outsiders appears in Gen 19:

> But before they lay down, the men of the city, the men of Sodom, both young and old, all the people to the last man, surrounded the house; they called to Lot, "Where are the men who came to you tonight? Bring them out to us, so that we may know them." (vv. 4–5)

Interpreters of this passage have often viewed all the residents of Sodom as pathologically immoral, as evidenced by this demand to Lot. In that view, the residents of Sodom exhibit no dissonance between their morals and actions, and hence no moral injury. Consideration of Gen 14 and group-orientation, however, offers other possibilities for interpreting the men's actions. If the king of Sodom (Gen 14) or the elders of the city were among the men, their actions could easily be interpreted as those of civic leaders seeking information about the strangers who had entered their city in order to determine whether they posed a threat.[5] Even so, it is not an individual or a small group of leaders who show up, but a large crowd. The language of vv. 4–5 emphasizes the group's size. The repetition of "men" implies they are adult men. The "old" men might include survivors of the war in Gen 14. Additionally, because of the ambiguity of "know," although it is possible to interpret the men's question as a way to assess a potential threat to the community by gaining sufficient knowledge, if we interpret "know" as a euphemism for "sexual intercourse" (cf. Gen 4:1, 17; 1 Sam 1:19), the men's intent is gang rape. Biblical commentators generally claim that the men of Sodom sought to violate social norms against male-male intercourse and hospitality's sacred duty to protect guests. In this reading, the dissonance required for moral injury to occur would be present.

Through the lens of group-orientation, gang rape, immoral as it is, could provide a protective function for the community of Sodom. For the men of Sodom, these messengers represented hostile foreign kings. Raping them would strip them of their dignity and honor, as well as result in lasting harmful, psychological, and physical effects. After being raped, the messengers would probably be incapable of spying and certainly in their shamed condition they would be incapable of reporting their information to their leaders.[6] Shaming the envoys would also provide an opportunity to take a modicum of revenge against the eastern kings for the humiliations they had inflicted upon the men of Sodom in the war described in Gen 14. Unable to take revenge directly against the eastern kings and their armies, their alleged envoys become the scapegoat.

It is important to emphasize that moral injury can occur even when the action was unavoidable or warranted at the time. Even if the men of Sodom viewed their threat of gang rape as the "right thing to do" at the time, they might have experienced it later as an act of perpetration.

The size of the group ("all the people") suggests a large crowd of men. After Lot's unsuccessful intervention (see next unit), the aggression escalates as they attempt to break down the door of Lot's house (v. 9). Their threat to do "more evil against you [Lot], than them" (author's translation) suggests their violence had risen to lethal levels. In today's language we would describe this as "mob violence." One of the dynamics Jonathan Shay discusses in his foundational works on moral injury is the "berserk state," a state of blood-lust in which abuse after abuse is committed.[7] The key aspect he found in soldiers in this state is the absence of any restraint. Soldiers described doing things they normally would not do, demonstrating the dissonance necessary for moral injury to occur. "All the diversity and multiplicity of social morality have been replaced by the single value of revenge."[8] Berserk seems to be the state the men of Sodom have reached. Shay describes the berserk state as ruinous. If the person survives, there are lifelong psychological and physiological injuries. "Once a person has entered the berserk state, he or she is changed *forever*."[9] I find myself wondering if the blindness inflicted by the angels (v. 11) might not be the symbol of that ruinous change.

With respect to the men of Sodom, the consequences of moral injury sustained during the war with the eastern kings seem evident in their reaction to the messengers, which can be interpreted as lack of trust and anger, leading to a dehumanizing of the enemy. Their previous moral injury leads to potential further moral injury in the threat of gang rape and going berserk. Unfortunately, there is no opportunity for moral repair as the men are killed and the city destroyed (Gen 19:24–25).

GENESIS 19:6–8

When Lot goes outside his house to intervene, what is his goal and what are his choices? From the perspective of group-orientation and self-preservation, he should give in to the men, which would ensure his safety by aligning himself with the insiders against the outsiders, but which would violate expected codes of hospitality. Yet, Lot states his goal as providing protection for the messengers whom he has sheltered in his house (v. 8), which may violate his responsibilities to the community where he resides as a resident alien. Protecting the messengers would surely increase the men of the city's suspicions and possibly threaten Lot and his family. As with the initial decision regarding whether to offer hospitality to these strangers, Lot finds himself caught in a dilemma. Either choice violates a moral code.

Perhaps to mitigate taking the side of the messengers, Lot tries to bond himself with the men of the city by referring to them as "my brothers" (v. 7). He then makes a puzzling counteroffer to give his two daughters to the mob bent on violence. Lot's motivation remains unclear. No rationale mitigates the possible moral injury that both Lot and his daughters might suffer as a consequence.

For Lot, the offer of his daughters would mean an act of failure to protect them. Depending on the men's response, he might be unable to save his daughters from death. For the daughters, it would be an act of disillusionment in authority when the father who was supposed to protect them does not. Their father was willing to exploit their bodies for his own purposes.

GENESIS 19:12–26

The messengers now tell Lot that he is to bring any immediate and extended family who are in Sodom "out of this place" (v. 12). The messengers' ability to rescue Lot and to blind the men reveals they were not from hostile kings but from Yhwh. They reveal to Lot they have been sent to destroy "this place" (v. 13).

We discover that Lot's daughters were betrothed and their soon-to-be spouses reject Lot's plea to leave. Why did they not take Lot seriously? Perhaps they considered that Lot's performance with the men of the city deprived him of any respect or believability. Should the man who offered to surrender his daughters to a group bent on assault be taken seriously? Did they also experience the moral injury of failing to protect their brides-to-be when they heard Lot offer up the women for whom they were legally responsible? Does their assessment that Lot was joking (v. 14) reflect an inability to trust others with regard to acts of morality? Furthermore, for Lot, these were men that he had found acceptable for marriage to his daughters and leaving them behind would leave his daughters without husbands, and therefore with less security. Another moral dilemma presents itself.

As dawn breaks, the angels "urge" Lot to take his wife and two daughters and leave "or else you would be consumed" (v. 15). Despite the clear urgency, Lot delays. Why he delayed is a missing piece of information in the story. He seems to be dallying, indecisive, and anxious. If we think of moral injury as the disruption of an individual's ability to make moral decisions, then Lot's delay may be indicative of that disruption. He now had to decide whether to stay or leave. While staying would certainly be disastrous if the messengers are to be trusted, maybe certain death would be preferable to an uncertain future. He would finally be an insider as he shared the fate of his adopted city. Leaving will save his wife and two daughters, but at what cost? After all, neither his decision to offer hospitality to the messengers nor his attempt to defuse the threat of violence ended well. He might be paralyzed by the inability to decide what is good and what is evil. Maybe he has become demoralized by all that has happened from his captivity in Gen 14 until now, and perhaps the delay is indicative of his confusion and the futility of moral actions.

Finally, the angels drag Lot and his family out of the city. Once outside, the angels instructed them: do not look back, and escape to the hills (v. 17). From the war story in Gen 14, we know the hills are a place of safety (14:10). But again, despite the imminent danger, Lot delays and argues with the messengers. Even though the hills represent safety, Lot is afraid that the disaster will overtake him before he is able to reach them, and he requests to flee to the city of Zoar instead (vv. 19–20).

There are several ways to interpret Lot's response as a consequence of moral injury. One interpretation is that it reflects demoralization. Lot's assessment that the "disaster will overtake me and I die" may reflect thoughts and feelings of being condemned. In his shame, Lot perhaps believed there was some sort of evil clinging to him as a stain, making him a target at which God had taken aim. Interpreting Lot's delaying as a lack of faith suggests he doubts God's ability to save him. Perhaps Lot believed in that divine ability once upon a time, but, in the wake of the disasters of captivity and the attack by the men of Sodom, he has lost that belief.

Though Lot reached physical safety in Zoar, disaster came upon him. Lot's wife, as is often the case in biblical narrative, has been there all long only by inference. For example, it was likely she who prepared the meal and bread for the messengers (see Gen 18:6–7; 19:3). She exists as Lot's "wife," and though never stated, as the mother of the daughters. The angels had warned not to look back (v. 17). That warning in Hebrew is in the masculine singular, addressed to Lot. Did Lot share the information with his wife? In the ancient patriarchal world, are we to assume that the command to Lot included her? Her knowledge of the command is another piece of missing information in the story, but the writer assumes she had that knowledge and violated the decree. The text states succinctly that she "looked back, and she became a pillar of salt" (v. 26).

One potential for the wife to experience moral injury would be in what may have occurred when she was taken captive in the previous story (Gen 14:16). Furthermore, from experiences of war, captivity, and the terror of the mob, she would have witnessed and experienced the kind of intense suffering and evil that can result in despair and hopelessness. She had no voice in Lot's offer of her daughters to the men of Sodom, even though women had nearly equal status and authority with men in their role as mothers. This would result in an act of failure to protect her daughters, similar to a mother who fails to protect her daughter from her father's sexual abuse.

We do not know why she looked back. One of the consequences of moral injury is emotional isolation and withdrawal from relationships. For Lot, this isolation and withdrawal is symbolized by the cave he will inhabit (v. 30). The wife's transformation into a pillar of salt may be similarly symbolic. She becomes immobilized, unable to move forward into any kind of new life. Less symbolically, she died and was permanently removed from the family, a kind of ultimate isolation from relationship. The most heartbreaking way to read her turning back, assuming she knew of the prohibition not to turn back, is as a suicide attempt because she failed to see a path toward renewal. Maybe what she chose was not disobedience, but a way out of her shame and despair. Suicidal tendencies are common with moral injury, and Lot's wife was successful in her attempt.[10]

GENESIS 19:30–38

The disaster that overtook Lot added another act of failure to his moral injury, as he was apparently unable to help his wife or prevent her death. After Sodom was destroyed, Lot—as leader of his family—appears overwhelmed by the enormity of the situation and unable to guide and protect his family. The final scene begins in a cave in the hills (v. 30), where Lot had fled with his daughters from Zoar. From the perspective of moral injury, we should consider the cave as an expression of Lot's extreme withdrawal. He has removed himself as far as possible from any extrafamilial relationships, expressing his loss of capacity for intimacy.

Lot's daughters accompanied Lot to the cave, perhaps also an expression of withdrawal from life and capacity for intimacy. At this point in the story, they have experienced captivity, their father's willingness to sacrifice their bodies without their consent, the loss and deaths of the men to which they were betrothed, the destruction of cities, and the bizarre death of their mother. Possible moral injury includes disillusionment in authority and having witnessed and experienced the kind of intense suffering and evil that can result in despair and hopelessness. The daughters would have experienced what amounts to the end of the world. The elder daughter notes two things in v. 31. First, their father is old, perhaps acknowledging he is unlikely to remarry and have descendants. Second, "there is not a man on earth to come into us." The meaning of the following phrase, "that we may preserve offspring" (literally, "to make seed live"), is ambiguous. Options include the expression of a global concern about repopulating the earth, a more local concern to ensure the continuation of Lot's family, a desire for love and life around them, or an effort to reconnect Lot to his capacity for intimacy as an attempt at moral repair.

The result is an ironic reversal. Earlier Lot was willing to use his daughters for sexual purposes without their consent. Now they will use him for sexual purposes without his consent. In vv. 32–38, it is not Lot who takes action, it is the daughters. As their father, Lot should be the one making plans for their survival. Given Lot's accumulated moral injury, however, his passivity might be interpreted as a loss of his capacity to make *any* decision.

The daughters' behavior can be interpreted as either reprehensible or heroic. If you think the daughters have fallen to the same level of moral depravity as Sodom, then no moral injury would occur. But the tactic of getting Lot drunk suggests the daughters viewed their behavior as shameful, though the reason is not given. Even though father-daughter incest is never explicitly prohibited in the biblical legal materials, it is prohibited in other legal codes in Western Asia. Perhaps they knew Lot would not agree to their proposal. Even though their plan may be viewed as justified or necessary, their sense that it was taboo would further add to the daughters' own accumulation of moral injury.

The story ends with the announcement of the births of the two sons (vv. 36–38). Since the sons become the eponymous ancestors to the Moabites and Ammonites, the daughters' stated goal "to make seed live" was accomplished. We know nothing more of Lot and his daughters.

MORAL INJURY IN GENESIS

This analysis has considered how concepts of moral injury illuminate the characters and dynamics within the story of the city of Sodom and the family of Lot. One way this exercise might be helpful for faith communities is as a case study to explain and illustrate concepts of moral injury. The Bible becomes a mirror that reflects dynamics that are also at work in our own context. This is similar to how Shay uses the Greek stories of the *Iliad* and the *Odyssey* to identify and explain concepts of moral injury. Perhaps this can be a way for active military and veterans in our communities to remain connected to their faith traditions by letting them see that they are not alone. Their ancient ancestors in the faith knew only too well the moral injuries they live with today. And it could help those of us who have not been to war to better understand those who have by studying the stories of moral injury in our own faith tradition.

MORAL REPAIR: THE BOOK OF RUTH

The story of Ruth is connected with Gen 19 through the opening scene set in Moab and the character of "Ruth the Moabite." Recall that Lot's daughters gave birth to sons who would become the eponymous ancestors to the Moabites and Ammonites. The lens of moral injury provides a new way to consider Ruth as a story of moral repair.

The story of Ruth can be viewed as a corrective life experience. When Elimelech and his family arrive in Moab, much like Lot and his family initially in Sodom, they live peaceably as sojourners with the Moabites. Perhaps the sons' marriages to Moabite women are expressions of care and love and not strictly based on economics (Ruth 1:4). When the sons tragically die, both daughters-in-law express their love for Naomi, and Ruth makes a covenant vow to stay with her (1:7–10, 14–17). In Bethlehem, Ruth cares for Naomi by going out to glean (2:2). Boaz acknowledges that Ruth's status as a Moabite woman makes her vulnerable to sexual violence, so he protects her (2:8–9). We see both Israelites and Moabites doing what they know to be good and right.

The scene of Ruth and Boaz at the threshing floor (ch. 3) mimics the scene between Lot and his daughters. The daughters waited until Lot passed out from drinking and then went to "lay" (Hebrew root, *šākav*) with him (Gen 19:33, 35). Similarly, Ruth waited until Boaz passed out from drinking and then "lay down" (Hebrew root, *šākav*) with him (Ruth 3:7). Given the parallels between the two stories, readers may assume that Ruth and Boaz had intercourse. Unlike Lot who "did not know" what happened to him, Boaz woke up. There are no clear taboos against Boaz and Ruth having sex, since Ruth was a widow and not an unmarried girl. The fact that Boaz sent Ruth away before it was light enough for "one person to recognize another" (3:14), however, suggests a level of inappropriateness to the encounter. But Boaz promises to pursue established channels and their encounter is not stigmatized. Only after they are later married does Ruth conceive (4:13), and instead of becoming the eponymous ancestor of a hated nation, she gives birth to a son who would be a direct ancestor of King David (4:18–22) and Jesus (Matt 1:5–6, 16). In psychological terms, the story of Ruth and Boaz "draws a firm line around the past and its related associations, so that the mistakes of the past do not define the present and the future and so that a preoccupation with the past does not prevent possible future good."[11]

As with Gen 19, reading Ruth this way might be helpful for faith communities as a case study to explain and illustrate concepts of moral repair. The Bible becomes a mirror that reflects dynamics that are also at work today. In considering Ruth as a story of moral repair, we can also say to those suffering from moral injury that a moral future is possible. The Moabite, Ruth, and the Israelites, Naomi and Boaz, show that good and moral deeds are possible even in the aftermath of moral injury. For veterans who belong to Jewish or Christian faith communities, Ruth might be used as a witness to the possibility of moral repair. What happened in Gen 19 is every bit as horrific and injurious as what occurs today in war. Yet on the other side of all that is a story that does not try to fix or change the past but moves toward a hopeful future through good actions, providing a path toward reconciliation and renewal.

POSTSCRIPT

The story of Sodom has often been used in Christian tradition to condemn homosexuality. I would note that those who condemn the men of Sodom often act just like them. The men of Sodom viewed the messengers as outsiders and "others." Likewise, some Christians have viewed homosexuals as outsiders and "others." The men of Sodom threatened violence against the messengers and Lot. Likewise, some Christians threaten LGBTQIA+ persons with violence. The men of Sodom's violence rose to lethal levels. Likewise, some Christian violence against gays and lesbians is often lethal, especially in countries where homosexuality is criminalized. I think of the torture and death of Matthew Shepard, as well as the deaths of so many African American trans women.

In the treatment of moral injury, psychologists contend that therapists need to be able to listen to a patient's story of what they did, did not do, suffered, or witnessed without censure, disgust, or disdain, since those dynamics are at the core of moral injury. "Without trust, details, responses, and meaning elements will remain hidden, and in order to promote healing, concealment needs to be avoided at all costs. To encourage disclosure, the therapist must portray unconditional acceptance and the ability to listen to difficult and morally conflicted material without revulsion."[12]

Reading Gen 19 through the lens of moral injury allows us to read the story without censure, disgust, or disdain, and instead with empathy for the characters, including the men of Sodom. We can see the actions of the various characters as dependent on context, a result of exigencies and extraordinary demands. A current area of research within moral injury concerns "communalization." According to Shay, "communalization" means "being able safely to tell the story to someone who is listening and who can be trusted to retell it truthfully to others in the community."[13] Christians should tell the story of Sodom, Lot, and his daughters in this truthful way to our communities. Perhaps then Christians can also learn to listen, without censure and with empathy, to the stories of moral injury in their own communities.

NOTES

1. This is a revision of Nancy R. Bowen, "Sodom and Lot's Family: Moral Injury in Genesis 19," in *Exploring Moral Injury in Sacred Texts*, ed. Joseph McDonald, Studies in Religion and Theology (London: Jessica Kingsley, 2017), 47–68. Used here with permission.

2. Lot and his family were originally a part of Abraham's extended family (Gen 12:4–5). Lot separated from Abraham (Gen 13:5–11) and resided in Sodom as a sojourner or resident alien (Gen 19:9). The Hebrew word *gēr* refers to someone who is a non-native with respect to where they live, thus the traditional English translation of "alien" or "resident alien." As such, the *gēr* did not possess landed property and required special structures of support (Deut 24:17–21; 26:5; 27:19).

3. This was more an incident of trauma than moral injury.

4. Discussion on group- and individual-orientation is based upon Lyn M. Bechtel, "A Feminist Reading of Genesis 19:1–11," in *Genesis*, ed. Athalya Brenner, Feminist Companion to the Bible, Second Series (Sheffield: Sheffield Academic, 1998), 108–28; Lyn M. Bechtel, "Boundary Issues in Genesis 19:1–38," in *Escaping Eden: New Feminist Perspectives on the Bible*, eds., Harold C. Washington, Susan Lochrie Graham, and Pamela Thimmes (Sheffield: Sheffield Academic, 1998), 22–40.

5. Similar to how the King of Jericho inquired after the men who entered Rahab's house in Josh 2:2–3.

6. Bechtel, "Boundary Issues," 28.

7. Jonathan Shay, *Achilles in Vietnam: Combat Trauma and the Undoing of Character* (New York: Atheneum, 1994), 77–98.

8. Shay, *Achilles,* 90.

9. Shay, *Achilles,* 98. Emphasis original.

10. I did not expect to interpret the transformation of Lot's wife into a pillar of salt as a successful suicide attempt until the words appeared on my computer screen. It stopped me in my tracks and left me almost as immobile as she for a moment. Then I wept for five minutes for this character, and for all others who have been unable to see a way forward to moral healing and a future.

11. Brett T. Litz et al., "Moral Injury and Moral Repair in War Veterans: A Preliminary Model and Intervention Strategy," *Clinical Psychology Review* 29 (2009): 704.

12. Litz et al., "Moral Injury," 702.

13. Shay, *Achilles,* 4.

BIBLIOGRAPHY

Bechtel, Lyn M. "A Feminist Reading of Genesis 19:1–11." Pages 108–28 in *Genesis*, Feminist Companion to the Bible, Second Series. Edited by Athalya Brenner. Sheffield: Sheffield Academic, 1998.

Bechtel, Lyn M. "Boundary Issues in Genesis 19:1–38." Pages 22–40 in *Escaping Eden: New Feminist Perspectives on the Bible*. Edited by Harold C. Washington, Susan Lochrie Graham, and Pamela Thimmes. Sheffield: Sheffield Academic, 1998.

Bowen, Nancy R. "Sodom and Lot's Family: Moral Injury in Genesis 19." Pages 47–68 in *Exploring Moral Injury in Sacred Texts*. Edited by Joseph McDonald. Studies in Religion and Theology. London: Jessica Kingsley, 2017.

Litz, Brett T. et al. "Moral Injury and Moral Repair in War Veterans: A Preliminary Model and Intervention Strategy," *Clinical Psychology Review* 29 (2009): 695–706.

Shay, Jonathan. *Achilles in Vietnam: Combat Trauma and the Undoing of Character*. New York: Atheneum, 1994.

Part III

Engaging Moral Injury (Diverse Perspectives and Resources)

Chapter Eight

Addressing Moral Injury in Psychotherapy and Counseling

Joseph M. Currier and Wesley H. McCormick

The emergence of the concept of moral injury since 2010 represents one of the most important developments in clinical research and practice with persons struggling to recover from the potentially multifaceted consequences of human-perpetrated acts of violence, betrayal, and harm. While psychology and other mental health fields have historically overlooked moral aspects of trauma, themes of moral injury were reflected in art and literature dating back to the earliest records of human societies.[1] Focusing on the Old Testament as just one example, Deuteronomy 20 highlights the potential turmoil of soldiers entering and returning from battle. When considering the possible extent of moral injury (directed at self or others), the psalms also attest to the debilitating shame and guilt that may emerge from moral violations that lead to death or serious harm of another individual (e.g., Ps 51), as well as the profound sense of anger and betrayal from being victimized by another's morally transgressive behavior (e.g., Ps 22). Drawing on Homer's tragedies to understand the suffering of Vietnam veterans entrusted to his care as a psychiatrist, Jonathan Shay first introduced the notion of moral injury into the mental health literature.[2] Even so, partly in response to waves of veterans from recent conflicts in Iraq and Afghanistan seeking treatment for trauma-related issues, widespread interest in moral injury among mental health professionals arguably did not begin until the publication of Brett T. Litz et al.'s seminal review article nearly a decade after 9/11.[3]

Since then, moral injury has increasingly garnered attention from psychologists and other mental health professionals as well as physicians, chaplains, educators, lawyers, theologians, and philosophers. Depending on one's professional discipline, diverse stakeholders approach moral injury from varying angles and grapple with different types of questions. From the vantage point of religion or theology, areas of interest could revolve around practices for forgiveness and reconciliation, theodicy or relationship with God, reestablishing patterns of moral living, and reintegrating with faith communities. From a philosophical view, persons may wonder about the justness of war in general, justifiability of certain wars and wartime actions in particular, moral responsibility of political parties and personages for wartime events, and the implications for activism as related to past, present, and future engagement in different wars. Within psychology and other mental health fields, the moral injury conversation has largely targeted diagnostic and therapeutic aims in which researchers and clinicians are diligently attempting to define and assess the construct of moral injury, identify its mechanisms and outcomes, and develop treatments to promote recovery from potential emotional, relational, and spiritual wounds of morally injurious events. To date, nearly the entirety of this work has focused on military veterans and service members (SM/Vs). More recently, however, mental health professionals are beginning to explore the clinical utility of the construct for civilian traumas as well (e.g., refugees, first responders, violent offenders).

Mental health professionals currently lack a paradigmatic definition of moral injury to guide research and practice. Nevertheless, in the absence of definitive answers to basic questions (e.g., What is moral injury? How does it compare and contrast with PTSD, depression, or other conditions? Should it become a mental health diagnosis?), several psychotherapies have been identified as promising options for promoting healing with morally injured persons. Before introducing these treatments, it is important to highlight that we write as psychologists with a strong commitment to evidence-based practice and interests in caring for SM/Vs. As such, in addressing moral injury in therapy or counseling, we implement approaches that have demonstrated effectiveness in clinical research whenever possible, while also honoring our patients' beliefs, values, circumstances, goals, needs, and preferences for care. The brevity of this chapter precludes us from offering a comprehensive discussion of all therapy approaches that have received scientific scrutiny and discussion in the mental health literature.[4] Instead, drawing on material from a recent case of the second author (McCormick) with a morally injured veteran, the goals of this chapter are to provide (1) an overview of promising treatments for moral injury, and (2) a discussion of important concerns that may emerge in the therapeutic process with morally injured patients.

CASE EXAMPLE: THE PRESENTING PROBLEM

"Mr. G." was a sixty-four-year-old, Caucasian who was self-referred for psychotherapy at a university-based outpatient mental health clinic. Upon arriving for his initial appointment, he quickly asserted his only motivation for seeking treatment was an ultimatum from his significant other. As we discussed his history and presenting concerns, he narrated how approximately five years prior he developed a romantic relationship while stateside during a short reprieve from his work as a military contractor. While the relationship had progressed fairly effortlessly despite his rotating schedule between the United States and Iraq, he described increasing emotional and interpersonal struggles since retiring one year prior. In detailing these concerns, Mr. G. recounted serving in the Army during Vietnam and working in the civilian sector for more than twenty years before becoming a military contractor after 9/11. Though he denied any struggles in the years after Vietnam, Mr. G. narrated how witnessing abuses of Iraqi militants and civilians on multiple occasions had left him feeling disillusioned about the Iraqi conflict, US government, and humanity at large. In keeping with morally injurious phenomenology emerging from betrayal events, he expressed a breadth of highly cynical beliefs, including mistrust of others, especially persons in authority, and viewing humanity as wholly irredeemable. Mr. G. also reported a loss of theistic faith as a result of trauma exposures in Iraq, and went on to describe how he could no longer believe in the god of his evangelical Christian upbringing because, "How can God exist and allow people to suffer like that?"

In terms of mental health symptoms, Mr. G. reported experiencing symptoms consistent with PTSD due to repeated exposures to trauma while working in war-zone environments in the Middle East for the better part of a decade. For example, intrusive thoughts and memories (e.g., visualizing scenes where individuals were mistreated, ruminating on his inability to intervene), avoidance-based coping (e.g., behaviorally inactive, social isolation), negative alterations in cognitions and mood (e.g., increased anger, cynicism toward the government and humanity), hypervigilance (e.g., repeatedly checking windows and doors of his home, scanning rooms while in public), and hyperarousal (e.g., difficulty sleeping, elevated heart rate, muscle tension). Since retirement, he described how his issues had proliferated, affecting his relationships with friends, family, and his partner. In particular, he described grappling with persistent anger toward God and humanity, an inability to connect meaningfully with other people, and frequent emotion dysregulation (e.g., arguing with his partner, becoming easily frustrated while grocery shopping and seeking refuge in his car until his partner was finished). As a result of his increasing social isolation and emotional hostility, Mr. G.'s partner demanded he seek help or face the dissolution of their relationship.

APPLICATION OF EXISTING THERAPIES FOR PTSD

From a mental health standpoint, one of the most pressing scientific priorities for advancing clinical practices for morally injured patients is to clarify whether and how moral injury fits with PTSD and other existing mental health diagnoses. Although numbers of moral injury stakeholders are growing exponentially, Brett T. Litz and Patricia K. Kerig rightly stated we "should not assume without evidence that moral injury, as a mental or behavioral health outcome, has explanatory validity and clinical utility beyond concepts more widely recognized, such as PTSD."[5] Further, even if strong evidence supports the validity and utility of morally injurious phenomena, the condition could share similar features with existing trauma-related syndromes. For example, in keeping with the diagnostic criteria for PTSD, Litz et al. suggested moral injury will likely similarly emerge following exposure to an emotionally challenging event in which common clusters of symptoms will ensue.[6] Many experts therefore believe that therapists should rely on proven procedures useful for PTSD unless there is clear evidence they do not work with moral injury.

Cognitive Processing Therapy

First developed to treat survivors of sexual assault, Cognitive Processing Therapy (CPT) is a manualized, trauma-focused, and scientifically-supported approach for PTSD and comorbid symptoms that has been recommended as a first-line treatment from the Department of Veterans Affairs (VA), Department of Defense (DoD), and American Psychological Association (APA).[7] Although CPT was not developed for moral injury per se, its theory and research base may support its application for posttraumatic symptomatology emerging from exposure to morally injurious events. CPT is based on a constructivist, social-cognitive model of PTSD emphasizing cognitive conditions of the trauma and their role in shaping emotional responses and behavior. Drawing on primarily cognitive therapy techniques, the goals of CPT are to (1) encourage expression of natural emotions (e.g., sadness) and reduce manufactured emotions (emotions resulting from unhelpful cognitions such as "I am solely to blame for this event") related to the trauma; (2) identify and challenge unhelpful ways of thinking about the trauma, as well as current thoughts about self, others, and world; and (3) promote a more balanced set of beliefs about oneself, others, and the world. In keeping with the notion of PTSD as a disorder of nonrecovery, it is assumed persons will experience distressing thoughts and emotions following a morally injurious event, which will naturally abate via attempts to make meaning on the basis of reflective capacities, social relationships, and other psychosocial resources. However, when the event greatly undermines a survivor's global meaning system and he or she overly relies on avoidance-based coping, PTSD and/or moral injury may emerge. In turn, whether during or outside of sessions, CPT predominantly utilizes exercises that attempt to disrupt this cycle such that meaning-making and consolidation of the traumatic memory become possible.

Prolonged Exposure

Prolonged Exposure (PE) is another trauma-focused intervention that has been identified as a highly effective approach for PTSD in clinical guidelines of professional organizations that also have a significant interest in moral injury work (e.g., VA, DoD, APA).[8] Whereas CPT focuses on cognition, PE focuses on behavior therapy principles and strategies. Historically, PE emerged out of emotional processing theory,[9] which proposes PTSD develops from a fear network of mental structures in memory (e.g., event stimuli, responses, and situational meanings) associated with the trauma that contribute to avoidance-based coping and limit meaning-making processes. PE then attempts to revise the fear network via activating these maladaptive structures and providing information that is discrepant from the fear network in the safety of the therapeutic relationship and other nontraumatic situations. Practically-speaking, PE includes three basic components: (1) confronting people, places, and possible activities that are somehow reminiscent of the morally injurious event the survivor has been avoiding (i.e., in vivo exposure); (2) repeatedly revisiting the central traumatic memory, engaging with painful emotional content in sessions, and listening to recordings of the exercises at home (i.e., imaginal exposure); and (3) working through the emotional content and situational meanings of the trauma via open-ended discussions after imaginal exposure exercises with the clinician. In combination, these interventions may promote emotional processing and consolidation of painful feelings and thoughts in a manner that may enhance self-efficacy and values-based living for morally injured patients.

Acceptance and Commitment Therapy

Acceptance and Commitment Therapy (ACT) is a third type of cognitive and behavioral intervention that has also been applied to moral injury.[10] As opposed to CPT and PE, ACT focuses on changing the sufferer's relationship to painful thoughts and emotions rather than reducing or changing the form or content of morally injurious phenomena. Inspired by relational frame theory,[11] moral injury could serve as a salient reminder of sacred values (e.g., closeness with family or God) and impetus for recovery and pursuing a purposeful life in ACT. Hence, the goal is to not to "feel better," but instead to increase willingness to experience painful emotions and thoughts for the sake of reconnecting with violated values and responding to life's inevitable stressors in a more psychologically flexible manner. From a procedural standpoint, ACT then pursues these aims through two means: (1) teaching psychological skills with metaphors and in-session exercises; and (2) helping patients clarify values that might guide, inspire, and motivate the development of goals and commitment to values-guided action that enriches their lives. These procedures are governed by behavioral principles situated within six core processes that might apply to moral injury: (1) "contacting the present moment," or consciously connecting with internal and external phenomena in the moment; (2) "defusion," or stepping back and detaching from unhelpful thoughts and emotions; (3) "acceptance," or willingness to encounter and make room for painful thoughts and feelings; (4) "self as context," or conceptualization of one's self as able to experience and yet transcend both positive and negative thoughts and emotions; (5) "values clarification," or identifying meaningful directions for one's life; and (6) "committed action," or taking effective action in the service of sacred values.

DEVELOPMENT OF NEW THERAPIES FOR MORAL INJURY

Even in the absence of a paradigmatic framework and definition of moral injury, several researchers have developed and evaluated new therapies for moral injury. In this regard, clinical researchers combine and repackage existing therapeutic approaches to address mental health concerns in new ways. When applied to moral injury, several research teams have identified a need to augment or bolster evidence-based treatments for PTSD with additional components from other theoretical models. For example, in most cases, these novel therapies are based in a general Cognitive Behavioral Therapy (CBT) model. Nevertheless, beyond a reliance on focal components of existing approaches (e.g., imaginal exposure, revising unhelpful patterns of thinking or cognition), they also draw from more experiential approaches to therapy (e.g., existential, gestalt) that are heavily emphasized in emotion-focused therapy (EFT).[12] Rather than being applied as a primary treatment, these new therapies frequently serve as complementary strategies for addressing specific aspects of moral injury that might warrant further attention after the completion of another evidence-based approach (e.g., forgiveness, struggles with faith or spirituality).

Adaptive Disclosure

Litz and his colleagues initially developed Adaptive Disclosure (AD) for active-duty military settings to address the potentially distinct psychological symptoms that may emerge from three prominent types of military traumas (life-threat, traumatic loss, and moral injury) by combining evidence-based strategies from CBT and EFT.[13] From the outset, treatment was developed to be time-limited, honor the military ethos, establish a foundation for healing over the long-term, leverage military values and customs, and encourage meaning-making within the context of military roles and values. From a procedural standpoint, AD primarily entails imaginal exposure and subsequent strategies to facilitate experiential processing and meaning-making. Depending on the type of traumatic event and resulting symptoms, patients may participate in different tracks according to their needs. In cases of moral injury in which they are struggling with profound shame and guilt from perpetration-based events, AD may start with imaginal revisiting exercises that align with the PE protocol. As treatment proceeds, AD could shift to reliance on interactive interventions or imaginal dialogues that specifically address forgiveness issues, moral conflicts, and other possible perpetuating factors for moral injury. For example, patients might confess the morally injurious event to a safe caring moral authority (e.g., God, parent) to promote hope and forgiveness, as well as to generate alternative meanings for the event. In addition, as treatment progresses, they may engage in real or symbolic making of amends and engagement in the larger social community. In so doing, the overall aim of AD is to rebalance the moral scales, reduce the prominence of painful moral emotions, and engender room for hope, purpose, and corrective emotional experiences in the social world.

Impact of Killing

Drawing upon research on the psychological costs of killing in wartime,[14] Impact of Killing (IOK) addresses these specific issues in a complementary manner with existing evidence-based interventions for PTSD.[15] When considering the profound shame, self-condemnation, and social isolation that defines a self-directed moral injury that may emerge from taking another's life, IOK begins with CBT strategies and incorporates elements of EFT, as well as existential and relational psychotherapies. In addition to therapeutic exposure and cognitive therapy techniques, IOK incorporates experiential and narrative assignments to foster empathy between SM/Vs and civilians, as well as inner healing and resolution of moral conflicts. For example, in keeping with AD's reliance on EFT-based exercises, IOK might similarly attempt to overcome barriers to self-forgiveness by facilitating an imaginal dialogue with a younger version of themselves or fellow veteran who is also struggling with moral injury related to killing in combat. Given the common stigma and fears of being negatively judged or condemned by others for killing, the therapeutic relationship can serve as a powerful catalyst for challenging those beliefs and experiencing acceptance and compassion from a trusted person. Further, as treatment progresses, IOK encourages conciliatory behaviors, social connections, and community integration through an "amends plan" to counteract withdrawal and isolation. Again, in keeping with AD, engaging in such prosocial activities (e.g., serving others) in one's family and community may bolster a sense of worth and moral identity in a manner that leads to further belonging and meaning after the completion of treatment.

Building Spiritual Strength

Building Spiritual Strength (BSS) is an eight-session intervention designed to facilitate the resolution of spiritual struggles commonly reported among morally injured SM/Vs (e.g., emotional tension with God, guilt and shame about not living up to religious standards of morality).[16] Often used in conjunction with other evidence-based approaches (e.g., PE, CPT), BSS can be facilitated by appropriately trained chaplains or mental health professionals in the VA or community-based settings. The therapeutic material can accommodate a wide range of religious faith identifications (including atheistic), and does not aim to change religious commitments or affiliations. Rather, the overall goal of BSS is to help SM/Vs resolve spiritual struggles that may contribute to PTSD or other trauma-related conditions, and to make more effective use of possible faith resources for restoring a sense of meaning in life and healing a damaged relationship with God. Both within and outside of sessions, BSS makes liberal use of silence, journaling, and narrative components to facilitate this healing process. Like a reliance on EFT strategies in AD and IOK, one of the most innovative in-session interventions in BSS entails imaginal dialogues with God in which SM/Vs can work through painful thoughts and emotions in this possible attachment relationship for the purpose of meaning-making. Patients may also share their faith histories, identify and resolve areas of conflict or lost relationship with God, increase awareness of and communication with God in a manner that is consistent with their religious faith affiliation (e.g., conversational prayer or meditation), address any issues of theodicy, build skills for effective understanding and implementation of forgiveness processes, and develop community resources for spiritual support following the completion of treatment.

CLINICAL CONCERNS IN MORAL INJURY TREATMENT

The increasing value placed on evidence-based practices in mental health professions over recent decades has contributed to an individualistic medical approach to therapy and counseling. In keeping with the metaphor of a physician prescribing a psychotropic medication to alleviate distress symptoms and improve function (e.g., sleep quality), psychologists in particular might be in danger of pursuing a transactional relationship with morally injured patients that overemphasizes the selection and implementation of treatment methods compared to the therapist-patient relationship, extratherapeutic factors, and attitudes and skills of the therapist. For example, for any of the aforementioned procedures to facilitate healing and growth, therapists need to cultivate a collaborative, empathic, and trusting bond in which patients feel honored, understood, and respected. Given the inherent social aspects of human morality in general, however, therapists should not underestimate the role of intimacy, social relatedness, and community engagement outside of sessions in the course of treating moral injury. Further, when considering specific therapist factors, therapists need to cultivate the ability to tolerate possible moral ambiguity and disclosure of emotionally distressing experiences without resorting to false reassurance that might invalidate the patient's sense of remorse or dissonance. Knowledge of military customs, ethics, norms, and various operational procedures (e.g., Rules of Engagement) can provide rich contextual information that may facilitate expression and processing of painful thoughts and feelings related to moral injury.

Consistent with contemporary emphases on culturally competent and patient-centered health care, mental health professionals also need to understand patients' religious and spiritual backgrounds in treating moral injury. Given the interplay between religion and morality in the United States, moral beliefs are often based on a sacred text (e.g., Bible, Koran) or central authority (e.g., pastor, pope, imam) that explicates certain patterns of thinking, feeling, and behaving.[17] Although religious traditions rely on varying authority structures and modes of interpretation, they typically ascribe to a set of writings as a source of revelation for how people should live and relate with themselves, God or the divine, and others—both inside and outside of their social group. In turn, these beliefs can inform the core of one's identity and serve as a nexus for pursuing fundamental needs for belonging and purpose in life. When confronted with morally injurious events, however, patients could suffer more severe symptoms when these sacred or transcendent aspects of life are perceived as damaged or lost. In addition, these events might not be easily equated with traditional mental health conditions that are framed in terms of psychological distress or behavioral dysfunction (e.g., PTSD, depression). Instead, in such cases, moral injury might come to represent a violation of a person's faith system or spiritual center. In turn, chronic issues might limit his or her motivation to draw on the repertoire of relationships, lifestyle practices, rituals, and coping strategies that once supported resilience and flourishing in earlier chapters in life. Clinically speaking, religious and spiritual concerns may therefore contribute to both problems and solutions in moral injury treatment.

Drawing on a continuum model of spirituality integration,[18] therapists at a minimum need to practice *spiritually conscious care* in which they can assess the importance of faith and conceptualize the influence of resources and struggles in this cultural domain on moral injury-related issues. Depending on different training backgrounds, many therapists might not be equipped to target religious beliefs and practices if they emerge as a treatment issue. In such cases, they might refer and collaborate with chaplains, clergy, or other pastoral professionals. Alongside this basic degree of spirituality-mental health integration, two other types of competence require specialized training that is not usually offered in graduate programs.[19] First, a competence in *spiritually integrated care* may be needed when religion and spirituality have factored prominently in identity development, social support, and coping, and when patients prefer to include their cherished beliefs and practices in their therapeutic interventions and goals.[20] This competence explicitly targets spiritual beliefs and practices in the process of alleviating a moral injury. Second, depending on the spiritual resources or struggles of particular patients, a competence in *spiritually directive care* might be needed. In such cases, therapists may utilize the same intervention procedures; however, beyond achieving psychological outcomes, morally injured patients seeking spiritually directive care also focus on transforming or conserving their faith systems (i.e., improving spiritual outcomes).

CASE EXAMPLE: TREATMENT SUMMARY

In collaboratively discussing evidence-based treatments for addressing Mr. G.'s other-directed moral injury and related issues (e.g., PTSD symptoms, anger, spiritual struggles), we agreed CPT afforded the best opportunity to attend to the cognitions and beliefs underlying his struggles. During the initial sessions of CPT, an overview of PTSD and moral injury was provided before we began identifying and challenging Mr. G.'s unhelpful thoughts and beliefs. Having identified anger and betrayal as important targets for his treatment, the impact of natural and manufactured emotions was emphasized. Specifically, we discussed how anger can arise from perceived mistreatment of self or others (natural emotion) or in response to feelings of sadness, uncertainty, or fear (manufactured emotion). As we progressed, Mr. G. was encouraged to differentiate thoughts based upon the antecedents of his anger, including anger toward God, and examine patterns associated with natural and manufactured anger, respectively. By doing so, CPT was intentionally utilized to challenge unhelpful thoughts related to his other-directed moral injury and address the profound sense of betrayal associated with Mr. G.'s traumatic experiences. While treatment did not focus exclusively on anger, processing the thoughts and behaviors associated with anger played a prominent role in assisting Mr. G. to make meaning of his experiences in Iraq and promote adaptive emotional coping regarding the past and present.

To help further process his divine struggles, a special "Theistic Beliefs Module" was incorporated as a stand-alone session after the CPT modules on Safety, Trust, Power/Control, Esteem, and Intimacy. Before implementing this exercise, Mr. G was informed of the adjunctive nature of the session as it related to CPT, the mental health provider's training and background as a Christian pastor, and the purpose of the session (i.e., processing theistic beliefs within his own meaning system as opposed to imposition of the provider's theological tradition). Similar to the topic of anger, thoughts and beliefs related to spirituality emerged naturally in sessions and were processed using a combination of Socratic questioning and CPT worksheets, as they arose. Notwithstanding the attention given to spiritual concerns throughout the treatment, the Theistic Beliefs Module was used to discuss the roles of God found within the Christian Bible (e.g., king, judge, father, shepherd) and their influence on the nature of God's relationship with humanity, both individually and collectively.[21] The session included discussion of Mr. G.'s perception of God at various points in his life, including as a young adult, prior to his morally injurious experiences, and at the time of treatment. With the therapist's help, he then considered the potential meanings that could be made for the traumatic event and his life based upon the various roles of God (e.g., God as judge or God as father). Throughout the session, Mr. G. generated a list of potential thoughts that he needed to challenge between sessions. In the final session, he reviewed his theistic thought challenges and so-called second Impact Statement, processing how his thoughts and beliefs had changed through the course of treatment.

In the case of Mr. G., CPT was an effective approach for addressing his struggles with PTSD and moral injury, particularly issues stemming from a sense of betrayal and manufactured anger. As Mr. G. mastered the CPT framework for challenging unhelpful thoughts, his painful other-condemning emotions endorsed on the worksheets steadily decreased, and he reported less frequent interpersonal conflict from "pausing to think for a minute before I act." Although the treatment is not designed to address spirituality per se, the reflective skills facilitated through CPT provided Mr. G. an opportunity to process his struggles with God. During the latter portion of treatment, he reported engaging in a variety of spiritual practices in addition to the worksheets, including prayer, reading the Bible, and having spiritual discussions with trusted friends and family. By incorporating a spiritually integrated approach to CPT, the treatment was optimized to address Mr. G.'s presenting concerns through the promotion of cognitive flexibility and meaning-making. At the end of treatment, Mr. G endorsed a seventeen-point decrease in PTSD symptomatology on the PTSD Checklist for DSM-5,[22] with the greatest changes occurring in avoidance and negative alterations in cognitions and mood.

CONCLUSION

The construct of moral injury will likely continue to evolve dynamically as stakeholders from a wide array of professions and backgrounds contribute to its theoretical, philosophical, and empirical underpinnings. As our understanding of moral injury increases from such efforts, mental health treatments will become more nuanced in how they assess and ameliorate posttraumatic symptoms. At present, a variety of evidence-based treatments for PTSD and empirically supported therapy techniques provide a foundation from which to address mental health concerns associated with emerging definitions of moral injury. Looking ahead, by being attentive to the unique cognitive, emotional, behavioral, and spiritual struggles of each SM/V, professionals from a variety of backgrounds can utilize their skills and current knowledge base to identify and assist individuals hampered by moral injury.

NOTES

1. Marc-Antoine Crocq and Louis Crocg, "From Shell Shock to Posttraumatic Stress Disorder: A History of Psychotraumatology," *Dialogues in Clinical Neuroscience* 2 (2000): 47–55.

2. Jonathan Shay, *Achilles in Vietnam: Combat Trauma and the Undoing of Character* (New York: Simon and Schuster, 1994).

3. Brett T. Litz, Nathan Stein, Eileen Delaney, Leslie Lebowitz, William P. Nash, Caroline Silva, and Shira Maguen, "Moral Injury and Moral Repair in War Veterans: A Preliminary Model and Intervention Strategy," *Clinical Psychology Review* 29 (2009): 695–706.

4. For more discussion, see Joseph M. Currier, Kent D. Drescher, and Jason A. Nieuwsma, eds., *Addressing Moral Injury in Clinical Practice* (Washington, DC: American Psychological Association, in press).

5. Brett T. Litz and Patricia K. Kerig, "Introduction to the Special Issue on Moral Injury: Conceptual Challenges, Methodological Issues, and Clinical Applications," *Journal of Traumatic Stress* (2019): 344.

6. For example, re-experiencing of traumatic memories, behavioral avoidance, trauma-related cues and reminders, emotional numbing, negative changes in beliefs/attitudes. See Litz et al., "Moral Injury and Moral Repair in War Veterans," 695–706.

7. Patricia A. Resick, Candice M. Monson, and Kathleen M. Chard, *Cognitive Processing Therapy for PTSD: A Comprehensive Manual* (New York: Guilford Publications, 2016).

8. Edna B. Foa, Elizabeth A. Hembree, and Barbara O. Rothbaum, *Prolonged Exposure Therapy for PTSD: Emotional Processing of Traumatic Experiences, Therapist Guide* (New York: Oxford University Press, 2007).

9. Edna B. Foa and Michael J. Kozak, "Emotional Processing of Fear: Exposure to Corrective Information," *Psychological Bulletin* 99, no. 1 (1986): 20–35.

10. Jacob K. Farnsworth, Kent D. Drescher, Wyatt Evans, and Robyn D. Walser, "A Functional Approach to Understanding and Treating Military-Related Moral Injury," *Journal of Contextual Behavioral Science* 6 (2017): 391–97.

11. Steven C. Hayes, Dermot Barnes-Holmes, and Bryan Roche, eds., *Relational Frame Theory: A Post-Skinnerian Account of Human Language and Cognition* (New York: Plenum Press, 2001).

12. Leslie S. Greenberg, *Emotion-Focused Therapy: Coaching Clients to Work Through Their Feelings* (Washington, DC: American Psychological Association, 2015).

13. Brett T. Litz, Leslie Lebowitz, Matt J. Gray, and William P. Nash, *Adaptive Disclosure: A New Treatment for Military Trauma, Loss, and Moral Injury* (New York: Guilford Press, 2016).

14. Shira Maguen, Thomas J. Metzler, Brett T. Litz, Karen H. Seal, Sara J. Knight, and Charles R. Marmar, "The Impact of Killing in War on Mental Health Symptoms and Related Functioning," *Journal of Traumatic Stress* 22, no. 5 (2009): 435–43 and Shira Maguen, Thomas J. Metzler, Jeane Bosch, Charles R. Marmar, Sara J. Knight, and Thomas C. Neylan, "Killing in Combat May Be Independently Associated with Suicidal Ideation," *Depression and Anxiety* 29 (2012): 918–23.

15. Shira Maguen, Kristine Burkman, Erin Madden, Julie Dinh, Jeane Bosch, Jessica Keyser, Martha Schitz, and Thomas C. Neylan, "Impact of Killing in War: A Randomized, Controlled Pilot Trial," *Journal of Clinical Psychology* 73 (2017): 997–1012.

16. J. Irene Harris, Timothy Usset, Cory Voecks, Paul Thuras, Joseph Currier, and Christopher Erbes, "Spiritually Integrated Care for PTSD: A Randomized Controlled Trial of 'Building Spiritual Strength,'" *Psychiatry Research* 267 (2018): 420–28.

17. See Brad E. Kelle, *The Bible and Moral Injury: Reading Scripture Alongside War's Unseen Wounds* (Nashville: Abingdon, 2020).

18. Stephone M. Saunders, Melissa L. Miller, and Melissa M. Bright, "Spiritually Conscious Psychological Care," *Professional Psychology: Research and Practice* 41, no. 5 (2010): 355.

19. Saunders, Miller, and Bright, *Professional Psychiatry*, 355. .

20. Ibid.

21. Allan Coppedge, *The God Who Is Triune: Revisioning the Christian Doctrine of God* (Downers Grove, IL: IVP Academic, 2007).

22. Frank W. Weathers, Brett T. Litz, Terence M. Keane, Patrick A. Palmieri, Brian P. Marx, and Paula P. Schnurr, "The PTSD Checklist for DSM-5 (PCL-5)." National Center for PTSD 2013. http://www.ptsd.va.gov.

BIBLIOGRAPHY

Coppedge, Alan. *The God Who Is Triune: Revisioning the Christian Doctrine of God*. Downer's Grove, IL: IVP Academic, 2007.

Crocq, Marc-Antoine and Louis Crocg. "From Shell Shock to Posttraumatic Stress Disorder: A History of Psychotraumatology." *Dialogues in Clinical Neuroscience* 2 (2000): 47–55.

Currier, Joseph M., Kent D. Drescher, and Jason A. Nieuwsma, eds. *Addressing Moral Injury in Clinical Practice*. Washington, DC: American Psychological Association, in press.

Farnsworth, Jacob K., Kent D. Drescher, Wyatt Evans, and Robyn D. Walser. "A Functional Approach to Understanding and Treating Military-Related Moral Injury." *Journal of Contextual Behavioral Science* 6 (2017): 391–97.

Foa, Edna B., Elizabeth A. Hembree, and Barbara O. Rothbaum. *Prolonged Exposure Therapy for PTSD: Emotional Processing of Traumatic Experiences, Therapist Guide*. New York: Oxford University Press, 2007.

Foa, Edna, B. and Michael J. Kozak. "Emotional Processing of Fear: Exposure to Corrective Information." *Psychological Bulletin* 99, no. 1 (1986): 20–35.

Greenberg, Leslie S. *Emotion-Focused Therapy: Coaching Clients to Work Through Their Feelings*. Washington, DC: American Psychological Association, 2015.

Harris, J. Irene, Timothy Usset, Cory Voecks, Paul Thuras, Joseph Currier, and Christopher Erbes. "Spiritually Integrated Care for PTSD: A Randomized Controlled Trial of 'Building Spiritual Strength.'" *Psychiatry Research* 267 (2018): 420–428.

Hayes, Stephen C., Dermot Barnes-Holmes, and Bryan Roche, eds. *Relational Frame Theory: A Post-Skinnerian Account of Human Language and Cognition*. New York: Plenum, 2001.

Kelle, Brad E. *The Bible and Moral Injury: Reading Scripture Alongside War's Unseen Wounds*. Nashville: Abingdon, 2020.

Litz, Brett. T. and Patricia K. Kerig. "Introduction to the Special Issue on Moral Injury: Conceptual Challenges, Methodological Issues, and Clinical Applications." *Journal of Traumatic Stress* (2019): 341–49.

Litz, Brett T., Leslie Lebowitz, Matt J. Gray, and William P. Nash. *Adaptive Disclosure: A New Treatment for Military Trauma, Loss, and Moral Injury*. New York: Guilford, 2016.

Litz, Brett. T., Nathan Stein, Eileen Delaney, Leslie Lebowitz, William P. Nash, Caroline Silva, and Shira Maguen. "Moral Injury and Moral Repair in War Veterans: A Preliminary Model and Intervention Strategy." *Clinical Psychology Review* 29 (2009): 695–706.

Maguen, Shira, Kristine Burkman, Erin Madden, Julie Dinh, Jeane Bosch, Jessica Keyser, Martha Schitz, and Thomas C. Neylan. "Impact of Killing in War: A Randomized, Controlled Pilot Trial." *Journal of Clinical Psychology* 73 (2017): 997–1012.

Maguen, Shira, Thomas J. Metzler, Brett T. Litz, Karen H. Seal, Sara J. Knight, and Charles R. Marmar. "The Impact of Killing in War on Mental Health Symptoms and Related Functioning." *Journal of Traumatic Stress* 22, no. 5 (2009): 435–43.

Maguen, Shira, Thomas J. Metzler, Jeane Bosch, Charles R. Marmar, Sara J. Knight, and Thomas C. Neylan. "Killing in Combat May Be Independently Associated with Suicidal Ideation." *Depression and Anxiety* 29 (2012): 918–23.

Resick, Patricia A., Candice M. Monson, and Kathleen M. Chard. *Cognitive Processing Therapy for PTSD: A Comprehensive Manual*. New York: Guilford, 2016.

Saunders, Stephone M., Melissa L. Miller, and Melissa M. Bright. "Spiritually Conscious Psychological Care." *Professional Psychology: Research and Practice* 41, no. 5 (2010): 355–62.

Shay, Jonathan. *Achilles in Vietnam: Combat Trauma and the Undoing of Character*. New York: Simon and Schuster, 1994.

Weathers, Frank W., Brett T. Litz, Terence M. Keane, Patrick A. Palmieri, Brian P. Marx, and Paula P. Schnurr. "The PTSD Checklist for DSM-5 (PCL-5)." National Center for PTSD. 2013. http://www.ptsd.va.gov.

Chapter Nine

Spiritual Care for Veterans and Their Families Affected by Moral Injury

How Faith Communities Can Help

Nancy J. Ramsay

Veterans of several generations participate in nearly every faith community in the United States—Jewish, Christian, Muslim, and more. Most of them will acknowledge familiarity with the wounds of conscience war inflicts on combatants now described by the term, "moral injury." It is a new term for an ancient insight: the moral trauma of war forever changes the lives it touches. Millenia ago we see this insight whether in the Old Testament/Hebrew Bible (e.g., Num 31:19–20), when soldiers remained in the field for a time of cleansing before going home after war, or in the first centuries of Christianity when returning soldiers spent a year in penance before they took the Eucharist again.[1] Somehow we lost this ancient wisdom that the trauma of war changes us.

The term "moral injury" describes what many call "wounds of conscience." Moral injury arises from situations in which troops may witness or be implicated in actions that violate their deepest convictions about protecting human life. They may be ordered to act in ways that violate their conscience, such as to leave wounded civilians behind; or in the context of battle, they may find it necessary to act in ways that violate their conscience in order to defend comrades or themselves.[2] Research continues to suggest that moral trauma, like the psychological trauma of posttraumatic stress, has lasting consequences.[3] Often both moral and psychological conflict arise for veterans and may coincide.

Since the latter half of the twentieth century, evidence of the consequences of the moral trauma of war has mounted. Several factors in the current wars in Iraq and Afghanistan appear to contribute to the increase in the numbers of those affected by moral injury. For example, these current conflicts regularly involve close combat in urban areas and often includes exposure to civilians—some of whom may include combatants, and all of whom may become fatalities. For instance, is that young teen preparing to throw a rock at the truck carrying troops, or is it a grenade? Close urban contact includes these ambiguous situations in which it is hard to distinguish civilians from insurgents. Decisions are required quickly to protect a unit. In close combat, soldiers are also more likely to have a higher awareness of responsibility for taking a life in combat. And they are more likely to see the consequences for innocent persons. They also frequently and unexpectedly see the remains of women and children or wounded civilians whom they may not be able to help. It is also the case that many serve more than one tour of duty, so they experience multiple exposures to such events. Veterans also describe the difficulty of shifting political rationales for these long wars. Troops that made a commitment to risk their lives based on one rationale may encounter different situations and subsequent political explanations that are not compelling in the midst of conflict zones. In contrast to the most recent previous war in Vietnam, troops in the current wars often experience the challenging emotional juxtaposition of very difficult conflict with all the possibilities described above and a phone or Skype call home later that day when their own family is visibly present to them. Their contact with family presents a drastically different emotional world and meaning-making frame than the military worldview that is their daily context. For pastors at home, this means that families experience this brief connection, and sometimes spouses or parents overhear the stressors without the capacity to be present. This is a strain for intimate relationships.

In addition to the consequences of the conditions of combat, the current wars arise in a very different cultural context than those that occurred earlier in the twentieth century. It is hard to imagine a more morally and spiritually difficult experience than combat. No faith tradition can blunt the horror of war. Yet, the decline in active participation in faith communities in the United States means that troops who experience the horror of war now more often do so without even the tools of a critically reflective faith tradition to help them voice their pain, anger, and fear, or provide some possibility that the brutality of war is not the last word. Ironically, those who come with clear and firm religious ideas may also be vulnerable to the brutal ambiguities of war raised by realities such as civilian casualties, especially if their imagination of God's control makes such suffering inexplicable.

In basic training, the military inducts recruits into a carefully constructed moral-orienting frame of meaning intended to supply values, beliefs, and behaviors that will prepare and support them in the context of intense combat where they are ordered to kill.[4] Two complications arise for some: this combat frame may not prevent the intrusion of earlier foundational moral obligations for preserving human life, and, at the end of military service, no sustained military program is offered for helping troops returning to civilian life deconstruct this militarized interpretive framework.

Finally, troops returning home realize quickly that this is not a war that impacts the experience of civilians in the United States, nor do most civilians understand the conditions described above. "Thank you for your service" is at once well-intentioned and highly problematic for most veterans.

IMPLICATIONS FOR PRACTICES OF CARE IN FAITH COMMUNITIES

For those of us who offer care to veterans, active duty military personnel who return from deployment, and their families, it is important to consider the likely implications of the contributing factors noted above that make moral injury such a potent wound. The relational scope of moral injury is individual, familial, relational, and generational. Caregivers will need to attend not only to those who incur moral injury in conflict but also to the ways their moral injury will likely alter the fabric of intimate relationships and capacities to engage once again in wider networks of friendships and work. These factors will require religious leaders to make systemic and programmatic preparations within faith communities, as well as to identify and develop networks of effective resources to whom we can refer.

Religious leaders also need to be attentive to the possibilities for responding to spiritual dimensions of moral injury, including the ways it predictably prompts deep questions about experiences of a Divine presence (e.g., whether the Divine is accountable for such deadly violence or whether the Divine can forgive a soldier's actions). There is a close emotional and spiritual reciprocity between how we imagine God and how we imagine ourselves.[5] War puts at risk foundational assumptions about self, as well as a divine presence ordering the world. Engaging in battle poses a profound spiritual and thus existential crisis that may include questioning the moral grounding of this world. In other words, moral injury can unravel ways of imagining not only one's own goodness but one's imagination about the moral foundations of the world. It is no wonder that the Department of Veterans Affairs suggests moral injury contributes to the staggering estimate of twenty-two suicides a day among combat veterans. Neither is it surprising that veterans may not speak readily of such wounds of conscience. We should remain alert in caring for veterans across their lifetimes because, while we may help ease the pain of moral injury, it does not go away. It is important also to remember that while current conflicts may exacerbate the likelihood of moral injury, veterans of World War II, Korea, and Vietnam are equally vulnerable to the moral injury of war, although they may not have experienced an opening in which to share their pain.

Military chaplains regularly remind us of one further aspect of moral injury that is often overlooked. Especially in the current context when most civilians do not experience any daily connection to the American military involvement in Iraq and Afghanistan, the response "Thank you for your service" often betrays what is likely an unreflective distancing from the fact that these troops put their lives at risk at the behest of this country's government. Their experience of moral injury was incurred as they acted on our behalf. Military chaplains such as Captain Beth Stallinga (US Navy) invites civilians to reflect on ways moral injury also implicates them.[6] Captain Stallinga helps us realize that in bearing witness to the pain and grief of veterans who have come home from a war they fought on our behalf, we may discover that we as civilians have our own moral wounds to tend. War, it seems, changes all of us.

Even this brief summary of the implications of military moral injury highlights some predictable themes we may encounter among veterans coping with moral injury. First, as Larry Kent Graham put it, innocence lost in moral injury cannot be regained; it can only be mourned, and, at best, one hopes to reestablish moral integrity.[7] The brutality of war puts at risk our hope in a world where moral order is secure. Healing moral injury requires daring to step into a future in which there can be again hope in love and goodness, as well as meaningful commitments.

Other themes in the lives of veterans and their families who are part of our faith communities may particularly include grief—a predictably prominent theme in the stories we hear. But the origin and cause of the grief can alter how we experience it and what strategies we use to address it. Grief that mourns innocence that cannot be recovered differs from grief that mourns the death of a loved one. It is often experienced as more ambiguous, harder to name, and calling for different strategies for modifying its impact. Pauline Boss, a marriage and family therapist, has written about grief that reflects the impact of moral injury. She uses the label "ambiguous loss" to describe the experience of being physically present but psychologically absent.[8] Many veterans and their spouses and families would affirm that moral injury creates this sort of grief. One is physically back from war, but the moral and relational consequences of war may still be very real and complicate being fully present at home. Similarly, seeing the brutality of war may forever complicate any easy confidence about the power of hope and love in the future. It will take courage and companions on the journey to reclaim a personal, relational, and spiritual or moral future shaped by hope. In the lives of the veterans we encounter in our faith communities, we are likely to overhear stories that echo the experience of ambiguous loss and concerns about ever again experiencing a hopeful future story. Boss suggests that persons who imagine themselves as able to control their environment, and likewise imagine a world shaped by forces for good, will be especially vulnerable to grief that arises from war—an event that discloses the cracks in such certainty about human goodness. Ironically, military service typically attracts persons who have strong self-confidence. Further, the military's programs to induct and orient recruits into a unified sense of identity and moral purpose for using deadly force without hesitation to achieve military goals encourage precisely such unambiguous confidence in their purpose and success. But for many, earlier foundational moral lessons about protecting human life surface in haunting ways. Boss suggests that when we walk beside persons forced to question their earlier certainty about their own goodness and the power of goodness generally, we can help them develop a more reflective sense of the limits of their control over the forces that confronted them. The goal, she suggests, is a more realistic way of imagining one's ability to be in control of situations and to respond as hoped. Similarly, for persons of faith, the goal is a more reflective way of imagining how God engages with the realities of human violence against one another. Her term, "resilience" is a helpful way of imagining an outcome of accompanying veterans on a journey toward a spirituality that will be able to sustain them in the wake of moral injury.[9]

In response to the implications of moral injury and the themes that spiritual caregivers may encounter among veterans, people of faith are able to draw on a number of practices that offer guidance in difficult situations. Two particularly helpful resources especially prominent in Jewish and Christian scriptures assist us when experiences of hope are challenged: practices of lament and multiple reminders that we worship a God who pursues those in need of forgiveness to offer hope for a new future. Surely Jacob's wrestling match at the Jabbok described in Genesis 32, and his opportunity to wrestle through the night with one who longed for him to claim a new future albeit with a limp, may be understood through the frame of moral injury. Scripture texts describe both lamentation and hope as profoundly relational. As we explore practices for walking beside veterans and their families as people of faith, we will uncover ways the communal context of faith, as well as ancient spiritual practices and rituals, can be used creatively to promote healing.

MORAL INJURY IN FAITH COMMUNITIES: A CASE STUDY

What follows is a composite, fictionalized story of moral injury in a Protestant (Christian) congregation. Such a story of grief and pain could be as easily told through the frame of a Jewish or Muslim community. We will focus on a young adult combat veteran reservist returning to his family and congregation. It is important to remember, however, that the themes in this story could also arise from the experience of others who were in conflict zones. For example, we could as easily hear the anguish of a nurse who worked in a field hospital or medivac unit accompanying terribly wounded veterans out of Afghanistan. She could be haunted by the mutilated bodies of troops and innocent civilians that she could not save, or the devastation of war that challenges her earlier sense of God's power and saving presence. We also could hear the themes of moral injury as we sit with an aging veteran who knows his life is nearing an end, and he shares the burden of his guilt hoping somehow he might experience forgiveness. Military moral injury touches all who enter zones of conflict, and it lasts a lifetime. Caregivers will overhear it from varied sources.

Our case focuses on Damon, a returning combat veteran reservist whose spouse, Linda, and young children and parents are long-time members of an African Methodist Episcopal (AME) congregation. Damon is twenty-seven. He identifies as a Black American. He is married to Linda, who also identifies as a Black American and who works part-time at a local insurance firm. They have been married six years. Damon's grandfather was a World War II veteran, and his father, Sam, is a recently retired career Army Vietnam veteran, who now owns a successful heating and cooling business. Damon's mother, Barbara, also works full-time in the family company. Damon attended college using his military benefits and entered the reserves as a commissioned officer to supplement his family's income as he and Linda began their family. Damon is returning after a seven-month tour in Afghanistan. He and Linda decided he would leave the reserves after this tour. He is returning to a position in his father's company. Damon and Linda have a four-year-old son, Samuel, and a two-year-old daughter, Lydia. The family participates in an AME congregation in which a number of active duty military personnel and reservists worship not far from a base. Damon's family has long been active in the congregation, and Damon grew up in it. Prior to his recent tour of duty, he was a youth group sponsor.

During his tour in Afghanistan, Damon was an officer in the infantry. In their Skype calls, Damon began to share with Linda the ways scenes of close conflict haunted him, especially the terror on the faces of women and young children, some of whom became casualties in the crossfire between his unit and enemy troops as their towns and homes were co-opted by the enemy. Especially as an officer, he struggled with those deaths and with deaths and serious injuries of several men in his unit who were close friends when their vehicle was blown up by an improvised explosive device. As his tour was coming to an end, he haltingly spoke of his inability to pray to a God who would allow such violence. In the last conversation, he wondered aloud if Linda could love him as before knowing he had innocent blood on his hands.

Linda was unnerved by these conversations and shared them with her pastor. She also sought support from the small group of military wives who are part of a congregational ministry for spouses of those serving combat tours. They helped her manage her work and the preschool children and especially offered psychological support, as Damon's absence meant Linda carried extra childcare duties along with her own job. They talked with her about the challenges of the transition once Damon returns. The pastor encouraged her to continue to use the support network for spouses at the nearby base. He promised he would walk with her and Damon and also encourage Damon to use the expert resources at the base. He hoped that Damon would be willing to meet with some recent and older veterans in the congregation who were familiar with the struggle he was describing. Linda also had an occasion to share cautiously some of her concerns with her mother-in-law, Barbara, when she was at the house helping with the children. She wondered if Barbara recalled Sam sharing such worries when he returned from Vietnam. Barbara confirmed that she had worried that Damon would know this grief, and she was grateful he trusted Linda with it. She knows Sam is haunted by memories of the brutality of the conflict in Vietnam, and she sometimes senses the distance such pain can create, but Sam rarely speaks of it with her. She thinks he does with veterans in the congregation, and she is grateful that group exists.

When Damon came home, the transitions were very hard for him, for their marriage, and for Damon's reconnection with his son and daughter. Seven months is a long time in the life of a four-year-old and nearly half the life of a two year-old. How could they make sense of a father at once glad to see them and sometimes distant because he is haunted by memories of children in the battle-scarred villages of Afghanistan? Marriage patterns also needed adjustment because Linda quickly realized that she would continue to bear more of the work at home while Damon tried to re-enter family and work life. She had become used to making family and household decisions, which would require some renegotiation of former patterns with Damon. It was stressful for Damon to engage at work, which was complicated since his father was his boss.

Effective care with veterans and their families involves several important elements that we see in this situation. First, religious leaders need to learn about the experience of moral injury. For example, the easily accessible, award-winning film, *Almost Sunrise*, which draws on the experience of two veterans of the war in Iraq, helps viewers better understand experiences of moral injury and journeys toward healing.[10] Religious leaders in faith communities also need to identify skilled professionals who will be knowledgeable allies in the work of healing. We need to make contact with them and establish good referral practices in advance of calling on their help.

Additionally, there is work internal to a congregation. Practices of care include programmatic and educational work, as well as relational skills. Note how Damon's pastor put in place structures that assist congregants to walk beside each other in stressful times (e.g., support teams made up of other spouses of veterans who know what support is needed during deployment and afterward). Their pastor also approached veterans in the congregation who could be counted on to walk beside someone in the throes of returning from combat and welcome them into a community of veterans who would be able to understand their pain while also demonstrating that the future could be different. The pastor insightfully encouraged other experienced veterans to reach out to invite Damon to consider attending their monthly conversation times with veterans in the congregation. This pastor could also then draw on earlier work in building a referral base to point Linda and Damon toward a marriage and family therapist knowledgeable about the challenges for returning veterans and their spouses and to review the process and contacts for Damon to take advantage of skilled resource persons at the base. These psychological and relational caregiving referrals support the spiritual care the pastor will offer. This support reflects best practices in marital and individual therapy such as Boss's guidance in responding to ambiguous loss.

In our case study, the pastor is aware that Damon is shaken personally and spiritually by combat experience and the violence in which he participated. Clearly, Damon's confidence has been shaken both in himself as a moral person and in God's power to control and prevent such evil. Gently, the pastor looked for openings for Damon to share the ways his tour was affecting him in relation to his faith. The pastor avoided making assumptions about Damon's experience, or valorizing it. He listened carefully and did not yield to problem solving. Gradually, with this gentle but steady availability, Damon began to share his moral anguish about experiences he had witnessed and in which he had sometimes been implicated, such as combat in populated areas that took the lives of civilians including children the ages of his own. The pastor sought to address his questions: How could he ever be forgiven for this? How could he live with himself? How could Linda love him or trust him if she knew about this? How could he trust a God who would allow such violence?

Clearly, this spiritual care journey would involve efforts to help Damon reimagine the relationship of God's power to God's love. What if Damon could come to imagine that God's power is in the service of love?[11] Psalm 23, for example, suggests a table in the presence of enemies where the power of God's love is certain even in the midst of the realities of deadly human violence.[12]

For the pastor, conversations with Damon sometimes resonated with the laments so common in the book of Psalms. Because laments invoke a listener or witness to validate the pain of the one voicing the lament, the pastor stepped into that role to recognize and respond to Damon's deep pain and to represent God's faithful presence when Damon imagined he was forgotten or abandoned.[13] Hope, it seems, is linked precisely with voicing one's fear or anger at the experience of God's absence because, ironically, such complaints presume God is listening. The response of the pastor's witness to the lament helped reconfirm the value of Damon's life and experience. In Jewish and Christian sacred texts, hope is sustained relationally. When Damon can break his silence and speak his pain, the seeds of hope are sown. To deepen healing and hope, the pastor may encourage Damon to write a lament and perhaps to bring it back to share if he wishes. Others have encouraged veterans to write "witness poetry" to express their pain amidst witnesses and experience the validation of such a hearing.[14]

Drawing on the ancient spiritual practice of *lectio divina*, the pastor invited Damon to spend time reading the story of Jacob as he returns to meet his brother Esau after committing such consequential moral violations of trust.[15] They talked together about the night Jacob wrestles with the angel or with God. What blessing did Jacob want? What blessing did God hope to give? What could it mean that Jacob walked with a limp and a new name into a future full of blessing?[16]

Remembering Boss's encouragement to respond to ambiguous loss by revising hope that relies on unrealistic images of control (human or divine) and fostering resilience through images of strength that are less absolute, the pastor and Damon considered the story in John's gospel when Jesus returns to the disciples after his resurrection. The disciples are terrified for their own safety. The doors are locked, but the risen Jesus comes among them with his body showing the gaping wound in his side and the wounds on his hands and feet. What might this Gospel passage suggest about the power of God's love to resist the finality of the violence humans do to one another and sustain Damon in the afterlife of war?[17] Maybe, in time, this passage invites Damon to imagine that the devastation he witnessed does not question the power of God's love. Maybe it will encourage his resilience in the journey to live faithfully after war. Perhaps with this insight into God's presence in the midst of the worst humans can do to one another, the Eucharist may once again convey forgiveness, empowering presence, inclusion, and renewed possibilities for a life of witness and service.[18]

Forgiveness is such a prominent theme for veterans like Damon. In Jewish theology, this pastor could find a welcoming perspective, because in that tradition forgiveness must include some act of repair toward the one harmed. Together, Damon and the pastor could explore ways Damon might engage in this restorative practice even though it is not possible to help the villagers in Afghanistan. Here we see another insight that, even as we attend to the pain of moral injury, we can also recognize and encourage the gifts of leadership and other skills that veterans learned or honed in the military to help provide care and resources for those who are rendered vulnerable or in need in their communities.[19] In this case, Damon cannot give back to villagers halfway around the world, but he can commit to share his energies and compassion by joining with other veterans to contribute funds and knowledge for restoring housing and recreational resources for at-risk children and families in his community.

This journey with one veteran, his family, their pastor, and congregation has offered us a chance to observe how religious leaders and faith communities can engage in structural, systemic, and relational practices to support healing for veterans and their families. The afterlife of war is real and long-lasting, but faith communities have resources for spiritual care that can restore possibilities for lives shaped by resilient hope.

NOTES

1. Bernard J. Verkamp, *The Moral Treatment of Returning Warriors in Early Medieval and Modern Times,* 2d ed. (Scranton, PA: University of Scranton Press, 2006), 1–8.

2. Jonathan Shay, *Achilles in Vietnam: Combat Trauma and the Undoing of Character* (New York: Touchstone, 1994), 3; Brett Litz et al., "Moral Injury and Moral Repair in War Veterans: A Preliminary Model and Intervention Strategy," *Clinical Psychology Review* 29 (2009): 695–706.

3. William P. Nash, "Commentary on the Special Issue on Moral Injury: Unpacking Two Models for Understanding Moral Injury," *Journal of Traumatic Stress* 32 (June 2019): 465–70.

4. Zachary Moon, *Warriors between Worlds: Moral Injury and Identities in Crisis.* Emerging Perspectives in Pastoral Theology and Care (Lanham, MD: Lexington, 2019), 56–69.

5. John Calvin famously noted the interrelation of knowledge of self and God as the opening of his *Institutes of the Christian Religion.* See John T. McNeill, ed. *Calvin: Institutes of the Christian Religion*, translated and indexed by Ford Lewis Battles; The Library of Christian Classics Vol. XX (Philadelphia: Westminster, 1960), 35.

6. Beth Stallinga, "What Spills Blood Wounds Spirit: Chaplains, Spiritual Care, and Operational Stress," *Reflective Practice: Formation and Supervision for Ministry* 33 (2013): 28.

7. Larry K. Graham, *Moral Injury: Restoring Wounded Souls* (Nashville, TN: Abingdon: 2017), 78.

8. Pauline Boss, *Loss, Trauma, and Resilience: Therapeutic Work with Ambiguous Loss* (New York: Norton, 2006), 8.

9. For a fuller discussion of ambiguous loss and military moral injury, see Nancy Ramsay, "Moral Injury as Loss and Grief with Attention to Ritual Resources for Care," in *Military Moral Injury and Spiritual Care: Resources for Religious Leaders and Professional Caregivers*, eds. Nancy J. Ramsay and Carrie Doehring (St. Louis, MO: Chalice, 2019), 42–54.

10. Michael Collins and Marty Syjuco (directors), *Almost Sunrise* (United States: Veterans Trek Production, 2017).

11. Wendy Farley, *Tragic Vision and Divine Compassion: A Contemporary Theodicy* (Louisville, KY: Westminster John Knox, 1990), 127.

12. Patrick D. Miller, *Interpreting the Psalms* (Philadelphia: Westminster, 1986), 112–19.

13. Kathleen O'Connor, *Lamentations: The Tears of the World* (Ossening, NY: Orbisl, 2002), 107. See also Kathleen Billman and Daniel Migliore, *Rachel's Cry: Prayer of Lament and Rebirth of Hope* (Cleveland. OH: United Church Press, 1999), 104–5.

14. Shawn Fawson, "Sustaining Lamentation for Military Moral Injury: Witness Poetry that Bears the Traces of Extremity," in *Military Moral Injury and Spiritual Care: Resources for Religious Leaders and Professional Caregivers*, eds. Nancy J. Ramsay and Carrie Doehring (St. Louis, MO: Chalice, 2019), 142–68.

15. Elizabeth Liebert, "Accessible Spiritual Practices to Aid in Recovery from Moral Injury," in *Military Moral Injury and Spiritual Care: Resources for Religious Leaders and Professional Caregivers*, eds. Nancy J. Ramsay and Carrie Doehring (St. Louis, MO: Chalice, 2019), 155–78.

16. Arthur Frank, *The Wounded Storyteller: Body, Illness, and Ethics* (Chicago: University of Chicago Press, 2013), 181–82.

17. Shelly Rambo, *Resurrecting Wounds: Living in the Afterlife of Trauma* (Waco: Baylor University Press, 2017), 145–54.

18. Nancy J. Ramsay, "Moral Injury as Loss and Grief."

19. Zachary Moon, *Coming Home: Ministry that Matters with Veterans and Military Families* (St. Louis, MO: Chalice, 2015), 35–52.

BIBLIOGRAPHY

Billman, K. D. and D. L. Migliore. *Rachel's Cry: Prayer of Lament and Rebirth of Hope*. Cleveland, OH: United Church Press, 1999.

Boss, P. *Loss, Trauma, and Resilience: Therapeutic Work with Ambiguous Loss*. New York: W.W. Norton, 2006.

Collins, Michael and Marty Syjuco (directors). *Almost Sunrise*. Veterans Trek Productions, 2017.

Farley, Wendy. *Tragic Vision and Divine Compassion: A Contemporary Theodicy*. Louisville, KY: Westminster John Knox, 1990.

Fawson, Shawn. "Sustaining Lamentation for Military Moral Injury: Witness Poetry that Bears the Traces of Extremity." Pages 142–68 in *Military Moral Injury and Spiritual Care: Resources for Religious Leaders and Professional Caregivers*. Edited by Nancy J. Ramsay and Carrie Doehring. St. Louis, MO: Chalice, 2019.

Frank, A. *The Wounded Storyteller*. Chicago: University of Chicago Press, 2013.

Graham, L. K. *Moral Injury: Restoring Wounded Souls*. Nashville, TN: Abingdon, 2017.

Liebert, Elizabeth. "Accessible Spiritual Practices to Aid in Recovery from Moral Injury." Pages 55–78 in *Military Moral Injury and Spiritual Care: Resources for Religious Leaders and Professional Caregivers*. Edited by Nancy J. Ramsay and Carrie Doehring. St. Louis, MO: Chalice, 2019.

Litz, Brett T. et al. "Moral Injury and Moral Repair in War Veterans: A Preliminary Model and Intervention Strategy." *Clinical Psychology Review* 29 (2009): 695–706.

McNeill, John T., ed. *Calvin: Institutes of the Christian Religion*. Translated and Indexed by Ford Lewis Battles. The Library of Christian Classics Vol. XX. Philadelphia: Westminster, 1960.

Miller, Patrick D. *Interpreting the Psalms*. Philadelphia: Westminster, 1986.

Moon, Zachary. *Coming Home: Ministry That Matters with Veterans and Military Families*. St. Louis, MO: Chalice, 2015.

Moon, Zachary. *Warriors between Worlds: Moral Injury and Identities in Crisis*. Emerging Perspectives in Pastoral Theology and Care. Lanham, MD: Lexington, 2019.

Nash, William P. "Commentary on the Special Issue on Moral Injury: Unpacking Two Models for Understanding Moral Injury." *Journal of Traumatic Stress* 32 (June 2019): 465–70.

O'Connor, Kathleen. *Lamentations and the Tears of the World*. Ossining, NY: Orbis, 2002.

Rambo, Shelly. *Resurrecting Wounds: Living with the Afterlife of Trauma*. Waco, TX: Baylor University Press, 2017.

Ramsay, Nancy J. "Moral Injury as Loss and Grief with Attention to Ritual Resources for Care." Pages 42–54 in *Military Moral Injury and Spiritual Care: Resources for Religious Leaders and Professional Caregiveres*. Edited by Nancy J. Ramsay and Carrie Doehring. St. Louis, MO: Chalice, 2019.

Shay, Jonathan. *Achilles in Vietnam: Combat Trauma and the Undoing of Character*. New York: Scribner, 1994.

Stallinga, B. "What Spills Blood Wounds Spirit: Chaplains, Spiritual Care, and Operational Stress." *Reflective Practice: Formation and Supervision for Ministry* 33 (2013): 13–31.

Verkamp, Bernard J. *The Moral Treatment of Returning Warriors in Early Medieval and Modern Times*. Chicago: University of Chicago Press, 2006.

Chapter Ten

Spiritual Formation and Pastoral Care Approaches to Moral Injury

Duane H. Larson

Spiritual formation and pastoral care always presume a faith tradition and a faith community. The tradition teaches that the community is extensive over space and time. The community reminds that the tradition is effective insofar as it is translated through the community, including the breadth and depth of its contextuality. Though against the grain of American individualism, spiritual formation and pastoral care do not and cannot go it alone. A faith community always participates in pastoral care, if often indirectly. For formation and care to go deep, they require a community.

How might spiritual formation and pastoral care today work with morally injured persons? I approach this question from the perspective of how faith-based communities address the challenge with their best practices. I take this approach primarily because I understand the human being as a person in communion—this theological anthropology theme being the most commonly held in Christianity since, at least, the writing of the Cappadocian fathers in the fourth century. I presume that conviction with a turn to the practical question of what effective faith-based community models of caring for the morally injured look like.

Regrettably, there are not many examples among Christian congregations in North America, and I do not here explore the numerous practices in other religious traditions or countries. The examples I describe here are richly suggestive, however, of practical and spiritual predicates for effective spiritual formation and pastoral care of morally injured persons. And while I do so with the focus on military service members and veterans, the shapes of care surely do not apply only to military cases. Abounding implications already are recognized in emerging communal caregiving for women service members; traumatized women outside the military; police and other community protectors; medical doctors, nurses, and administrators; and many others, perhaps uniquely including a subset of people not yet addressed in the literature: military service members who were less than honorably discharged. All these and more deserve caring attention.

PASTORAL INTUITION, A CONGREGATION'S HOSPITALITY, AND LOCAL GEOGRAPHY

The few cases I describe have much to teach. One effective retreat program sponsored by a Christian congregation takes advantage of a beautiful resort setting to offer graciousness to veterans. Led by a wise pastor, Paul Palumbo, his congregation, set in a vacation setting in the northwest, offers a retreat program two to three times a year. The retreats are of modest size and ambition. Three to four veterans with their partners are hosted for a four-day/three-night retreat. Congregation members are selected by the pastor on the basis of their spiritual maturity, sense of hospitality, and ability to relate easily with others. Each volunteer is assigned to accompany a retreat guest and partner. Their job is to relate, to listen, and to share from their own vulnerabilities when contextually appropriate. There is no cost to the attending veterans and their partners. The leading goal for the retreat producers is to shower the attendees with grace and "see where it goes."

The retreat begins with an upscale restaurant dinner that includes mutual introductions and orientation to the weekend. The next day is dedicated to leisure and recreation. Attendees choose whether to hike, fish, enjoy a helicopter tour, or more. The evening offers another fine dinner and informal conversation. It might happen that conversation turns more serious, as the guests have become more confident in a new safe space.

Such a turn routinely happens the next day, when the guests are taken to a spacious log mansion atop a mountain with ample private acreage all around. It is the ideal "private bunker" getaway that so many vets have fantasized having for themselves. Here the personal stories begin to flow. Previous suspicions are confessed; struggles shared; traumas divulged, perhaps even for the first time with listeners other than battle buddies. Congregation volunteers practice disciplined appreciative listening. No judgments or solutions are offered. Volunteers might offer their own trauma stories, too, in recognition that their own task of internal reconciliation partners with the guests' quest for healing. There is no script, no formula to be followed. There will be a "soft" conclusion, however, that evening. The community will gather around a ritual bowl. The pastor will wear the clerical collar. There will be a ritual handwashing. Words of grief and lament are said over the hands. Then the guests are anointed with oil. No explicitly Christian language is used at any time throughout the retreat. "God" suffices.

When the guests leave after the next morning, the farewells and expressions of gratitude have their own ad hoc liturgical character. The guests share often that, "This community loves me. Therefore I can love myself, too," even, "Maybe I can believe that I'm forgiven." As one vet said some weeks after the event, "I realize that it was the first time in forty years that I could actually enjoy life."

This program is characterized by informality and hospitality, with no ready knowledge of clinical protocols. Indeed, it is the pastor's prior experience in a different congregation with individual crises that readied him for this iteration of care. In particular, in that other ministry, it was a member's disclosure of his own invisible war wounds to the pastor, the first time in more than thirty years of sharing his trauma with anyone, which helped Pastor Palumbo thereafter to recognize moral injury symptoms. But there are premises, winnowed from experience, to which the retreat sponsors must be dutiful. There is to be no patronization, no "thank you for your service," no invocation of patriotism. There is to be an unflinching leaning into listening and receiving "the hard stuff" with no judgment, only compassion and vulnerability. It takes spiritual maturity to do this. And it was all inductively learned from many conversations with the war-wounded.

Though he had believed this program was duplicable, Pastor Palumbo since has concluded otherwise. Having failed at another congregation that was sociologically, but not spiritually, like his, Pastor Palumbo believes that the host faith community itself must be deeply rooted in ritual and prayer, like his own congregation. It takes a spiritual generosity long nurtured in communal practices to fund the finances and to commit oneself to deep listening and wise midwifing of soldier stories. It takes a special lay spiritual maturity to know how and when to offer forgiveness in non-churchy, uncondescending ways to a suffering soul.

FORMAL RESEARCH-BASED RETREAT PROGRAMS

A similar program has completed five retreats over four years and has a university-based research component. Each retreat is led by a team of ten to twelve trainers. This program, located in the Upper Midwest, is led by Reverend John Sippola, a parish pastor and retired Navy chaplain. The program differs from the previously cited in that it is structured to generate more such trained teams and healing events. While service members are integral, of course, as participants, the "trained trainers" (of many ages, mixed gender, clergy and lay, etc.) bring two or three new participants who themselves aspire to multiplying the venues for similar retreats. The total number of participants has ranged from twenty-five to forty at each retreat. The intended primary audience is blue-collar vets and families, following an adapted Alcoholics Anonymous style, and consciously structured with Brett Litz's criterion that professional therapy must be transferred into practical, informal, and communal settings, with spiritual accompaniment.[1]

While moral injury is a central concern, the retreats reveal and address many vivid trauma narratives. In this respect the communal vulnerability and sharing embeds military service members in a trusting environment. Everybody shares and participates in each other's healing. The trainers have learned profoundly hereby that healing is a process to be repeated, and not a one-and-done experience.

The immersive retreat program is scheduled for five days and begins with each participant sharing a piece of memorabilia that connects to military experience. This is part of the first evening's introduction and orientation. On subsequent mornings a more formal presentation is scheduled, the first focused on posttraumatic stress disorder (PTSD) and moral injury. The latter half of the morning then is dedicated to large group discussion. The trainers' responsibility is to practice "eavesdropping," in deliberate accord, per Sippola, with Soren Kierkegaard's observation that "just listening" to stories reveals the essence of a person and nurtures the trust that enables deeper sharing yet. In subsequent large group sessions, trainers will "tell on themselves," sharing stories relating to PTSD and moral injury. Afternoons are for free time. Many one-on-one conversations start then and continue through the retreat. It is important that the trainers come from a wide variety of professions/disciplines. Differing identities—religious and non-religious—are necessary and scattered among the participants. This furthers the trusting environment. Indeed, this diversity is discovered to be essential to clergy and chaplains who are notorious for not addressing their own moral injury.

These retreats are intended to exemplify Jonathan Shay's observation that trauma stories must be resolved through the "communalization" of both the injured and the caregivers.[2] American Indian communities excel at this with their rituals of warrior return. Thereby the entire community accepts the morally injured peer with honor rather than shame and simultaneously resist hero worship. This means, too, that though stories will show a confessional character, the terms "confess," "confession," and "confessional" are avoided. They are too ambiguous, too laden with denominational and even pejorative meaning. Such terms cannot be used until the individual's background and disposition are well understood. Thus, the retreat modality must be nonsectarian and large enough that any religious tradition might find itself at ease in it. This means that proselytizing, no matter how seemingly innocuous, is never appropriate.

Interesting implications issue from a formal assessment of this program. The research and evaluation component, located with Sara Buehler at the

University of Minnesota, Duluth Medical School, identified early how important a focus on team training is. This must include follow-up, perhaps monthly, to do the necessary problem-solving, especially after the face-to-face experiences at retreats.

Significant psycho-social and theological insights arise in this program's repetitions. Participants realize that "grieving the grievances" is lifelong, as is forgiveness.[3] Forgiveness comes to be understood as a process of personal reconciliation. But this process of forgiveness requires that there always be an active community (a "priesthood of all believers") in this work. The work is a "joint-op," not a matter for individualized stoicism. Partners in less formal conversation are necessary. As the goal is always the communalizing, therapists often miss that the real work happens in the private conversations after the formal group session. Later those private stories come back into the communalization. Again, all is best conducted in non-parochial language and with the inclusion of non-Christians who appreciate community.

Scott Hutchinson and Chris Antal—a parish pastor and veteran's hospital chaplain, respectively—have nurtured several effective programs that address moral injury from a more holistic communal vision. Hutchinson's program began from St. Andrew's United Church of Christ in Perkasie, Pennsylvania, in 2006, when a congregation member/military veteran (Roger) shared in a worship service his deepening faith struggle with conscience after his deployment during Desert Storm. He regarded his service as a duty and honor, and still does. But reflecting upon the dehumanization of the soldier in training and the concomitant dehumanization of the enemy, Roger struggled with how he could be both soldier and Christian. Upon the congregation's embrace of Roger's witness, Roger and Pastor Hutchinson explored what it would mean for a congregation not only to have room for veterans, but to be open to hearing and "owning" veterans' experiences along with their own. Full welcome would mean that a whole faith community commits to exploring their support of veterans' honorable duty and confesses complicity in sending the veteran into morally dubious situations.

Hutchinson's previous training in trauma care led him to recognize what soon would be labeled "moral injury." With a small team of congregation members, he partnered with the local expression of the STAR program[4] for orientation to veteran issues and with Eastern Mennonite University for peacemaker training. Through the latter, Hutchinson and his emerging program linked with Chris Antal at the Corporal Michael J. Crescenz VA Medical Center in Philadelphia. Chris, himself a former front-line chaplain with the Army in Afghanistan and Unitarian Universalist minister, provided coaching to the congregation-based program. In turn, Hutchinson has significantly enriched the program at the VA. The collaboration led to Hutchinson establishing a "Veteran's Ministry Team" at his parish. This was the first faith community to be directly informed and fostered by Edward Tick's

"Soldier's Heart" program.[5] Since 2014, they have sponsored "Soldier's Heart" retreats and committed further to developing a "Circle of Trust" in the larger community beyond the congregation in partnership with the Veteran's Community Network inspired by John Schluep's "Warriors' Journey Home."[6] This faith-based community program was preceded by robust due diligence of research and partnership with numerous formal and informal agents. Many different kinds of support were engaged, thus affording a holistic and deeply personalized approach to the recommunalization of the returned warrior and the home faith community.

For a congregation to honor its returned warriors and commit to the hard work of listening, sharing the burden of morally injured memory, and making repentance for the civilian sector's sending of the warrior into physical and moral harm's way requires a complex practice of vulnerability. Christian congregations in the United States rarely combine prophetic preaching, a deeply prayerful-liturgical attitude, and public love for the military service member and veteran in one unified communal habitus.[7] The most common problem congregation leaders face is the initial question of how to identify and attract the military service member who may suffer moral injury (or, of course, many other struggles) into a program. Part of the problem may be an incipient "we/they" congregational disposition. Granting credibility to a healing agency—especially if it is religious—may be off-putting for the soldier who has long been hardened into suspicion of civilians who do not and generally will not try to understand military culture and experience. The presence of civilian faith leaders in places such as the American Legion, veteran care agencies, the VA hospital, and grassroots outreach agencies may help in this regard. Public efforts, with great care not to appear opportunistic and paternalistic, may also help, as long as they refuse the civil religious shape of only thanking military service members and veterans for their service. Public services of gratitude and communal rededication to a healthier and more peaceful common life—not unlike the practices of the Greek city-states of ritualized return and reinstatement into the civic life of their warriors—can lead to smaller, group-oriented caregiving.

Consider one congregational annual practice called "The Witting Tree." Each morning of the eleven days up to and including Veterans Day, the congregation hosts a brief morning prayer service at a large tree in public view. With psalmody and contemporary liturgical expressions, twenty-two dog tags are placed on the tree each morning, representing the average number of suicides that occur each day among American service members and veterans. The public time is devoted to remembering, giving thanks, and committing to better care for veterans with all their challenges. The church then hosts an inter-religious service on Veterans Day evening. Again, it centers on the same goals: to root all present—civilian and veteran—into healthier community wherein all are nurtured toward deeper listening, stronger solidarity, and a sense of purpose together in the hope offered by the Holy. A similar community service is sponsored on Memorial Day. These are not merely about celebrating and honoring veterans. Lament is spoken with the concentric circle practice of the Lakota. A representative inner circle of warriors speaks and the outer circle of representative civilians listens. Then they change place and role. The large assembly watches, listens, and silently ponders. These practiced community events communicate the mission of the local congregation and invite service members and veterans into more focused small-group associations through the year.

Hutchinson's work includes one of these small-group associations called a "Compass Healing Circle." In the early months, many veteran families participated along with their spouses. More recently, the shape has been mostly of veterans with lay volunteers. Volunteers receive formal training concerning how to hold compassion and discipline tightly together. They must listen compassionately to stories of horror that would drive the undisciplined listener to flee the room. They must bear in a new way the pain of the warrior. Indeed, they must bear not only that individual's burden, but many others', because the veteran brings all the victims of war into the room in a spiritual manner more palpable even than the physical and historic. Volunteers also assume a key role in calling the larger community to repentance. Working with veterans' invisible wounds brings the volunteer to realize how ruptured the social contract with the warrior is. The covenant of support is broken every time society and government do not respect the restorative principles first committed to when sending the serviceperson to war. Such a holding close of a warrior's memories and pain within select members of a larger faith community also inspires a deeper spirituality within the faith community as a whole. It becomes a larger sign of promise for the wider community.

THE EMERGING LEADERSHIP OF THE VETERANS ADMINISTRATION

Over the past decade, chaplains serving within the structure of the Veterans Administration (VA) hospital system have become more aware of the necessity for collaboration between spiritual care providers and mental health care providers. A seminal paper, "The Pew vs. the Couch," summarizes the antipodal relationship between religious and medical-psychiatric care approaches over the last two millennia.[8] Recognizing the lack of time and expertise, outreach by the VA to clergy began in earnest in the early 2000s, mostly as a matter of developing mutual recognition and respect, and to orient clergy in how to access VA support for certain pastoral care situations. Notably, this VA outreach, particularly informed by a project in rural Arkansas, recognized the importance of learning from spiritual leaders as well as providing expertise to them. For example, the US Department of Veterans Affairs Office of Rural Health provides ongoing orientation and training for rural clergy.[9] This program reflects the fact that twenty-four members of the average rural congregation are veterans. Video curricular supplements are donated by the commercial sector (e.g., Bristol Myers), an expression of a larger collaborative effort to bring resources to bear on veterans' health. Moral injury is always discussed and embedded in four key points for training: 1) description of military culture and wounds of war; 2) the character of pastoral care with vetereans and families; 3) mental health references and resources; and 4) building broader community partnerships. While clergy express sincere initial interest and participate in the orientations, their disparate responsibilities rarely allow for long-term direct involvement in moral injury healing. Subsequently, theirs is more of a cheerleader and overseer approach, commending leadership to non-clergy mental health leaders who lead community action boards. This approach has generated eight congregation community-based sites in Arkansas, serving as inspirations for other rural settings across the country. The biggest success in this effort has been to draw congregational interest, notwithstanding religious and political differences, for the further purpose of attracting veterans back into faith communities.

"LOOSER" NETWORKS FOR FOSTERING FAITH COMMUNITY CARE

For the last six years, General James Mukiyama (Ret.) has practiced a more personal outreach to addressing moral injury. He has done so with a tactical, multigoal approach by forging a network of organizations (Military Outreach USA).[10] This network includes private businesses and nonprofit organizations that sponsor mini-retreats for veterans and their families, as well as collaborations with the VA. The strategic ends are explicitly threefold: 1) that the serviceperson and families understand their struggles; 2) that they experience forgiveness; and 3) that self-worth is rebuilt by serving others. Faith communities have the programs to perform this kind of service, and veterans respond well when they are given a mission; *doing* is integral in the regaining of self-worth. Mukiyama sees himself as a catalyst for communal efforts—faith-based or otherwise—to care for military service members. He recognizes that his own evangelical faith gave him the resilience to deal with moral injury after certain traumatizing experiences in war. He does not resist sharing his faith. But he recognizes, with others noted above, that a kind of "non-religious" retreat language is necessary. Whatever the setting, the civil religious discourse of ultrapatriotism is countereffective.

Chris Antal's work, mentioned above, is another example of establishing a "looser" network of care for the morally injured on "their turf" (i.e., in the

VA setting). Noting that congregations do not have the capacity to do the healing work alone, his model, while VA centered, means to move toward congregational collaboration. We noted this above with reference to his collaboration with Pastor Hutchinson. Antal facilitates ongoing moral injury groups throughout the year. Each iteration culminates with a Community Healing Ceremony that has become so well-attended that the chapel space is filled and ticketed reservations are required. The ceremony has become central to the culture of the VA community there and is attended by many beyond the immediate community. This success, in itself, provides a platform for further training over the next two days for spiritual leaders wanting to build their own capacities for similar work. Key words shape the program, such as communal, spiritual, religious, social, non-pathologizing, and spiritual-resiliency. There is no holding back, too, with political and sociocultural analysis that examines and exposes civilian/state complicity and vulnerability regarding moral injury. Civilian culture is often morally disengaged and thereby both the military and civil sectors may even deny moral truth. But Antal takes to heart the conviction that the community is vital for moral repair. The hard work of recognizing how war affects all our common life must be done by all commiserating people together. Antal (and Hutchinson) ensure that the communalizing goal is more than intuitive.

CONCLUSION

All the above examples of spiritual care and formation for morally injured persons are attuned to the recovery side of injury. They would also apply to the front side—the "before the bang" preparatory time that nurtures resilience. Best faith community practices already include the common spiritual formation emphases of confession, forgiveness, renewed promise of prophetic purpose, self-and-neighborly love, deep-listening, and the ritualized non-identical repetition that celebrates and rehearses these formative themes. We have observed how they all are practiced in informal and formal ways, in larger worship contexts and in small groups, and with secular and interreligious language.

The importance of such positive reinforcement on the front side is underscored in a recent study of more than four hundred service members who had seen combat. The study notes that there is a virtual 100 percent correlation between the experience of an unjust war event and moral injury. On the other hand, there is a very strong correlation between the just killing of enemy combatants and warrior satisfaction. Of the former sample, those who professed a strong moral/spiritual foundation did not exhibit as severe a sense of moral damage as those who could not so identify. The counsel to command, then (of many implications), is that more attention should be given to situations that contradict the warrior ethos, including the toll of witnessing traumatic events and being unable to intervene. More emphasis on leadership and training, the report advises, can positively influence warrior choices and ability to cope with war's tragic consequences.[11]

The classic task of any spiritual "system" is not only to form individual spirituality but also to shape persons into a communal spirituality. This is the role of liturgy and traditional education (catechesis). Whatever Peter did with Cornelius, it meant simultaneous work with his congregation (Acts 10:1–11:18). The same goes for Augustine with Bonifacius, and thereby a whole church tradition. John Sippola shares a sweet story of a teenage boy who, in his confirmation class, had practiced for many weeks the announcement of forgiveness to the theoretical broken soul. That soul turned out to be the boy's own father. Years earlier in an auto accident, the father had caused the death of another person. One day, with his teenage son in the car, the father was overwhelmed when driving through the same intersection. The confirmation class gave the boy the ability "in the name of Christ" to help his father toward freedom.[12] Along these lines, catechism itself may be effective for resilience building and posttrauma care for service members and veterans. The classic Christian practices are more effective than merely the evocations of stoicism advised in military training. Even as terminology changes, the basic teachings—differentiated from civil religion—of God in solidarity with humankind, especially where there is suffering, truth-telling, forgiveness, prayerful listening, personal meaning in vocation, love of God, love of self, and love of neighbor, constitute the things to be reinforced for faithful persons-in-community before and after moral injury.

In the end, those of us interested in spiritual care need to provide contextualized spaces that are safe and restorative. We need small moral injury groups in places like the VA, where trust is established. We need eclectic borrowing and integration of inter-religious spiritual practices into Christian hospitality for the broader community. We need to recognize that women require their own shapes of nurture and formation, especially after trauma,[13] as do the less-than-honorably discharged. We need the discipline of researching, networking, and risk-taking so that we can be available to sorrowing souls as spiritual communities and leaders. And we will no doubt find that we are as broken as the soldiers and society around us, and that we have as much, if not more, of a need for healing than the morally injured persons who welcome us into their community.

NOTES

1. Brett T. Litz et al., "Moral Injury and Moral Repair in War Veterans: A Preliminary Model and Intervention Strategy," *Clinical Psychology Review* 29 (2009): 695–706.

2. Jonathan Shay, "The Birth of Tragedy—Out of the Needs of Democracy," *Didaskalia* 68:2 (1995). https://www.didaskalia.net›issues›shay.

3. The quotation is from a conversation with John Sippola (June 24, 2019).

4. STAR began as a Substance Treatment and Recovery program associated with the VA. It has since come to include posttrauma care.

5. See Edward Tick, *War and the Soul; Healing Our Nation's Veterans from Post-Traumatic Stress Disorder* (Wheaton: Quest, 2005). About the Soldier's Heart program, recently concluded, see www.soldiersheart.net.

6. See https://warriorsjourneyhome.org.

7. I use this term *habitus* intentionally. It recalls Pierre Bourdieu's important insights on how local history, subculture, geography, architecture, and express academic practices shape, often innocuously, a particular community's identity and praxis. See Pierre Bourdieu, *The Logic of Practice*, translated by Richard Nice (Palo Alto, CA: Stanford University Press, 1990).

8. Steve Sullivan, Anne M. Cheney, Jeff Pyne, Justin Hunt, "The Pew vs. the Couch," *Journal of Religion and Health* 53 no. 4 (June 2003). https://www.researchgate.net/publication/239734151.

9. Keith Ethridge and Steve Sullivan, "Rural Promising Practice Issue Brief: Training and Connecting Community Clergy Partners to Increase Access to Care for Rural Veterans, U.S. Department of Veterans' Affairs' Office of Rural Health," (November 2016). www.ruralhealth,va.gov .

10. www.militaryoutreachusa.org .

11. Steven W. Krause, Jeffrey Zust, and Amy B. Adler, "Killing Enemy Combatants, Unjust War Events and Moral Injury in US Service Members," Unpublished Manuscript; Study sponsored by the United States Army Medical Research and Materiel Command.

12. Duane Larson and Jeff Zust, *Care for the Sorrowing Soul: Healing Moral Injuries from Military Service and Implications for the Rest of Us* (Eugene, OR: Cascade, 2017) 228–29.

13. The Sisters of Mercy at the Cranaleith Retreat Center sponsor regular retreat opportunities named as "Coming Home, Becoming Whole" for veterans, and particularly retreats only for women veterans.

BIBLIOGRAPHY

Bourdieu, Pierre. *The Logic of Practice*. Translated by Richard Nice. Palo Alto, CA: Stanford University Press, 1990.

Ethridge, Keith and Steve Sullivan. "Rural Promising Practice Issue Brief: Training and Connecting Community Clergy Partners to Increase Access to Care for Rural Veterans." U.S. Department of Veterans' Affairs' Office of Rural Health. (November 2016). www.ruralhealth,va.gov .

Krause, Steve W., Jeffrey Zust, and Amy B. Adler. "Killing Enemy Combatants, Unjust War Events, and Moral Injury in US Service Members." Unpublished Manuscript. Study Sponsored by the United States Army Medical Research and Materiel Command.

Larson, Duane and Jeff Zust. *Care for the Sorrowing Soul: Healing Moral Injuries from Military Service and Implications for the Rest of Us*. Eugene, OR: Cascade, 2017.

Litz, Brett T. et al. "Moral Injury and Moral Repair in War Veterans: A Preliminary Model and Intervention Strategy." *Clinical Psychology Review* 29 (2009): 695–706.

Shay, Jonathan. "The Birth of Tragedy—Out of the Needs of Democracy." *Didaskalia* 68:2 (1995). https://www.didaskalia.net›issues›shay.

Sullivan, Steve, Anne M. Cheney, Jeff Pyne, and Justin Hunt. "The Pew vs. the Couch." *Journal of Religion and Health* 53 no. 4 (June 2003). https://www.researchgate.net/publication/239734151 .

Tick, Edward. *War and the Soul: Healing Our Nation's Veterans from Post-Traumatic Stress Disorder*. Wheaton: Quest, 2005.

Chapter Eleven

Moral Injury, Scripture, and Contemporary Biblical Studies

Brad E. Kelle

This chapter contributes to the efforts to engage moral injury from diverse perspectives. The goal is two-fold: to consider how perspectives from a particular area of study can contribute to those working on moral injury in other contexts and how insights from moral injury can shape ongoing work within the field of study in view here. My specific aim is to survey the ways that the Bible (in this case, the Christian scriptures of the Old and New Testaments) has intersected with moral injury work thus far and to consider ways it might possibly do so in the future.[1] Through this exploration, I hope to raise the larger questions of how the study of the Bible (both academically and devotionally/pastorally) might contribute to work being done on moral injury in a variety of contexts, and how insights from moral injury might impact the interpretation and use of the Bible. I propose that professional, critical biblical scholarship can stand alongside other academic disciplines such as psychology, ethics, moral philosophy, pastoral care, theology, and religious and cultural studies in the wider conversation about moral injury.

The present volume contains some specific engagements between biblical texts and moral injury (see the chapters by Bowen, Yandell, Cottrill, and Carter). As with most works published thus far concerning the Bible and moral injury, these chapters are not theoretical treatments or constructive proposals; rather, they are case studies that use moral injury as a lens through which to bring new understandings out of particular biblical passages. My survey that follows here will place the biblical studies chapters in this volume into the larger context of the past and present intersections of the Bible and moral injury.

To preview what follows, the survey begins by noting that some moral injury works from fields outside of biblical studies (e.g., psychology, military studies, moral philosophy, and even Christian theology and pastoral care and counseling) have already used the Bible in their discussions, albeit not usually in substantial, systematic, or sophisticated ways. The survey then focuses on the small but growing number of works within the specific discipline of biblical studies per se that have very recently engaged elements of moral injury in dialogue with biblical interpretation. These works within biblical scholarship evidence two primary trajectories concerning their use of the Bible with moral injury: 1) creative rereadings of biblical stories and characters informed by insights from moral injury; and 2) explorations of the post-war rituals and symbolic practices found in biblical texts and how they might connect to the felt needs of morally injured persons. Both of these trajectories within biblical studies reflect long-established practices evident within general moral injury research. Both trajectories also suggest that the engagement between the Bible and moral injury generates a two-way conversation: On the one hand, moral injury can be an interpretive lens that brings new meanings out of biblical texts, especially those associated with war and violence; on the other hand, the critical study of biblical texts can make substantive contributions to the ongoing attempt to understand, identify, and heal moral injury.

One additional introductory comment is in order. Readers of this volume who do not work in contexts that involve Christianity specifically, or faith and spirituality generally, may wonder why the efforts to understand and engage moral injury should consider the Bible. First, as mentioned above, it is not uncommon to find references to the Bible (in different ways and for different purposes) in works on moral injury that have appeared in various, even non-religious, contexts over the last decade or more. These references sometimes appeal to the Bible's cultural importance in Americans' lives and sometimes to its status as an ancient cultural text, but do not typically engage the methods and perspectives found within the academic discipline of biblical studies.

Additionally, regardless of their own religious sensibilities, caregivers and clinicians who serve people affected by moral injury will likely be working with some, if not many, who come from a Christian (or Jewish) background. Given the Bible's cultural and religious significance and the amount of US service members who identify as Christian, particular understandings of biblical ideas and texts will likely be at work in the self-understanding and worldview of many veterans and others seeking care. Consideration of the Bible, enhanced by perspectives from academic biblical studies, may provide additional insights into the elements, dynamics, and impact of moral injury as they manifest themselves within the meaning systems of persons and communities.[2] Perhaps, however, the Bible is most immediately relevant within moral injury for those who work as Christian ministers, chaplains, and counselors. Members of these groups often look to the Bible as Christian scripture to find teachings, stories, poems, and perspectives to put into dialogue with other resources that inform their work as Christian moral healers and guides. Several recent publications have addressed moral injury care for chaplains and Christian ministers, but deeper examination of the contributions of biblical studies may yield specific textual resources.[3]

MORAL INJURY AND THE BIBLE: PAST WORK AND PRESENT TRAJECTORIES

As a starting point for this survey, I assume a generally shared, even if provisional, understanding of moral injury and its key elements (for definitional discussions, see the chapters by McDonald, Litz, and Lettini).[4] Moral injury has functioned primarily as a working label meant to highlight certain unspecified, and often ill-defined, effects of war participation not covered by clinical diagnoses such as posttraumatic stress disorder (PTSD), and those working within biblical studies have primarily engaged moral injury in this general sense. Although many formal definitions have appeared, especially in clinical and research-based studies, any single description masks the complexity and diversity present within current moral injury literature. In a general sense, I understand the label "moral injury" to describe the result of the violation of a person's core moral beliefs (by oneself or others). Put more technically, moral injury refers to the deleterious effects of war participation on moral conscience and ethical conception—the wrecking of a person's fundamental assumptions about "what's right" and how things should work in the world that may result from a sense of having violated one's core moral identity and lost any reliable, meaningful world in which to live.

My survey of the intersections between the Bible and moral injury begins with works outside of the discipline of biblical studies that engage biblical texts in some way in their discussions of moral injury.[5] As noted above, some moral injury works from fields such as psychology, military studies, moral philosophy, and even journalism have referred to biblical texts, often in their discussions of the effects and healing of moral injury. Sometimes these references have been minor, simply drawing principles from the teachings of scripture and applying them to moral stress and repair. For example, Grimsley and Grimsley used the biblical principle of forgiveness as a key for healing moral injury.[6] More frequently, however, moral injury works have employed references to the Bible in discussions of the potential role of rituals and symbolic practices in moral repair. Several psychologists and other researchers have identified rituals from biblical (as well as other ancient) texts as possible models. In this regard, for example, writers have highlighted the

Israelite post-battle purification ritual described in Num 31, along with similar post-battle biblical passages.[7] Other psychologists, approaching the Old Testament writings as artifacts of an ancient culture, have identified certain biblical characters, especially Saul, David, and Job, as allegories for soldiers' experiences, not unlike Shay's initial use of the ancient Greek mythological characters of Achilles and Odysseus.[8]

Not surprisingly, moral injury works from fields such as pastoral care, theology, and Christian ethics, while remaining outside of the discipline of biblical scholarship strictly speaking, have made more use of the Bible in their discussions. The method of engaging the biblical texts, however, is similar: these works, too, tend simply to draw principles from the teachings of scripture (e.g., hope, forgiveness) and apply them to moral stress and repair, while some point to biblical rituals and characters as potential models and lessons. Many of these works have particularly referenced the Old Testament psalms, especially the so-called lament and penitential psalms, as potential resources for the elements of grief, confession, honesty, and forgiveness in moral repair. Others have mentioned the reading of certain psalms as ways to express feelings of shame, guilt, betrayal, and anger, or the incorporation of lament into corporate rituals and public memorials related to moral injury.[9] From within pastoral care, for example, Ramsay suggests the laments found in the Old Testament psalms as key resources for facilitating grieving and building resilience both for the sufferer and for those who would bear witness to the sufferer's testimony.[10] A recent study of moral injury in relationship to the Bible and classical Jewish writings surveys biblical stories and characters, as well as Jewish rabbinical and liturgical texts, for references to spiritual brokenness and wounds, although most of the examples involve nonmilitary contexts (e.g., Cain and Abel in Gen 4).[11]

These examples show that the Bible has been a part of the conversation about moral injury in various fields and contexts. Yet they also reveal that works from fields such as psychology and pastoral care have often referenced biblical texts in insubstantial and cursory ways, and without engaging the perspectives and approaches of professional biblical scholarship. Very recently, however, a small but growing number of works from within the discipline of biblical studies per se have engaged elements of moral injury in dialogue with the interpretation of biblical texts. Overall thus far, biblical scholars have primarily used moral injury as a heuristic (interpretive lens) to bring out new meanings for biblical passages. In other words, for the most part, the focus has remained on the interpretation of the biblical texts themselves, rather than on what or how the biblical texts might contribute to the formulations of moral injury and its healing.

As mentioned above, however, the full range of works emerging within biblical scholarship evidences two primary trajectories concerning the use of the Bible with moral injury.[12] The first, and most prominent, trajectory reflects the tendency noted above to use moral injury as a heuristic for interpreting biblical passages. This trajectory undertakes creative rereadings of biblical stories informed by the experiences of moral injury, often portraying biblical characters in these stories as morally injured warriors. As those working on moral injury will recognize, these works within biblical scholarship follow a practice long-established in general moral injury research of using ancient texts as conversation partners. They are, for instance, akin to what Shay did with the characters of Achilles and Odysseus as metaphors for the experiences of contemporary soldiers both in warfare and homecoming in his foundational works on moral wounds.[13] A number of other moral injury works have followed suit, especially with regard to the ancient Greek myths and tragedies and their characters such as Heracles, Ajax, and Philoctetes.[14] And, as mentioned above, recent moral injury works from various, even non-religious, fields have included references to certain biblical characters (e.g., Job, Saul, David) as possible allegories and analogues, often approaching the Bible as a cultural artifact in touch with the realities of war.[15]

Within biblical scholarship, several recent works have attempted to do with biblical characters and stories what Shay and others have done with Achilles, Odysseus, Heracles, and more. The most recent, book-length collection containing these kinds of works is the volume entitled, *Exploring Moral Injury in Sacred Texts*.[16] For example, in this collection, Bowen reconsiders the disturbing acts in the Sodom story in Gen 19 as the possible consequences of previous moral injury suffered in the war described in Gen 14. She also rereads the subsequent reconnection between some Israelites and Lot's descendants (in Moab) described in the book of Ruth as a narrative example of moral repair.[17] Similarly, Blumenthal reinterprets David in the books of Samuel and Kings as a basic model of the experiences of return and repair after morally injurious actions.[18] As another resource, my new monograph entirely devoted to the intersections between the Bible and moral injury contains an extended example of this first trajectory using the character of King Saul from the Old Testament.[19] I ask if the story of King Saul (1 Sam 9–31), in which Saul has often been interpreted as a psychologically disturbed or tragic figure, might be read as the tale of a morally wounded warrior showing the effects of moral trauma on character, social trust, and personal survival.

Concerning New Testament texts, Yandell's chapter in *Exploring Moral Injury in Sacred Texts* interprets the Gerasene demoniac in Mark 5 as a veteran of the Roman military and explains the man's isolation, self-harming, and aggression in terms of the consequences of moral injury through war participation.[20] Likewise, Carter reads the portrayals of Peter and Judas in the gospels of Matthew and John as stories of moral injury in nonmilitary contexts experienced through the act of betrayal of one's own moral code and values.[21]

The second trajectory of the engagement of moral injury by works within biblical studies explores the identification, importance, and implementation of postwar rituals and symbolic practices found in biblical texts (and their ancient Near Eastern contexts) and connects them to the experiences of moral injury, especially the felt needs of morally injured persons. As with the first trajectory, the biblical studies works in this trajectory follow a practice long-established within moral injury research in general. Various moral injury works have looked to rituals and practices from ancient and traditional societies and their surviving writings for models. The moral injury discourse has often connected these rituals and practices with the felt needs of forgiveness, purification, communalization, and hope.[22] Some works within moral injury have even appealed to researchers to look for other potentially useful models among rituals and practices in ancient writings. The proposed postwar rituals and practices that have appeared in general moral injury works cover a wide range of types from general to specific, communal to individual, religious to nonreligious, and more. Some of the symbolic acts proposed in moral injury discussions involve positive, redemptive actions of well-being designed to counter involvement in war's destructiveness (e.g., community service projects, disaster relief, or other acts of kindness). Most of the discussed rituals, however, involve acts that symbolize cleansing or forgiveness for the sake of transitioning out of combat contexts. Additionally, as noted above, some moral injury works from various, even non-religious, fields have specifically referenced—albeit only in cursory ways—the Bible (usually the Old Testament) as a potential source for the needed postwar rituals and practices.[23]

Within biblical studies, this trajectory has been less prominent than the first one, but some biblical scholars have attempted to further the conversation about possible Old Testament rituals and symbolic practices that might be reexamined with moral injury in mind. The goal is to analyze the relevant passages in their textual, historical, and cultural contexts in ancient Israel and the ancient Near East, as well as through the use of ritual theory, as academic biblical studies would typically do. But the goal also includes consideration of how the ancient rituals described in the biblical writings might, in turn, be resources for understanding the dynamics of moral injury or for developing contemporary practices of moral repair. My recent book provides detailed analyses of biblical texts in this regard.[24] For example, I survey the postwar rituals and symbolic acts in the Old Testament and identify five categories that appear: 1) purification of warriors, captives, and objects; 2) appropriation and redistribution of spoils; 3) construction of memorials and monuments; 4) celebration or procession; and 5) lament (often corporate). These rituals appear quite frequently in texts from other ancient Near Eastern cultures, but the Old Testament and other texts do not provide any sustained reflection on the significance of these post-battle practices or on what they might have meant to those who engaged in them, or, at least, preserved their memory.

From this starting point, I explore how insights from moral injury might illuminate these unstated symbolic functions, as well as how the rituals and practices described in the biblical and extrabiblical sources might provide concrete examples for moral injury research to consider. Note, for instance, the Old Testament references to the most widely attested postwar practice in the biblical and extrabiblical sources—namely, the division of spoils after battle. Two types of the division of spoils after battle appear in Old Testament texts: the redistribution of spoils among combatants and noncombatants, and the dedication of spoils into sanctuaries. In both cases, I explore possible ways that these redistribution rituals might have served, even implicitly, to reframe and communalize the local and specific encounters of combat within larger communal perspectives. My analysis also includes a special focus on the biblical laments found in war-related contexts and the book of Psalms.[25] As mentioned above, certain perspectives and emphases related to lament—understood as a passionate, sometimes public, expression of grief—have appeared in moral injury research from its beginnings in psychology and veterans' care to its present formulations in chaplaincy and Christian ministry.[26] And some general moral injury works have referred to the Bible's laments in particular.[27] The biblical lament poems that feature the honest expression of pain, loss, grief, as well as sometimes pleas for forgiveness and cleansing, connect with emerging moral injury approaches such as "Adaptive Disclosure," which emphasizes the use of confession and dialogue with a compassionate moral authority who can grant forgiveness.

PATHWAYS FOR FUTURE WORK

In summary, there have been many and varied intersections between the Bible and moral injury over the last decade or so. Some have been from the side of moral injury works in fields such as psychology and military studies with no explicit connection to biblical, theological, or religious studies. Others have been from works dealing with moral injury from within theology, pastoral care, and Christian counseling. From within the academic discipline of biblical scholarship per se, the engagements with moral injury, while fewer and more recent than those within the other disciplines, have tended to fall along two primary trajectories: 1) creative rereadings of biblical stories and characters informed by insights from moral injury; and 2) explorations of the postwar rituals and symbolic practices found in biblical texts and how they might connect to the felt needs of morally injured persons.

The various intersections surveyed above suggest, in my view, that the mutual engagement of the Bible, biblical studies, and moral injury, even when done from very different perspectives and contexts, can generate a two-way conversation. On the one hand, moral injury can be an interpretive lens that brings new meanings out of biblical texts, especially those associated with war and violence; on the other hand, the critical study of biblical texts can make substantive contributions to the ongoing attempt to understand, identify, and heal moral injury. I conclude this chapter by highlighting some of what I believe is needed for fruitful future engagement between the Bible and moral injury, including what contributions moral injury study may make to biblical interpretation and what biblical scholarship has to offer to ongoing work on moral injury.[28]

First, I see no reason to doubt that moral injury work can continue to contribute to biblical interpretation, especially by providing a particular interpretive lens by which to reread stories, characters, rituals, poems, and more with an eye for what these biblical writings offer to our thinking about moral conscience and consciousness. When we read the Bible through the lens of moral injury, we can become better attuned to characters and stories that resonate with issues raised by moral injury—characters who display the characteristics of violating their moral conscience or experiencing betrayal, and stories that illustrate the consequences of and attempts to deal with these experiences. We can look for war-related rituals, poems, or prayers that connect to experiences of moral injury and attempts to come to grips with them. In all these ways and more, the moral injury frame of reference can help us see things we might have missed in our readings of biblical characters, stories, rituals, and prayers—most especially, the human experiences, realities, and dynamics that stand behind these sacred texts and the communities that created and preserved them, particularly the reality of human pain caused by loss, death, moral violation, and betrayal.

More specifically, insights from moral injury may encourage future biblical interpreters to pay more attention to several areas of study concerning the Bible's often-troubling texts related to war and violence in particular. For example, moral injury perspectives encourage biblical interpreters to study the reception history (or history of interpretation) of the Bible's stories, rituals, and poems related to war and violence. These studies might try to determine, for instance, whether previous interpreters of these texts (even in premodern contexts) expressed similar concerns about war, morality, ethics, and self-understanding to those raised by moral injury. Additionally, biblical interpreters might seek connections between moral injury and specific genres (types of literature), motifs, or scenes within biblical writings (e.g.: Do biblical poetic texts have special characteristics that encourage engagement with moral injury perspectives? Do scenes depicting endangered daughters and wives reflect experiences associated with moral injury?). An interest in moral injury may also prompt more sustained attention to the rituals depicted in biblical texts, as well as the potential contributions made by ritual theory from within anthropology to understanding the functions of rituals in warfare contexts in particular.[29]

In this conclusion, however, I am especially keen to register a plea for those working on moral injury in a variety of settings to take biblical studies seriously as a potential contributor to their ongoing work, whether they are working in religious or non-religious contexts. Toward that end, I highlight here some contributions that the study of the Bible, especially as done within the field of academic biblical scholarship, might make to the work on moral injury being done by psychologists, veterans workers, moral philosophers, chaplains, and others. Clearly, the use of the Bible can contribute perspectives related to faith and spirituality, which may be sought especially by the US service members who self-identify as Christians, come from Christian backgrounds, or at least express interest in spirituality.[30] For those who operate from these faith-based contexts, particular understandings of the Bible might even constitute the source (or one of the sources) of a person's starting moral sense of the self and the world—the very core moral identity and ethical framework that gets violated in moral injury and that counselors are working to help repair.

Beyond the more obvious dimensions of faith and spirituality, however, biblical studies might contribute additional resources to efforts already underway within general moral injury work. For instance, moral injury discourse in general has begun to think critically about the moral dimensions of many different types of violence, environments, and social and political dynamics, and has begun to apply the notion of moral injury to nonmilitary settings.[31] Biblical interpretation can contribute resources to this recent broadening beyond military contexts by offering a broader range of biblical passages that are not related to war, soldiers, or military violence. Additionally, the use of the Bible might contribute resources to the effort to use moral injury as a larger critique of some of the social dynamics and practices that are associated with war and the military in the wider culture—a potential function moral injury has had since its inception around issues of betrayal by authorities.[32] The Old Testament prophets, for example, challenged the morals and ethics of the people of ancient Israel at both personal and communal levels, questioning contemporary notions of the social body and pushing them to reconsider who they were as a people and how they should have lived out that identity in the world. Even more, the stark depictions of war and its effects in the Bible, along with the laments given in response and the rituals that relate to the aftermath, may provide resources for honest discussion about the negative impact on individuals and communities that results even from legal or sanctioned violence.

In my view, however, biblical studies can make perhaps its most important contribution to moral injury work underway in all contexts by virtue of its nature as a discipline within the so-called humanities (history, philosophy, language, literature, etc.). Biblical scholarship examines the Bible as one of the sacred texts of the world's religions, looking for the ways that these ancient writings reflect and shape aspects of human life, society, and culture past and present. For the most part, moral injury study thus far has been dominated by mental health, psychology, and related therapeutic contexts, resulting in a kind of "medicalization" of the topic. Academic biblical studies can contribute a particularly humanities-oriented dimension to this clinical and scientific reductionism—that is, the dimension of historians, philosophers, literary critics, artists, theologians, sociologists, and textualists. The human lives and experiences reflected in these ancient biblical writings, whether the lives and experiences of those who are portrayed in the texts or of those who authored and preserved the texts in various communities throughout history, point to the historical and cultural breadth of the moral struggles involved in war. And the biblical texts can place moral injury into contexts that clinical psychology and moral philosophy cannot—contexts of rituals, penance, confession, and narratives about complex moral agency and characters.

Seen in this way, the critical study of the biblical texts as ancient writings can provide a resource for pursuing the goal that Boudreau says we should seek when we talk about moral injury: "[W]e seek a deeper understanding of our humanity."[33] These ancient writings reflect not only the events but also the experiences of war for individuals and communities. The Bible's war-related stories, poems, and rituals stand as one manifestation of a human phenomenon known in diverse times and settings, and thus help veterans and others who feel alone in their struggles to see the moral wounds of war as part of a very ancient and human experience. Additionally, however, the Bible's reflections on the nature, purposes, and right ends of human living that stand alongside its war-related texts invite us to consider carefully how war affects our understanding of who we are as human beings, why we are here, and toward what ends we live—the very understandings of the self and the world that war's experiences can alter and even deform. The intersections of the Bible and moral injury invite us into a broader inquiry beyond diagnoses and treatments—an inquiry in which we study war and its moral effects in order to understand more fully what it means to be human.

NOTES

1. For the most comprehensive current treatment of the Bible and moral injury, see my recent book, Brad E. Kelle, *The Bible and Moral Injury: Reading Scripture Alongside War's Unseen Wounds* (Nashville, TN: Abingdon, 2020).

2. Zachary Moon (*Warriors Between Worlds: Moral Injury and Identities in Crisis* [Lanham, MD: Lexington Books, 2019]) has recently argued that understandings of moral injury must consider the broad and complex "moral orienting systems" that veterans develop from their backgrounds and experiences. These systems include values, beliefs, behaviors, and rela-

tionships. For those from Christian backgrounds, notions of the biblical teachings would likely play a formative role in the moral orienting system.

3. For recent treatments of moral injury aimed at chaplains and Christian ministers, see, e.g., Larry Kent Graham, *Moral Injury: Restoring Wounded Souls* (Nashville, TN: Abingdon, 2017); Duane Larson and Jeff Zust, *Care for the Sorrowing Soul: Healing Moral Injuries from Military Service and Implications for the Rest of Us* (Eugene, OR: Cascade, 2017); Lindsay B. Carey et al., "Moral Injury, Spiritual Care and the Role of Chaplains: An Exploratory Scoping Review of Literature and Resources," *Journal of Religious Health* 55 (2016): 1218–45. In this volume, see the chapters by Nancy Ramsay and Duane Larson.

4. For some of the now-standard, clinical definitions of moral injury, see Brett T. Litz et al., "Moral Injury and Moral Repair in War Veterans: A Preliminary Model and Intervention Strategy," *Clinical Psychology Review* 29 (2009): 695–706; Kent D. Drescher et al., "An Exploration of the Viability and Usefulness of the Construct of Moral Injury in War Veterans," *Traumatology* 17 (2011): 8–13; and J. D. Jinkerson, "Defining and Assessing Moral Injury: A Syndrome Perspective," *Traumatology* 22 (2016): 122–30.

5. This discussion draws heavily from Kelle, *The Bible and Moral Injury*, ch. 2.

6. Charles W. Grimsley and Gaylene Grimsley, *PTSD and Moral Injury: The Journey to Healing through Forgiveness* (Mesa, CO: Xulon, 2017), 33–35. They also use Deuteronomy's teaching on remembering, and forgiveness in the passion narratives in the Gospels (p. 67).

7. See Jonathan Shay, *Odysseus in America: Combat Trauma and the Trials of Homecoming* (New York: Scribner, 2002), 152; Larson and Zust, *Care for the Sorrowing Soul*, 164; Graham, *Moral Injury*, 135–52.

8. E.g., Larson and Zust's (*Care for the Sorrowing Soul*, 164) use of Saul and David, as well as the Roman centurions in the New Testament (pp. 160–92). On Saul and David, see also Edward Tick, *Warrior's Return: Restoring the Soul after War* (Boulder, CO: Sounds True, 2014), 91–93, 111–15, 199–202.

9. See Rita Nakashima Brock and Gabriella Lettini, *Soul Repair: Recovering from Moral Injury after War* (Boston: Beacon, 2012), 26; Graham, *Moral Injury*, 135–57.

10. Nancy J. Ramsay, "Moral Injury as Loss and Grief with Attention to Ritual Resources for Care," *Pastoral Psychology* (Dec 2018). doi: https://doi.org/10.1007/s11089-018-0854-9.

11. Kim S. Geringer and Nancy H. Wiener, "Insights into Moral Injury and Soul Repair from Classical Jewish Texts," *Pastoral Psychology* 68 (2019): 59–75. https://doi.org/10.1007/sll089-018-0848-7.

12. See the full discussion in Kelle, *The Bible and Moral Injury*, ch. 2 from which the discussion here draws.

13. See, e.g., Shay, *Odysseus in America*.

14. E.g., Robert Emmet Meagher, *Herakles Gone Mad: Rethinking Heroism in an Age of Endless War* (New York: Olive Branch, 2006); Nancy Sherman, *Afterwar: Healing the Moral Wounds of Our Soldiers* (Oxford: Oxford University Press, 2015), 81–97, 114–24.

15. For the use of Joseph, see Grimsley and Grimsley, *PTSD and Moral Injury*, 36–49; for Saul and David, see Larson and Zust, *Care for the Sorrowing Soul*, 164 and Tick, *Warrior's Return*, 91–93, 111–15, 199–202.

16. Joseph McDonald, ed., *Exploring Moral Injury in Sacred Texts* (Studies in Religion and Theology; London: Jessica Kingsley, 2017).

17. Nancy R. Bowen, "Sodom and Lot's Family: Moral Injury in Genesis 19," in McDonald, *Exploring Moral Injury in Sacred Texts*, 47–68. See also Bowen's chapter in the present volume.

18. David R. Blumenthal, "Soul Repair: A Jewish View," in McDonald, *Exploring Moral Injury in Sacred Texts*, 33–46.

19. Kelle, *The Bible and Moral Injury*, ch. 3.

20. Michael Yandell, "'Do Not Torment Me': The Morally Injured Gerasene Demoniac," in McDonald, *Exploring Moral Injury in Sacred Texts*, 135–50. For an abridged and revised version of this study, see Yandell's chapter in the present volume.

21. Warren Carter, "Peter and Judas: Moral Injury and Moral Repair," in McDonald, *Exploring Moral Injury in Sacred Texts*, 151–68.

22. For examples, see Brock and Lettini, *Soul Repair*, xviii; Shay, *Odysseus in America*, 244–45; Larson and Zust, *Care for the Sorrowing Soul*, 164; Sherman, *Afterwar*, 161. For a chapter devoted to the use of rituals for moral injury from a Christian counseling and pastoral care perspective, see Graham, *Moral Injury*, 135–52.

23. See, e.g., Shay, *Odysseus in America*, 152; Tick, *Warrior's Return*, 194–98, 206–207; Larson and Zust, *Care for the Sorrowing Soul*, 164.

24. Kelle, *The Bible and Moral Injury*, ch. 4.

25. Kelle, *The Bible and Moral Injury*, ch. 5.

26. For example, Graham (*Moral Injury*, 135–57) offers an extended discussion of the use of lamentation ceremonies in the context of public memorials.

27. See Brock and Lettini, *Soul Repair*, 26; Ramsay, "Moral Injury."

28. For a fuller version of this discussion, see Kelle, *The Bible and Moral Injury*, chs. 1 and 7.

29. The lens of moral injury may also give new insights into the perennial challenge for biblical readers, especially those within Christian communities of faith, of how to deal with the Bible's passages that depict violence, war, and killing done by God's people at God's command, and sometimes directly by God. The frame of moral injury may give contemporary readers a new perspective from which to engage these ethically difficult texts, perhaps by asking, Do the biblical warfare and violence texts morally injure their readers? Perhaps the lens of moral injury indicates that the "theological problem" for many readers is how these texts violate their usual sense of a right and stable moral world—a world where God is good and works to bring life and where the chief moral values are "do not kill" and "love your neighbor." Insights from moral injury may allow contemporary readers to articulate in new ways why the biblical warfare texts are morally injurious, how they have been used throughout history to justify a variety of violent and hateful actions, and whether any of the proposed ways to heal moral injury in soldiers might also help with reading the texts. For a full discussion, see Kelle, *The Bible and Moral Injury*, ch. 6.

30. Some recent studies within moral injury work have indicated that veterans generally welcome the incorporation of religion and spirituality into psychological counseling concerning moral injury. See, e.g., Joseph M. Currier et al., "Military Veterans' Preferences for Incorporating Spirituality in Psychotherapy or Counseling," *Professional Psychology: Research and Practice* 49 (2018): 39–47.

31. For a recent application to prison settings, see Alice Lynd and Straughton Lynd, *Moral Injury and Nonviolent Resistence: Breaking the Cycle of Violence in the Military and Behind Bars* (Oakland, CA: PM Press), 2017.

32. Early on, see Shay, *Odysseus in America*, *passim*. More recently, see Joseph Wiinikka-Lydon, "Moral Injury as Inherent Political Critique: The Prophetic Possibilities of a New Term," *Political Theology* 18 (2017): 219–32.

33. Tyler Boudreau, "The Morally Injured," *Massachusetts Review* (Fall-Winter 2011–2012): 754.

BIBLIOGRAPHY

Blumenthal, David R. "Soul Repair: A Jewish View." Pages 33–46 in *Exploring Moral Injury in Sacred Texts*. Edited by Joseph McDonald. Studies in Religion and Theology. London: Jessica Kingsley, 2017.

Boudreau, Tyler. "The Morally Injured." *Massachusetts Review* (Fall-Winter 2011–2012): 746–54.

Bowen, Nancy R. "Sodom and Lot's Family: Moral Injury in Genesis 19." Pages 47–68 in *Exploring Moral Injury in Sacred Texts*. Edited by Joseph McDonald. Studies in Religion and Theology. London: Jessica Kingsley, 2017.

Brock, Rita Nakashima and Gabriella Lettini. *Soul Repair: Recovering from Moral Injury after War*. Boston: Beacon, 2012.

Carey, Lindsay B. et al. "Moral Injury, Spiritual Care and the Role of Chaplains: An Exploratory Scoping Review of Literature and Resources." *Journal of Religious Health* 55 (2016): 1218–45.

Carter, Warren. "Peter and Judas: Moral Injury and Moral Repair." Pages 151–68 in *Exploring Moral Injury in Sacred Texts*. Edited by Joseph McDonald. Studies in Religion and Theology. London: Jessica Kingsley, 2017.

Currier, Joseph M. et al. "Military Veterans' Preferences for Incorporating Spirituality in Psychotherapy or Counseling." *Professional Psychology: Research and Practice* 49 (2018): 39–47.

Drescher, Kent D. et al. "An Exploration of the Viability and Usefulness of the Construct of Moral Injury in War Veterans." *Traumatology* 17 (2011): 8–13.

Geringer, Kim S. and Nancy H. Wiener. "Insights into Moral Injury and Soul Repair from Classical Jewish Texts." *Pastoral Psychology* 68 (2019): 59–75. https://doi.org/10.1007/sll089-018-0848-7.

Graham, Larry Kent. *Moral Injury: Restoring Wounded Souls*. Nashville, TN: Abingdon, 2017.

Grimsley, Charles W. and Gaylene Grimsley. *PTSD and Moral Injury: The Journey to Healing through* Forgiveness. Mesa, CO: Xulon, 2017.

Jinkerson, J. D. "Defining and Assessing Moral Injury: A Syndrome Perspective." *Traumatology* 22 (2016): 122–30.

Kelle, Brad E. *The Bible and Moral Injury: Reading Scripture Alongside War's Unseen Wounds*. Nashville, TN: Abingdon, 2020.

Larson, Duane and Jeff Zust. *Care for the Sorrowing Soul: Healing Moral Injuries from Military Service and Implications for the Rest of Us*. Eugene, OR: Cascade, 2017.

Litz, Brett T. et al., "Moral Injury and Moral Repair in War Veterans: A Preliminary Model and Intervention Strategy." *Clinical Psychology Review* 29 (2009): 695–706.

Lynd, Alice and Straughton Lynd. *Moral Injury and Nonviolent Resistence: Breaking the Cycle of Violence in the Military and Behind Bars*. Oakland, CA: PM Press, 2017.

McDonald, Joseph, ed. *Exploring Moral Injury in Sacred Texts*. Studies in Religion and Theology. London: Jessica Kingsley, 2017.

Meagher, Robert Emmet. *Herakles Gone Mad: Rethinking Heroism in an Age of Endless War*. New York: Olive Branch, 2006.

Moon, Zachary. *Warriors Between Worlds: Moral Injury and Identities in Crisis*. Lanham, MD: Lexington Books, 2019.

Ramsay, Nancy J. "Moral Injury as Loss and Grief with Attention to Ritual Resources for Care." *Pastoral Psychology* (Dec 2018). doi: https://doi.org/10.1007/s11089-018-0854-9.

Shay, Jonathan. *Odysseus in America: Combat Trauma and the Trials of Homecoming*. New York: Scribner, 2002.

Sherman, Nancy. *Afterwar: Healing the Moral Wounds of Our* Soldiers. Oxford: Oxford University Press, 2015.

Tick, Edward. *Warrior's Return: Restoring the Soul after War*. Boulder, CO: Sounds True, 2014.

Wiinikka-Lydon, Joseph. "Moral Injury as Inherent Political Critique: The Prophetic Possibilities of a New Term." *Political Theology* 18 (2017): 219–32.

Yandell, Michael. "'Do Not Torment Me': The Morally Injured Gerasene Demoniac." Pages 135–50 in *Exploring Moral Injury in Sacred Texts*. Edited by Joseph McDonald. Studies in Religion and Theology. London: Jessica Kingsley, 2017.

Chapter Twelve

Moral Injury and Humanizing the Enemy in Judges 5

Amy C. Cottrill

Historian Jill Lepore says that war involves "wounds and words," acts of violence and their interpretation.[1] In order to make sense of the experience of warfare, humans generate narratives and poetry, among other creations, to negotiate their relationship to violence of warfare, the enemy, and themselves. Because the violence of warfare is often not easily undertaken and frequently presents ethical conflicts for all involved, texts are often essential to the process of providing an interpretive structure for the violence of war, both in preparation for warfare and in confronting its aftermath. Textual depictions of warfare, therefore, undertake complex work for individuals and communities as they struggle with the effects of violence in war, whether they are victims or perpetrators, or both.

In this chapter, I explore a particular instance of "wounds and words" in Judges 5 by focusing on the possibilities for ethical reflection in the particular way the text represents violence. Judges 5 celebrates an unlikely victory. Jael, a woman alone in her tent, kills the runaway military commander, Sisera, accomplishing a great triumph for Israel. Though this text no doubt affirms and celebrates Jael's act, there is also a moment in which the reader is offered a sympathetic glimpse of Sisera's mother waiting and hoping for her son's return.

The reader knows that Sisera has died an ignominious death at the hands of Jael and will not return to his mother ever again, a fate that the poet wishes for all God's enemies: "So may all your enemies perish, Yhwh (Judges 5:31)."[2] Though the poem ends on this note of triumph and celebration of Sisera's death, that brief glimpse of Sisera's mother abruptly interrupts the celebratory tone of the poem with a poignant and affecting image of maternal anxiety. Though the poet soon redirects the reader's attention toward the enemy's brutality, reinforcing the poet's feeling that Sisera's death was necessary, that humane moment of recognition of the enemy's grief and loss complicates the celebration of Sisera's death by offering new knowledge to the reader. Suddenly, Sisera is a human being with a mother. This encounter with Sisera's anxious mother makes it far more difficult to villainize her and her son. In a text that celebrates victory over an enemy, the poet includes an affecting moment of sympathy, creating a complex and ethically significant memorialization of the violence of war.

Why does the poet include such a moment of recognition of the enemy's humanity? How does that moment function in a poem that also celebrates Jael's victory? What opportunities for ethical reflection does this moment offer as an interpretation of the violence of the wounds of war? To explore these questions, I bring to bear current research on the role of humanizing the enemy in the experience of moral injury among those who witness and/or perpetrate violence in the context of war. Finally, I offer reflections about the ethical significance of this moment in the text.

JUDGES 5 AND THE HUMANIZATION OF THE ENEMY

At least part of the poet's intentions in Judges 5 are clear from the beginning of the account. This is to be a memorialization of triumph:

> Most blessed of women be Jael,
> Wife of Heber the Kenite,
> blessed of women in tents. (v. 24)

The narrator's hand is strong in guiding the reader's assessment of Jael's actions. Jael will be blessed. In ch. 5, we meet Jael the blessed woman before we meet Jael the woman warrior.

The subsequent description of her actions substantiates the poet's claim that Jael is worthy of blessing. The poet depicts Jael as empowered, brave, and in control, piercing the temple of a warrior who sinks before her as he dies. The intensity of Sisera's death is described with visual force in this poetic depiction:

> Her left hand reached for the tent pin,
> her right for the workman's hammer.
> She struck Sisera, crushed his head,
> smashed and pierced his temple.
> At her feet he sank, lay outstretched,
> at her feet he sank, lay still;
> he sank, there he lay—destroyed. (Judges 5:26–27)

Repeated three times, the poet insistently celebrates the image of Sisera sinking before Jael, a tent peg in his skull. Jael's penetration of Sisera's body is related here with zeal and enthusiasm. One could imagine Jael confronting Sisera on the battlefield as readily as in her tent.

The poem seems to be reaching its conclusion in v. 27 with the image of Sisera destroyed at Jael's feet, a fitting end to a song of triumph. In fact, the progress of the poem would not be impeded if the poet had skipped from this image of the slayed Sisera in v. 27 to the final verse in v. 31 in which the poet hopes for all of God's enemies to perish in such a way. In v. 28, however, the poet suddenly introduces a new character, Sisera's mother. In this verse, the poet dramatically shifts from a celebration of Sisera's death to a portrait of his mother, anxious for his safety and longing for his return:

> Through the window peered Sisera's mother,
> Behind the lattice she frets:
> "Why is his chariot so long in coming?
> Why so late the clatter of his wheels?" (Judges 5:28)

This image of Sisera's mother anxiously awaiting the return of her son complicates the memory of Sisera as an enemy. Suddenly, Sisera is not just an enemy warrior, but is someone with a mother who loves him and awaits his return. Further, the reader knows what the mother does not yet know, that she is about to experience wrenching heartbreak and grief. The effect is suddenly and unexpectedly to expand the emotional and affective range of the poem, creating emotional complexity for the reader in the awareness that Sisera is a mother's son and that his mother is on the precipice of enormous pain.

This moment of encounter with a mother at a window awaiting her son's return from war is certainly striking. The evocative potential of this moment is observed by several biblical scholars who note the way the portrayal of a mother at the window engenders sympathy for Sisera's mother. Danna Nolan Fewell and David Gunn observe, "The poignant image reveals another side of Sisera's world. Besides violence and conquest, there is home and family. He is a mother's son."[3] Jo Ann Hackett calls this moment a "touching detail in the poem," and acknowledges the way "the reader is moved by the suffering of these women, who do not yet know the fate of their men and who will be devastated by that knowledge."[4] Susan Niditch finds in this brief encounter with Sisera's mother a sympathetic critique of war that represents women's experience of battle "which creates heroes but eliminates sons and enslaves daughters."[5]

The potential for the reader's compassion for Sisera's mother is reinforced and encouraged by the sympathy of the companions who surround Sisera's mother. In another affecting and sympathetic moment, Sisera's mother does what many worried mothers might do; she seeks from trusted sources a narrative in which to contain her anxiety and provide some order in a chaotic world. The ladies comfort the worried mother and she accepts their comfort, internalizing her ladies' words as she verbalizes them for herself:

The wisest of her ladies give answer;
She, too, replies to herself: (v. 29)

The comfort the companions offer comes in the form of a story, a narrative in which to organize and interpret distress and disturbance. They offer her a narrative in which she can comfort herself and find assurance.

The poet does not allow the audience prolonged sympathetic exposure to Sisera's mother or her companions, however. In another abrupt shift, the poet provides access to the contents of the story Sisera's mother recites to herself as reassurance:

They must be dividing the spoil
they have found:
A womb or two for each man,
Spoil of dyed cloths for Sisera,
Spoil of embroidered cloths,
A couple of embroidered cloths,
Round every neck as spoil. (Judges 5:30)

The wise ladies offer a picture of Sisera as a plunderer of Israelite women and property, trophies of warfare that seem to be of equal value in their minds: "a womb or two for each man" (v. 30). The compassion the reader may have felt for an anxious mother is suddenly in conflict with the reader's sympathy with Jael and the Hebrew people who might have been the victims of such violence had Sisera won the battle. This description of women's experience in the aftermath of battle is disturbing enough, yet this image of rape and looting functions as comfort for Sisera's mother adding an additional layer of horror to this scene. That this mother perversely accepts the possibility that her son is raping and looting as comfort, so easily wishing upon other mothers the pain she is about to feel, is a source of moral repulsion. Israel may have won the war in Sisera's death, but his mother is firmly established as a source of violent threat herself, willing to achieve her own comfort by hoping for the sexual violation of other women. As Fewell and Gunn note, "poignancy gives way to revulsion," a revulsion felt more intensely by the reader because of the compassion the poet stirs in the tender image of the mother waiting for her son's return from war just one verse prior.[6]

How do these verses function in the memorialization and celebration of Jael's victory over Sisera? Many scholars have argued, I think rightly, that these verses are an incidence of gloating or mockery over Sisera and his family or that the scene serves as justification for the violence of the story. Hackett believes that the poem was written "largely as a final piece of gloating over the enemy, as a way to show how very much the Israelites had hurt Jabin, Sisera, and their people," the effect of which causes the reader to reread "in a less generous frame of mind" the portrayal of Sisera's mother that might have stirred sympathy.[7] Fewell and Gunn argue that this scene is justification for the violence of the story, especially, perhaps, that of Jael, who puts a tent peg through Sisera's skull.[8] Why should the reader feel sympathy for Sisera and his mother, when they clearly represent threat and so egregiously fail at compassion themselves?

There seems little doubt that at least one function of this text is to justify violence. Sisera's mother is more monster than mother by the end of this chapter. Moreover, this text could easily function as a taunt of the enemy; the enemy's family awaits Sisera when all along the reader knows that Sisera is dead. The poet allows the reader access to a private domestic scene of anxiety, effectively empowering the reader at the expense of the enemy. It is a humiliation of the enemy, not only celebrating his death at the hand of a woman, but eavesdropping on the family as they await notification of devastation. Justification of war by dehumanizing the enemy through mockery and portrayals that remove the possibility for sympathy is a long-standing theme in warfare, and this text seems to fall squarely in that tradition.

Yet the justification of violence does not exhaust the interpretive potential of this encounter with Sisera's mother and the poet's characterization of her attempts to comfort herself with visions of her own son's violence against the Hebrews. If these verses do, in fact, teach the reader to reject any sympathetic impulses they might have toward a mother and her son, why would the poet feel that was necessary? Why does the poet feel the need to justify Jael's acts by demonstrating how unworthy the enemy is of the audience's potential compassion? It is not clear. If the poem functions as justification, providing affirmation of the necessity of Jael's act and affirmation of the audience's celebration of the rightness of her actions, it is reasonable to assume that the poet felt the need to justify that celebration of violence. Why? Did the poet feel some misgiving about Jael's actions, some guilt about celebrating the death of an enemy combatant, whose mother grieves him? Did that guilt require justification of Jael's act of violence?

Perhaps one reason the poet provides justification for Jael's killing of Sisera and the celebration of that act is a simple one: killing in warfare is not easily undertaken. Human beings have developed ways over centuries of warfare to prepare themselves for the taking of human life in battle and interpreting it after the fact. One of the most common ways soldiers are prepared for killing in warfare is through dehumanization of the enemy other, imagistic and linguistic erasure of the humanity of the other that avoids the possibility of sympathy or compassion. On one level, this text does seem like a text that dehumanizes the enemy by erasing any possibility of readerly compassion for Sisera and Sisera's mother by the end of the poem.

Yet before dehumanizing Sisera's mother, the poet poignantly humanizes the enemy, portraying her maternal anxiety and generating sympathetic concern in the audience. Why does the poet create such a vivid and tender encounter with Sisera's mother to begin with? Why take the trouble to create such a possibility for sympathy with an enemy if one's intent is ultimately to counter that sympathy with justification for the enemy's suffering? Though the poet clearly wants the audience to come to the conclusion that the death of Sisera was right and necessary, and that Jael should be celebrated for killing him, this text does not accomplish that goal via a straight path, through images that only dehumanize and admit no recognition of Sisera's humanity. In fact, the poet introduces a level of humanity to the enemy that is not necessary if the poet's goal is only to celebrate Jael's actions and the death of Sisera. If the only goal of this text is to taunt the enemy and celebrate the actions of Jael, the introduction of a sympathetic moment of human recognition creates burdensome knowledge for the reader, offering an inconvenient opportunity for sympathy with a mother in a poem that ultimately celebrates the death of her son. Considering the few examples of access to sympathetically portrayed thoughts and feelings of enemies in biblical literature, this is a highly unusual portrayal. Why, especially in a text that functions as a war memorial, do the authors stir the sympathy of the reader for the conquered enemy, an emotion that seems highly inconvenient? Why not deny access to the humanity of the enemy altogether? Why is Sisera's mother humanized so sensitively and *then* portrayed as truly monstrous?

In order to explore this moment of humanization of the enemy within a text that also celebrates the enemy's death, I turn to the concept of moral injury, which provides a different set of questions to ask of this moment of human recognition embedded in a poem of war memorialization. The movement from humanization to dehumanization offers possibilities for reading Judges 5 beyond its role as justification for the violence perpetrated by Jael. The dynamics of this scene are complex and not easily explained as simple justification for acts of violence. The text is doing multiple kinds of work. Read through the lens of moral injury, this moment of recognition of the enemy's humanity is more than a literary manipulation by a narrator who evokes sympathy only to feel it revoked or who mocks a mother's pain in order to taunt a defeated enemy, but one that reflects the poet's struggle to negotiate the human cost of warfare and the reality of violence. In this poem, for a brief moment, the humanity of the enemy lies alongside the celebration of his death. Though this text does justify the violence of warfare, it does not *only* justify the violence of warfare, but also exposes the cost of that violence, especially to those who mourn. That moment of humanization of the enemy is not erased by her later portrayal, making the easy celebration of Sisera's death ethically fraught for readers in a way that invites ethical reflection about the human cost of violence and the tendency to mask that cost through dehumanization of the enemy.

MORAL INJURY AND HUMANIZING THE ENEMY

Moral injury refers to the damaging effects—psychological, moral, and ethical—of involvement in the violence of war. The concept of moral injury has emerged relatively recently as a way to understand and treat the effects of traumatic violence among veterans that were not recognized by the diagnosis of posttraumatic stress disorder (PTSD). PTSD is a clinical diagnosis that focuses on the intense fear and sense of threat that results from experiencing battle and affects the traumatized in a way that makes it difficult for them to return to a sense of safety and security. Moral injury captures another aspect of the experience of violence that comes from having witnessed, perpetrated, or approved of acts of violence that are in profound conflict with other deeply held moral convictions and values. Moral injury, therefore, refers to the painful experience of feeling one's self to have transgressed ethical values and commitments that mark the world as just and humane, leading to intense guilt, despair, shame, anxiety, and pain. As veteran and writer Tyler Boudreau describes, moral injury is the "damage done to our moral fiber when transgressions occur by our hands, through our orders, or with our connivance. When we accept these transgressions, however pragmatically . . . we sacrifice a piece of our moral integrity. That's what moral injury is all about."[9] Moral injury is emerging as an important approach that expands the ability to recognize the ways violence affects people who are close to it, whether as agents, witnesses, or supporters.

Though moral injury is a relatively recent term, many psychologists argue that it is not a new experience. Jonathan Shay, often credited with coining the term, relies heavily on the portrayals of warriors in the *Iliad* and the *Odyssey* in his discussion of moral injury among Vietnam veterans.[10] Because of the ubiquity of war in human history, ancient texts may be particularly useful as tools for recognizing the challenges individuals and communities face in reconciling war with other deeply held moral commitments.[11] The experience of trauma is an increasingly important lens through which to read biblical literature and has become essential to the conversation about the conditions under which the formation, transmission, and early reception of these texts occurred. As a corollary to recognizing that war and suffering were an ever-present factor in Israel and Judah's embattled history, moral injury is an additional concept to add to the examination of biblical texts as they depict and reflect the experience of war. In warfare, individuals both commit and endure violence. Psychologist Kent Drescher and colleagues observe that "combat is one of the very few experiences where trauma exposure comes not only through being the direct or indirect victim of violence and witnessing the aftermath and human toll of violence but also through inflicting (perpetrating) violence and destruction upon others (generally with social sanction)."[12] It seems inevitable that there should be examples in the biblical text in which characters and authors wrestle with participation in warfare, from the vantage point of the victim of violence, from that of the perpetrator, and even from the one who celebrates and affirms it years after the fact.

One set of biblical texts that reflect the process of contending with committing acts of violence in war is the so-called ban texts (Heb. *cherem*), those that command the extermination of all living things by divine order or sanction as an act of war. As described in the book of Joshua, "[The Hebrews] exterminated everything in the city with the sword: man and woman, young and old, ox and sheep and ass" (Josh 6:21). In Niditch's reading, this kind of extermination is part of the sacrificial system of ancient Israel; within the sacrificial framework, the killing of the enemy is treated as a gift to God in response to God's salvific acts on behalf of the Israelite warriors. The "ban," according to this understanding, is not an act of enraged and vengeful slaughter of combatants and noncombatants, but may instead be a way of attributing value and honor to the enemy killed in battle. As Niditch says, "Paradoxically, the ban as sacrifice may be viewed as admitting of more respect for the value of human life than other war ideologies that allow for the arbitrary killing of soldiers and civilians."[13] In this interpretation, the *cherem* texts do not depict the practices of a people with an overly zealous inclination toward violence; instead, they reflect the need of the Hebrew people to understand their actions in warfare in ways that treat the guilt and moral conflict that come from killing other human beings.

Niditch begins her analysis of these texts with the assumption that war is not easily undertaken by human beings. In order to engage in killing, most societies construct structures of meaning in which killing has value and purpose, thereby helping the warrior to negotiate moral conflict. Though she does not use the term "moral injury," Niditch identifies the particular understanding of *cherem* as one way that the biblical authors may have negotiated a rift between their ethical commitments and the violent practices of warfare. What is significant about Niditch's theory of *cherem* as sacrifice is the difference between this construal of the identity of the enemy and the process of dehumanization of the enemy, which is another possibly more familiar construction of the enemy in warfare. According to Niditch, the practice of the ban may, in fact, rely on the humanization of the enemy, an interpretation which reflects the difficulty soldiers had in participating in violent acts against enemies.[14] Recognizing the humanity of the enemy may have been one way warriors gave meaning to their violent acts and to the lives of those they killed.

If this is correct, the impulse to humanize while also celebrating victory over the enemy is particularly relevant to recognizing the dynamics of Judges 5. Moreover, the importance of humanizing the enemy is one that many researchers of moral injury recognize and is consequently emerging as an important part of treatment for moral injury. Shay says that honoring the enemies, which cannot be done without recognizing their humanity, is essential in the recovery from the trauma of war, and resisting the dehumanization of the enemies may be one way for warriors to come to terms with their violent actions.[15] Shay connects humanization of the enemy with recovering trust in one's self that is often deeply damaged in warfare: "The veteran's self-respect never fully recovers as long as he is unable to see the enemy as worthy."[16]

In a similar way as Shay, Vietnam veteran Karl Marlantes recognizes the deleterious effect of dehumanizing the enemy. Of his experience in the Vietnam War, Marlantes says,

> I didn't kill people, sons, brothers, fathers. I killed "Crispy Critters." It could have been krauts, nips, huns, boche, gooks, infidels, towel heads, imperialist pigs, yankee pigs, male chauvinist pigs . . . the list is as varied as human experience. This dissociation of one's enemy from humanity is a kind of pseudospeciation. You make a false species out of the other human and therefore make it easier to kill him.[17]

In light of the many ways people learn to dehumanize others, Marlantes laments the lack of rituals that recognize the enemy's life. He believes that recognizing and restoring the enemy's humanity is an essential part of limiting the violence of warfare.[18] Importantly, Marlantes believes those rituals could also include curses of the enemy and celebration of victory.[19] By recognizing the humanity of the enemy, however, the soldier is brought back to his own humanity; a moment of compassion for the enemy is one part of the soldier's resistance to being overwhelmed by the dehumanization—of the enemy and of the warrior—that has often led to unnecessary acts of depravity. Both Shay and Marlantes indicate that one way to recover one's own humanity after committing acts of violence is to restore the enemy to full humanity, resisting the objectification of the enemy *and* the soldier that is often part of preparation for war.

The concept of moral injury helps readers to see more clearly the complexity of the depiction of war and its aftermath; the impulse to humanize and dehumanize the enemy can exist alongside each other in memories of war. The impulse to humanize may not merely be set up for a more powerful dehumanization, but may reflect the author's or reader's attempts to negotiate genuinely conflicted responses to the experience of violence. In much the same way as Marlantes describes, perhaps there is a particular logic in a war memorial, such as the poem in Judges 5 that recognizes the humanity of an enemy in the same poem that celebrates the enemy's death. Specifically, restoring the humanity of the enemy in this memorial of victory, even for a moment, may be one way in which the poet offers individuals and communities who have affirmed acts of violence against others an opportunity to restore and maintain their own sense of humanity, even as they recognize their participation in the sometimes horrific practices of warfare. Recognizing the humanity of the enemy is perhaps a recognition of moral injury, a way to restore humanity to the enemy and to those who were part of the enemy's death or who affirmed it from afar.

This restoration of humanity provides an important avenue for interpreting the presence of Sisera's mother at the window in Judges 5. Something more than justification of violence is happening in this text. Through the lens of moral injury, this brief scene in Judges 5 brings into focus a poet who is cognizant of the humanity of the enemy and calls to mind a grieving mother aching for her son's return. Though he soon distances the reader—and perhaps himself—from this moment by transmogrifying the mother, he first evokes sympathy for this woman and her family. He does not allow the reader to forget her. The pain of the enemy is also memorialized in this poem, alongside Jael's bravery, heroism, and triumph. In this way, the poet offers the reader a chance to acknowledge the humanity of the other and perhaps offers the reader an opportunity to return to her own humanity, as well, by recalling that the violence of war creates wounds that are not always visible to the naked eye and are carried not only by those who are direct victims of violence, but also by those who perpetrate and celebrate those actions.

A small moment in an ancient text unleashes potent questions for readers today: How do texts assist readers to both remember and forget the pain of the enemy in warfare? How do texts assist readers in remembering violence in ways that generate compassion for the enemy and also create distance from the enemy, often in the same text? How do texts assist readers in negotiating moral and ethical commitments that are often in tension with one another?

CONCLUSION

Recognizing that there are even very small moments in the poem of Judges 5 in which the enemy is humanized does not solve any ethical problem related to human acts of violence. Moral injury as a construct does not directly engage abstract questions of the ethics of warfare or whether or not human beings should ever kill other human beings and neither does the book of Judges. What moral injury supplies is more particular, the perspective of those who have experienced and perpetrated acts of warfare and are familiar with its ethical and moral costs, as well as a set of questions to ask of texts that might elucidate the ways that human beings make sense of their participation in or celebration of those wars.

The portrait of Sisera's mother at the window longing for her son's return is a small moment. Most certainly, no ethical questions are solved by recognizing this brief moment as one that humanizes the enemy. The window at which Sisera's mother awaits her son reveals more than just an anxious domestic scene, however; through the lens of moral injury, it may also reveal a poet who acknowledges the aftermath of a violent act. The poet does not linger on the human costs of warfare for the enemy and quickly turns to justification of those effects. Yet that interruption in the justification of violence and celebration of triumph generates complexity and ambiguity that is ethically important.

Especially in a text that memorializes an act of violence, the inclusion of the enemy's mother is highly significant, offering the reader an opportunity to step outside the celebration of Jael's act and see Sisera from another perspective. Though the poet quickly distances the reader from Sisera's mother, the humanity of Sisera and his mother is anchored in the reader's mind and complicates the poet's attempt to create that distance. The effect is to create a space for ethical reflection about the identity of the enemy and the ways that those who commit violence negotiate their self-understanding in the context of that violence. That the poet of Judges 5 included a brief encounter with the enemy as human may provide readers the opportunity to ask about the construction of enemies in other texts, ancient and modern, where acts of violence are interpreted, sometimes in ways that distort the humanity of everyone touched by violence: Whose perspectives are included in our interpretations of violence? The appearance of Sisera's mother at the window offers readers an opportunity to ask their own questions about the effects of violence on all who encounter it. Though these verses undoubtedly serve to justify the violence against an enemy nation, they may also function in another way, offering a brief glimpse of the enemy as human and, by extension, offering to the reader an opportunity to acknowledge the humanity of all involved in war, including those who perpetrate violence, those who witness it or experience it from a distance, and those who interpret those events for later generations.

NOTES

1. Jill Lepore, *The Name of War: King Philip's War and the Origins of American Identity* (New York: Vintage Books, 1998), x.
2. All translations of the biblical text are by the author.
3. Danna Nolan Fewell and David M. Gunn, "Controlling Perspectives: Women, Men, and the Authority of Violence in Judges 4–5," *Journal of the American Academy of Religion* 58.3 (1990): 407.
4. Jo Ann Hackett, "Violence and Women's Lives in the Book of Judges," *Interpretation* 58.4 (2004): 359.
5. Susan Niditch, *Judges: A Commentary* (Old Testament Library; Louisville, KY: Westminster John Knox, 2008), 5.

6. Fewell and Gunn, "Controlling Perspectives," 407.
7. Hackett, "Violence and Women's Lives in the Book of Judges," 358–59.
8. Fewell and Gunn, "Controlling Perspectives," 408.
9. Tyler Boudreau, "The Morally Injured," *Massachusetts Review* (Fall-Winter 2011–2012): 746.
10. Jonathan Shay, *Achilles in Vietnam: Combat Trauma and the Undoing of Character* (New York: Simon and Schuster 1994); Jonathan Shay, *Odysseus in America: Combat Trauma and the Trials of Homecoming* (New York: Scribner, 2002).
11. See Brad E. Kelle, *The Bible and Moral Injury: Reading Scripture alongside War's Unseen Wounds* (Nashville, TN: Abingdon, 2020).
12. Kent D. Drescher, David W. Foy, Caroline Kelly, Anna Leshner, Kerrie Schutz, and Brett Litz, "An Exploration of the Viability and Usefulness of the Construct of Moral Injury in War Veterans," *Traumatology* 17 (2011): 8.
13. Susan Niditch, *War in the Hebrew Bible: A Study in the Ethics of Violence* (Oxford: Oxford University Press, 1993), 50.
14. Niditch, *War in the Hebrew Bible*, 21.
15. Shay, *Achilles in Vietnam*, 115.
16. Shay, *Achilles in Vietnam*, 115.
17. Karl Marlantes, *What It Is Like to Go to War* (New York: Atlantic Monthly Press, 2011), 41.
18. Marlantes, *What It Is Like to Go to War*, 78–79.
19. Marlantes, *What It Is Like to Go to War*, 79.

BIBLIOGRAPHY

Boudreau, Tyler. "The Morally Injured." *Massachusetts Review* (Fall-Winter 2011–2012): 746–54.

Drescher, Kent D., David W. Foy, Caroline Kelly, Anna Leshner, Kerrie Schutz, and Brett Litz. "An Exploration of the Viability and Usefulness of the Construct of Moral Injury in War Veterans." *Traumatology* 17 (2011): 8–13.

Fewell, Danna Nolan and David M. Gunn. "Controlling Perspectives: Women, Men, and the Authority of Violence in Judges 4–5." *Journal of the American Academy of Religion* 58.3 (1990): 389–411.

Hackett, Jo Ann. "Violence and Women's Lives in the Book of Judges." *Interpretation* 58.4 (2004): 356–64.

Kelle, Brad E. *The Bible and Moral Injury: Reading Scripture alongside War's Unseen Wounds*. Nashville, TN: Abingdon, 2020.

Lepore, Jill. *The Name of War: King Philip's War and the Origins of American Identity*. New York: Vintage Books, 1998.

Marlantes, Karl. *What It Is Like to Go to War*. New York: Atlantic Monthly Press, 2011.

Niditch, Susan. *Judges: A Commentary*. Old Testament Library. Louisville: Westminster John Knox, 2008.

—. *War in the Hebrew Bible: A Study in the Ethics of Violence*. Oxford: Oxford University Press, 1993.

Shay, Jonathan. *Achilles in Vietnam: Combat Trauma and the Undoing of Character*. New York: Simon and Schuster, 1994.

—. *Odysseus in America: Combat Trauma and the Trials of Homecoming*. New York: Scribner, 2002.

Chapter Thirteen

The New Testament and Moral Injury

Peter, Judas, and the Portrayals of Moral Harm and Repair

Warren Carter

Most work on moral injury and repair has been undertaken in the context of war. The groundbreaking work, insightful and very moving, is that of Jonathan Shay, who pioneered a narrative approach to moral trauma.[1] He brought together the narratives he had heard from Vietnam War veterans with Homer's *Illiad*, especially the character of the soldier, Achilles. Shay approached the *Illiad* as a story "about soldiers in war" and found a study of the betrayal, rage, and disintegration analogous to the moral trauma or injury experienced by Vietnam vets.[2] At the heart of the moral injury Shay parses is the notion of betrayal—when soldiers betray, in whatever circumstances, their personal moral code concerning what they deem to be right and wrong or have this code betrayed by those in authority.

How, then, might we read New Testament texts in relation to this experience of the betrayal of what is right? In what ways might New Testament texts function as a resource for addressing situations of moral injury and contributing to its repair?

In this chapter, I follow Shay's example of utilizing a narrative approach, informed by a moral injury and repair hermeneutic, to read New Testament texts, though other thematic approaches might also be employed. I begin by offering a justification for this inquiry and approach, identify some resources on moral injury and repair, provide a brief example from my previous work on Peter in Matthew's Gospel, and finally suggest some possible directions for working with parishioners or teaching a course with students in this area.

THE NEW TESTAMENT AND MORAL INJURY AND REPAIR

How might New Testament texts function as a resource for addressing situations of moral injury and contributing to its repair? Answering this question faces several immediate obstacles. One obstacle is that there are very few published efforts that seek to engage New Testament texts in this perspective.[3] In the absence of well-laid paths, this initial work takes on the positive and negative characteristics of all pioneering contributions.

Second, the New Testament writings, both the Gospels (my particular interests) and letters, are not stories about soldiers in war. While the New Testament writings include military imagery, themes, and personnel, they do not engage or describe the experiences of those involved in war and its aftereffects. They do not offer the psychological details, personal insights, and moral dilemmas that Homer offered to Shay. Therapy is not their primary orientation; they are neither clinically prescriptive nor descriptive.

The New Testament writings are concerned with making sense of life and its difficult experiences and situations in relation to central commitments, to understandings of what is right, to making moral decisions, to trying to live faithfully in relation to God. Religious beliefs, commitments, and actions are to the fore, sometimes faithful, sometimes betraying. Scholars of moral injury recognize that "many of the pre-existing morals and values that are transgressed in war stem from religious beliefs and faith practices. Religion and spirituality are critical components of moral injury."[4] Scholars working on moral repair also recognize the key role of spirituality ("an individual's understanding of, experience with, and connection to that which transcends the self") in repairing moral injury.[5] The New Testament writings affirm freedom from the past and new starts, and celebrate experiences of divine and communal love, mercy, and forgiveness. We might expect to find, amidst the Gospel narratives and the world-constructing rhetoric of the remaining New Testament documents, some resonances with both the betrayal of what is right and a way forward that is free from a traumatic past.

A third issue requires address. As I have noted above, discussions of moral injury and repair have focused on experiences of war. By attempting to read New Testament texts in the perspective of moral injury and repair, I am claiming that moral injury and repair is not only a matter of experiences of betrayal in war. I am suggesting that moral injury can occur in all sorts of areas of life where fundamental commitments are betrayed. I am thinking of interpersonal relationships, of the domestic arena, of personnel and colleagues in various professions (medical, legal, business, education, finance, construction, to name a few) where for various reasons such as ambition, jealousy, the need to dominate or exclude, greed, laziness, coercion by a supervisor or mentor, required displays of loyalty or toughness, institutional reward and so forth, people make decisions and take actions that betray what they know to be right.

Some working in this field would not necessarily agree with such an extension to these areas and would argue that war brings its own unique gravity and intensity of moral injury. Given the vastly elevated consequences of war, so the argument runs, that should be the focus. That war brings its own particular casualties is undeniable and, to be very clear, I do not want to undermine, undervalue, or deflect attention from the injuries of war or question its gravity. I see no need to create a contestive either-or situation whereby attention to one precludes discussion of the other. Rather, I want to recognize that human interactions in other spheres of life can also cause moral injury as people betray commitments and/or are betrayed by others.

UNDERSTANDING MORAL INJURY AND REPAIR FOR NEW TESTAMENT INTERPRETATION

Familiarity with the expanding research on moral injury and strategies of repair is the first step toward reading New Testament texts in this perspective. Since other chapters in this volume address this research in detail, I will mention only a few understandings that shape my work here. In addition to Shay's work noted above, Rita Nakashima Brock and Gabriella Lettini have collected numerous stories from soldiers and discussed the impact of combat, the experiences that constitute moral injury, and processes of repair. They describe moral injury as follows:

> [Moral injury] comes from having transgressed one's basic moral identity and violated core moral beliefs. [Consequences] include overwhelming depression, guilt, and self-medication through alcohol and drugs. Moral injury can lead veterans to feelings of worthlessness, remorse, and despair; they may feel as if they lost their souls in combat and are no longer who they were. Connecting to others becomes impossible . . . the only relief may seem to be to leave this life behind.[6]

Brett Litz and colleagues not only describe moral injury but also set out intervention strategies for moral repair. They argue that people construct a moral code or morals that comprise "rules for social behavior, either explicit or implicit . . . fundamental assumptions about how things should work and how one should behave in the world."[7] Emotions such as pride, embarrassment, and gratitude accompany and reinforce a moral code and sustain adherence to the code. Moral injury from breaking one's moral code can result in social withdrawal, "conflict, confusion and black-and-white thinking about whether one can be good and moral and deserving of a fulfilling life after having severely transgressed standards of conduct."[8] The strategies for intervention include a caring and empathetic therapeutic relationship, education about the therapeutic process and moral injury, exposure to or reliving of deployment experiences, examining maladaptive beliefs about the self and the actions of war, dialogue with a benevolent moral authority, repair and self-forgiveness through doing good deeds, fostering reconnection through positive and healing relationships, and identifying values and goals for the way forward.[9]

READING PETER AND JUDAS IN MORAL INJURY PERSPECTIVE

In this section, I offer a brief example of reading the characters of Peter and Judas in Matthew's Gospel in a moral injury and repair perspective.[10] Matthew's story of Peter can be read as a story of moral injury through betrayal—of his leader, his group, and himself—as well as a story of repair. Matthew's Gospel establishes Peter's moral code, his sense of right and wrong, the values and practices that constitute his worldview and identity. He is bold and loyal to Jesus, leaving all to follow (Matt 19:27), exemplifying the mastery over himself and others that constitutes constructions of dominating masculinity in the ancient world.[11] His house is a base for Jesus's actions (8:14). He is frequently the dominant voice of and among the disciples (15:15; 18:21; 19:27). He is commissioned to a special leadership role (16:16–19) and functions as a spokesperson for Jesus (17:24). There are momentary vulnerabilities (14:28–30; 16:32–33) but nothing diverts him.

In Matthew 19–25, Peter plays no active role in the narrative. He reappears in 26:33 once Jesus has entered Jerusalem. Following the last supper scene, Jesus declares that all his male followers will desert him (26:31). Peter strongly and confidently reasserts his loyalty to Jesus by boasting he will never desert Jesus and declaring that his commitment is superior to that of all the fallible and faithless disciples. Jesus rejects Peter's boast and declares that Peter will betray him three times (26:34). Still confident, loyal, and reasserting of his self-mastery, Peter declares that even if he must die, he will not deny Jesus. Underscoring Peter's social dominance, the other male disciples follow his lead (26:35).

The Garden of Gethsemane scene follows immediately. Peter's vulnerability emerges. Though one of three chosen to accompany Jesus while he prays, Peter cannot obey Jesus's repeated instructions to stay awake (26:40–45). In the following scene, Jesus is arrested (26:47–56). An unnamed disciple seeks to defend Jesus and cuts off the ear of the slave of the high priest when Judas and the large crowd arrest Jesus (26:47). Who is this disciple? While the disciple remains unidentified, two factors suggest that this unnamed disciple might be Peter. First, this disciple's action to defend

Jesus displays loyalty and courage, characteristics that have defined Peter's previous behaviors vis-à-vis Jesus and comprised his moral code. This self-assertion is consonant with Peter's previous actions.

Second, recall Peter's resistance to Jesus's previous announcement of his approaching death (16:21–23). His act of opposing those who arrest Jesus is consistent with his previous resistance. Peter indicates that he has not aligned himself with someone who will be dominated in this way. His moral code, his sense of right and wrong, involves an alignment with strength, domination, power, and success, not with weakness, subjugation, and arrest. To resort now to violence and counter-attack with a sword suggests an even greater assertion of this moral code against the threat of the crowd who would arrest and dominate Jesus. Peter's manly strategy is to dominate before being dominated, strike before being struck, kill before being killed.

> Yet when the arrested Jesus is taken before the high priest, Peter betrays his moral code "outside in the courtyard" (26:69). He is in the courtyard because, unlike the rest of the disciples, he did not run away (26:56). Rather, he had asserted his moral code of bold loyalty in following the arrested Jesus to the house of the high priest Caiaphas (26:57–58). "He sat with the guards in order to see how this would end" (26:58b).

This act of waiting in the high priest's courtyard "to see how this would end" is strange. At least five times previously, Jesus had spoken to the disciples, including Peter, about his imminent death in Jerusalem. He had described the sequence of events that would lead to his crucifixion in considerable detail (16:21; 17:22–23; 20:17–19; 26:1–2). Peter has had ample opportunity to know "how this would end"—namely, in Jesus's death. Yet his boldness and loyalty, as well as his refusal to be intimidated by imperial personnel, means he sits bravely with the guards. We might see in this action a display of Peter's moral code and worldview that do not embrace such an outcome for Jesus. Manly domination (and not being dominated by or submissive to others), along with commitment to success, leave no space for somatic defeat. Bold and loyal, Peter does not accept Jesus's version of reality.

Even so, interactions with two female slaves and some "bystanders" result in Peter betraying his moral code. Three times, in keeping with Jesus's previous prediction (26:34), they name Peter's allegiance to the arrested Jesus, and three times he betrays his commitment by denying any association. They make three statements (26:69–75):

> "You also were with Jesus the Galilean."
> "This man was with Jesus of Nazareth."
> "Certainly you are also one of them, for your accent betrays you."

Each assertion aligns Peter with Jesus. But each one brings a strong and escalating denial from Peter involving oaths and cursing. He completely betrays his relationship with Jesus:

> "But he denied it before all of them, saying, 'I do not know what you are talking about'" (26:70).
>
> "Again he denied it with an oath, 'I do not know the man'" (26:72).
>
> "Then he began to curse, and he swore an oath, 'I do not know the man!'" (26:74).

For whatever reason—the context, the company, the pressure—Peter's boldness and loyalty collapse in the company of the female slaves, soldiers, and other bystanders. As Shay observes concerning circumstances of moral injury, there is "shrinkage of his social and moral horizons" of support.[12] Peter is cut off from his familiar band of disciples and his leader and is alone. He is in an unfamiliar social context. He does not act as he usually does. In this context, he cannot be the self that he has constructed himself to be—neither bold nor loyal, dominant nor faithful. He is not in control of himself and is subjected to, not dominant over, others. He cannot live up to his boast that not even death could shift his loyalty to Jesus (26:35).

The narrative pauses with Peter's vulnerability and loss of self-mastery to describe his reaction. "At that moment the cock crowed. . . . Then Peter remembered what Jesus had said: 'Before the cock crows, you will deny me three times.' And he went out and wept bitterly" (26:75). Whereas previously the narrative had passed over Peter's vulnerabilities quickly (14:28–30; 16:21–23), here it describes his remembering of Jesus's prediction of his betrayal (26:31–35). From the perspective of a hermeneutic of moral injury, Peter's tears denote the shame of betraying his sense of what is right in a high-stakes situation. Peter has betrayed his moral code in the disparity between commitment and performance. His self-construction has collapsed under pressure. Jesus dies.[13]

Peter is not explicitly mentioned again in Matthew, yet he is not absent from Jesus's post-resurrection appearance. While Matthew does not narrate a reconciliation or repair scene between Peter and the resurrected Jesus, three factors suggest steps towards a reconstructed self and repaired moral code for Peter. First, the risen Jesus summons eleven male disciples to Galilee (28:16–20). Judas is not present because he has committed suicide after betraying Jesus (27:3–10). Peter would be one of the "eleven" disciples. He has been reincorporated socially into the group constituted by loyalty to Jesus. The work of Litz et al. emphasizes the importance of countering the social isolation and withdrawal that often follow moral injury with social "reparation, reengagement, and reconnection" in the process of repair.[14]

Second, Jesus gives this group a purpose in the form of worldwide mission (28:19–20). The incorporation of Peter in this commission means his past failure and betrayal no longer define or confine him. A future that includes doing new and good deeds is part of the strategy of repair that Litz et al. identify: "The mistakes of the past do not define the present and the future and . . . a pre-occupation with the past does not prevent possible future good."[15] Jesus counters a "maladaptive interpretation" that Peter's betrayal would define him forever.[16] Peter's failure to live his moral code is not the end. And this future has some continuities with the past. Peter's boldness and loyalty, features of his moral code, are reaffirmed as necessary for this new purpose and task.

Third, the task that Jesus gave Peter earlier in Matthew—"you are Peter and on this rock I will build my church" (16:18)—is not rescinded. This task also requires the boldness and loyalty he demonstrated before his betrayal. These qualities are not denied or revoked by ongoing life; they are redeployed. Again, the Gospel evidences an aspect of the process of repair that Litz et al. propose: Peter grows toward "a new synthesis-a new way to view the world and the self in that it takes into account the reality of the event and its significance without giving up too much of what was known to be good and just about the world and the self prior to the event."[17]

These three factors suggest the repair and reconstruction of Peter's moral code and the establishment of a new future not determined by the past.

The Gospel of Matthew, however, also includes another character, Judas, who betrays Jesus. Peter's embracing of a new role and future contrasts with Judas's sad demise after his betrayal of Jesus. Matthew introduces Judas last in the list of male disciples and describes him from the outset as "the one who betrayed him" (10:4). This descriptor, along with his inclusion on the list of male disciples, creates ambiguity in his presentation. He is both a disciple and a betrayer. Matthew offers no other explicit description of his moral code.

When Judas reappears in the narrative after this introduction, he is in the company of the chief priests in Jerusalem, conspiring to betray Jesus (26:14–16). The emphasis on his role and behavior as a betrayer continues in the scene of the Passover meal (26:21–25). Jesus predicts he will be betrayed by one of his disciples and Judas (again identified as the one "who betrayed him") questions him, "Surely not I, Rabbi?" Among the disciples, only Judas addresses Jesus as "Rabbi" in the gospel (26:25, 49), a term that Jesus discredits in Matthew (23:8); disciples typically address Jesus as "Lord" or "Master" (e.g., 26:22). Judas's next action is to lead "a large crowd with swords and clubs" to arrest Jesus, threatening violence, greeting him as "Rabbi," and kissing him (26:47–51). He betrays his identity and commitment to Jesus, but Matthew offers no insight on Judas's inner world concerning this act.[18]

Yet surprisingly, a very different Judas appears in his final scene in Matthew (27:3–5). Again Judas is explicitly identified as "his betrayer" but now also as one who "has changed his mind" or "has regrets in the sense that he wishes it could be undone and is very sorry."[19] He acknowledges his betrayal and regret by returning the "thirty pieces of silver" and with the words, "I have sinned" (27:4). These actions and words suggest an openness to a different future, both crucial aspects of moral repair.

Tragically, repair is not accomplished. The chief priests dismissively refuse any support for Judas: "What is that to us? See to it yourself" (27:4). Litz et al. emphasize in the repair process the crucial role of a "strong and genuinely caring and respectful therapeutic relationship," the use of "a caring and benevolent moral authority," and the need to foster a community of "positive and healing relationships."[20] The chief priests could supply such compassion, authority, and community, but their retreat from Judas isolates him. "Seeing to it himself" is exactly what the morally injured Judas cannot do. He needs the resources that the chief priests could supply but withhold. Nor does he seek out other disciples for compassion, authority, and community. Rejected by the chief priests, isolated and withdrawn from the community of disciples, and subjected to self-condemnation, he commits suicide. Keizer and Lettini note the prevalence of self-harming behaviors and "the loss of a desire to live" as consequences of moral injury.[21]

TEACHING A COURSE

In this section, I take up the pedagogical challenge involved in helping students (or, with appropriate modifications, parishioners) adopt this lens of moral trauma and repair in order to reflect on New Testament texts in relation to communities of faith, and facilitate pastoral conversations and interventions concerning moral injury and repair. I outline a possible course of study and I think in terms of three steps.

First, students need to understand the contours of moral injury and repair. I have suggested above some definitions of moral injury that assist in the process of constructing this hermeneutic. Input from veterans would be an especially important resource. Second, students need to engage some of the works which have read biblical texts from the perspective of moral injury and repair. These might include shorter chapters and full-length monographs.[22] Third, students should create their own readings of New Testament stories employing moral injury and repair approaches. Perhaps it is my failure of imagination, but, I do not think there is an endless supply of such scenes available in the New Testament. So I want to borrow a strategy that some earlier feminist work employed. This approach took New Testament scenes in which women characters appeared in all sorts of roles, minor or major, and it encouraged interpreters to elaborate the women's stories, to create narratives involving the women characters, to render them visible, and to imagine their possible life circumstances and roles in the emerging Jesus movement. By analogy, I propose having students engage in imaginative reworkings of references to some characters in the Gospels or Acts in keeping with perspectives from moral injury and repair. Such work would require an imagination informed both by moral injury and repair discussions, as well as by historical-cultural scripts appropriate to the first-century imperial world.

Some examples from Matthew's Gospel which we might imagine, and elaborate upon, include:

- King Herod, in hindsight, experiences moral injury in coming to regret deeply his order to kill the baby boys in the region of Bethlehem (2:16).
- The moral injury crisis that one of Herod's soldiers experiences after carrying out the order to slaughter the infants in the region of Bethlehem (2:16).
- The centurion in Capernaum who approaches Jesus for healing for his slave in crisis because he has injured his "beloved" slave with a whipping or rough sex and wants Jesus to heal him (8:5–13).
- The executioner of John the Baptist in a crisis of moral injury because he does not think he should have executed John but had no option but to follow orders (14:1–12).
- Herod or Herodias or the daughter as filled with regret at seeing John's head on a platter, or the crisis of some of the advisors who should have spoken up to prevent the execution (14:1–12).
- The characters in the parable of the wicked tenants, who seize the owner's heir and kill him, experiencing a crisis of moral injury for having violated their moral code (21:33–43).
- The citizens of the city in the parable of the wedding feast, who undergo great suffering (including loss of loved ones and property) when the king orders their city burned because he is angry with its leaders, experiencing a crisis of moral injury because they feel greatly betrayed by their king (22:10).
- The king in the parable of the wedding banquet, who sends troops to destroy the city's leaders and burn their city, experiencing a crisis for violating his moral code of care for his subjects after such a horrendous act (22:1–10).

This last instance raises an interesting theological question. For many interpreters, the king represents God; the act of burning the city represents Rome's destruction of Jerusalem and the temple in 70 CE, which the Gospel of Matthew—along with other Jewish texts—interprets as God's act of punishing the leaders of the city. Could we also imagine that God experiences regret for an act that caused loss of life and property for many, as well as much anguish and pain? Exploring this, here are two additional possibilities:

- From the parable of the weeds and wheat that the Son of Man who throws the weeds, the evildoers, and causes of sin into the furnace of fire and consigns them to weeping and gnashing of teeth, is now in a crisis of moral injury for a violation of the moral code of mercy and indiscriminate goodness to all (13:24–30).
- Jesus, after the harsh and merciless rhetoric of his sevenfold condemnation of the scribes and Pharisees as hypocrites, experiencing a crisis of moral injury for betraying his moral code of mercy for all (ch. 23; 9:13; 12:7).

The preceding lists are illustrative not comprehensive, picking some examples from parts of one New Testament book. My aim is to point to ways of engaging New Testament texts in this moral injury and repair perspective and thus ways of opening the possibility of discourse about such matters in communities of faith.

NOTES

1. Jonathan Shay, *Achilles in Vietnam: Combat Trauma and the Undoing of Character* (New York: Atheneum, 1994) and Jonathan Shay, *Odysseus in America: Combat Trauma and the Trials of Homecoming* (New York: Scribner, 2002).
2. Shay, *Achilles in Vietnam*, xiii.
3. See the New Testament chapters in Joseph McDonald, ed., *Exploring Moral Injury in Sacred Texts* (Studies in Religion and Theology; London: Jessica Kingsley, 2017).
4. Shira Maguen and Brett Litz, "Moral Injury in Veterans of War," *PTSD Research Quarterly* 23 no. 1 (2012): 2–3.
5. Brett Litz et al., "Moral Injury and Moral Repair in War Veterans: A Preliminary Model and Intervention Strategy," *Clinical Psychology Review* 29 (2009):704.
6. Rita Nakashima Brock and Gabriella Lettini, *Soul Repair: Recovering from Moral Injury after War* (Boston: Beacon, 2012), xiv–xvi.
7. Litz et al., "Moral Injury and Moral Repair," 699.
8. Litz et al., "Moral Injury and Moral Repair," 701.
9. Litz et al., "Moral Injury and Moral Repair," 702–4.
10. The example here summarizes the longer and more detailed discussion in Warren Carter, "Peter and Judas: Moral Injury and Repair," in McDonald (2017, 151–68).
11. Colleen Conway (2008, 21–9) remarks while discussing domination that a lack of self-control "calls into question one's masculinity" and creates a process of "sliding down the scale from man to unman" (24). On masculinity and self-control, see Craig Williams (2010, 151–56).
12. Shay, *Achilles in Vietnam*, 23–38.
13. It is interesting to note a difference between Matthew's account of Peter's instant response of tears and John's account where Peter's moral injury emerges in the subsequent narrative. John's narrative describes Peter's three denials of knowing Jesus without reference to any reaction. There are no tears or sudden departure (John 18:15–17, 25–27). That is, unlike Matthew's depiction of an instant moral injury, John constructs a delayed recognition. Herman Keizer and Gabriella Lettini (2012) observe that "moral injury has a slow burn quality that

takes time to sink in." In John, it is Jesus's post-resurrection questions to Peter that function to prompt his memory and open the way for his acknowledgment of his betrayal of Jesus. He tried returning to life as usual as a fisherman (Jn 21:1–3) but belatedly Jesus's questions expose his betrayal. Litz et al. (2009, 703) emphasize the importance of honest and forthright exposure in the repair of moral injury: "It is important to appreciate that holding onto the idea of a moral self or a moral code may require that a bad act be judged as such . . . precluding an easy forgiveness."

14. Litz et al., "Moral Injury and Moral Repair," 702.
15. Litz et al., "Moral Injury and Moral Repair," 704.
16. Litz et al., "Moral Injury and Moral Repair," 703.
17. Litz et al., "Moral Injury and Moral Repair," 703.
18. Contrast John's Gospel in which Judas is allied with the devil (6:70–71) and subject to the devil's influence (13:2, 27). Not only is he a betrayer (6:71; 13:2, 21–27), he is also a thief who steals from the common purse (12:5). When he betrays Jesus and accomplishes Jesus's arrest (18:1–12), John offers no indication of Judas's response. There is no recognition of moral injury, no self-destructive behavior, and no sign of moral repair.
19. The Greek verb used has two meanings. The first emphasizes regret or feeling sorry for a past action as the reason for the change of mind (see Matt 27:3). The second meaning recognizes a change of mind or having second thoughts but without a focus on regret [see Bauer, Danker, Arndt, and Gingrich (2000, 639)]. In the main text here, I paraphrase the first meaning.
20. Litz et al., "Moral Injury and Moral Repair," 102–4.
21. Keizer and Lettini, "Moral Injury: The Crucial Missing Piece."
22. For example, see McDonald (2020).

BIBLIOGRAPHY

Bauer, Walter, Frederick Danker, William Arndt, and F. Wilbur Gingrich, *A Greek-Englis Lexicon of the New Testament and Other Early Christian Literature*. Chicago: University of Chicago Press, 2000.

Brock, Rita Nakashima and Gabriella Lettini. *Soul Repair: Recovering from Moral Injury After War*. Boston: Beacon, 2012.

Carter, Warren. "Peter and Judas: Moral Injury and Repair." Pages 151–68 in *Exploring Moral Injury in Sacred Texts.* Edited by Joseph McDonald. Studies in Religion and Theology. London: Jessica Kingsley, 2017.

Conway, Colleen. *Behold the Man: Jesus and Greco-Roman Masculinity.* Oxford: Oxford University Press, 2008.

Keizer, Herman and Gabriella Lettini. "Moral Injury: The Crucial Missing Piece in Understanding Soldier Suicides." *Huffington Post*. July 23, 2012.

Kelle, Brad E. *The Bible and Moral Injury: Reading Scripture Alongside War's Unseen Wounds*. Nashville, TN: Abingdon, 2020.

Litz, Brett, Nathan Stein, Elaine Delaney, Leslie Lebowitz, William P. Nash, Caroline Silva, Shira Maguen. "Moral Injury and Moral Repair in War Veterans: A Preliminary Model and Intervention Strategy." *Clinical Psychology Review* 29 (2009): 695–706.

Maguen, Shira and Brett Litz, "Moral Injury in Veterans of War." *PTSD Research Quarterly* 23 no. 1 (2012): 1–6.

McDonald, Joseph, ed. *Exploring Moral Injury in Sacred Texts.* Studies in Religion and Theology. London: Jessica Kingsley, 2017.

Shay, Jonathan. *Achilles in Vietnam: Combat Trauma and the Undoing of Character.* New York: Atheneum, 1994.

—. *Odysseus in America: Combat Trauma and the Trials of Homecoming.* New York: Scribner, 2002.

Williams, Craig. *Roman Homosexuality.* 2d ed. Oxford: Oxford University Press, 2010.

Chapter Fourteen

Moral Injury, the Bible, and US War-Culture

Kelly Denton-Borhaug

During the summer 2019 Democratic debates, candidate Pete Buttigieg called out Republicans regarding supposed inconsistencies involving public policy and religious values:

> The Republican party likes to cloak itself in the language of religion. . . . And for a party that associates itself with Christianity, to say that it is O.K., that God would smile on the division of families at the hand of federal agents, that God would condone putting children in cages, has lost all claim to ever use religious language again.[1]

But Republicans, such as *Daily Wire* blogger Aaron Bandler, equally criticize Democrats for similar inconsistencies: "Indeed, the Democrat Party likes to invoke the Bible only when it comes to imposing their agenda onto the populace; otherwise they sneer at conservatives as bitter clingers."[2]

Both Republicans and Democrats are sensitized to the other party's hypocrisy regarding exploitation of biblical texts for political interests. When it comes to elements of US culture related to war, however, for the most part Democratic and Republican political leaders and parties are in sync regarding their reception of the Bible. Members of both parties regularly turn to the sacrificial framing of what I call "The War-Culture Bible." Why? This "Bible" provides sacred backup to extol military buildup, glorify military service, and justify and mystify the enormity of US coercive violence around the world.

To cite just one example, President Trump's first speech to congress in 2017 relied on a familiar Bible verse to tamp down protest of a military action that the new president approved. The action resulted in the death of elite Navy Seal William "Ryan" Owens, the deaths of more than twenty Yemeni civilians and combatants, and the loss of valuable military equipment. Sharp questions and protest ignited across media outlets, including criticism from the father of Ryan Owens, who also is a military veteran. But Trump and his advisors contained the tense and uncomfortable atmosphere by calling upon the power of presidential ritual and symbol, through a formal address to both houses of Congress. Inviting not Ryan's father, but his wife (now a widow), to a special seat in the balcony and turning to her at a pivotal moment in his speech, Trump rehearsed the well-trodden verse to promote a particular cognitive framework of what had taken place, and rouse emotion:

> Ryan's legacy is etched into eternity. Thank you. *As the Bible teaches us, there is no greater act of love than to lay down one's life for one's friends*. Ryan laid down his life for his friends, for his country, and for our freedom—we will never forget Ryan.[3] (italics mine)

Hearing the link between the Bible verse (Jn 15:13) and this military loss, listeners in the audience immediately burst into an emotional applause. And in an instant, the swirling controversy was successfully buried. Not only Trump, but politicians of all stripes and persuasions rely on these rhetorical strategies to transcendentalize war, promote an endless buildup of militarism, and mute the reality of US violence and destruction around the world.

In addition to political and media cultures, military cultures exhibit the same pattern. The "Luminary Initiative" of the Marine Corps encourages thousands of luminaries to be lighted on the last Sunday of September every year as a commemoration for those who have died and for those who grieve their loved ones. Like the first example, Jn 15:13 holds center stage on the website commemorating the event, and provides the sacrificial logic: "Greater love has no one than this, to lay down one's life for one's friends."[4]

As the above examples show, in diverse subcultures of the United States, biblical passages are interpreted to foreground sacrificial values and frameworks, and intermix with other civil religious sacrificial references. Currently, efforts are in place to create "Gold Star Family Memorials" in every state of the union. These memorials feature various scenes of military life and death, with sacrificial logic and practice as the justificatory glue. The memorial in Valley Forge, Pennsylvania, spells out the central message: "Gold Star Families: A Tribute to Those Who Sacrificed a Loved One for Our Freedom." The memorial depicts four different "scenes," including "Homeland, Family, Patriot, Sacrifice."[5]

Veterans' groups and organizations are shaped by the same frame. The "Wounded Warriors High Five Tour 2019" featured a "quintessential road trip" to thank Americans "for their appreciation and support of our nation's military families for the sacrifices that they make when America goes to war."[6] Military service, characterized as "sacrifice," is buttressed by Isa 40:31: "But those who hope in the Lord will renew their strength. They will soar on wings like eagles, they will run and not grow weary, they will walk and not be faint."

This chapter first draws on insights from the scholarly discipline of Bible reception history to explore how the Bible is "received" in US war-culture. I then extend these insights to develop an outline of the "US War-Culture Bible." Finally, I raise questions about how this "Bible" impacts the phenomenon of military moral injury among US service members, veterans, and the nation responsible for sending them to war.

US WAR-CULTURE

I use the terminology of "US war-culture" to describe the state of militarism (the centrality of military values, ethos, and culture) and militarization (the concomitant buildup of military and war-related institutions and social structures) in the post-9/11 era. "US war-culture" describes the ethos, institutions, and practices of war that interpenetrate with sites of civilian culture. In the institutions of government, education, religion, youth culture, as well as in practices of manufacturing, consumption, popular culture, and economy, the ethos of war impacts decision-making and culture. Dominant forms of religious practice, values, and frameworks invariably play a telling role in this reality. Moreover, the massive size and impact of war-culture in the United States are both sacralized and concealed through dominant forms of religious practice, values, and frameworks. A sacred canopy shields and promotes the ideology of the necessity of war-as-sacrifice. In other words, symbols, texts, practices, and cognitive frames of communication and understanding are borrowed from dominant religion (in this case, Christianity), and mobilized, creating a sacred frame that encircles US war-culture. The sacred frame protects war-culture from active criticism. It also naturalizes, legitimates, and even sacralizes war-culture, leading to citizens' lack of consciousness about their own reality.[7]

Three pieces of evidence demonstrate the existence of this war-culture. First, there is the amount of money spent to sustain the military's maintenance and unending growth. The United States spends more on war and militarism than the next seven to eight highest spenders of the world combined. The United States spends well over half of all its discretionary budget resources on things military or war-related (more than $0.65 out of every dollar).[8] Second, the United States has more than eight hundred military installations scattered across the globe. In comparison, sovereign nations with the next highest numbers of foreign military bases weigh in with three to five apiece.[9] This apparatus of structural violence correlates with direct violence; at the time of this writing, the "The Costs of War" research group confirms that the United States is involved militarily in no fewer than seventy-six countries around the world under the guise of so-called counter-terrorism activities.[10] Third, the ethos, practices, and institutions of war are tightly interwoven with and impact most of the sites of everyday life in the United States to such an extent that citizens mostly are inured to this impact and understand it as a given and natural reality.

Given these realities, how is military moral injury impacted by the sacred canopy over US war-culture, and what role does the Bible play? Can these knotted threads be disentangled so that we can better understand our own reality? To respond to these questions, I will first provide an overview of the disciplinary method called biblical reception history as a way of analyzing Christian sacred text and culture. Then I will focus on the role of the "US War-Culture Bible" in military moral injury.

SOCIAL MEMORY THEORY AND BIBLE RECEPTION RESEARCH

US war-culture is perpetuated and concealed from critical consciousness by collective assumptions and formations of memory in the wider culture. As Chris Keith explains, "collective memory" refers to how human beings "recall and reconstruct the past in public forms."[11] These memories are crucial to the shaping and maintenance of group identity.

But scholars of social memory theory disagree about the degree to which social constructions of memory in the present obliterate trustworthy historical reconstructions of the past. Some thinkers claim that the pressing urgency of immediate interests means that the past largely will be exploited, as those in the present "exercise their will over it" (the "constructivist perspective"). Other scholars emphasize the "continuity perspective," which sees more of a mutual influence between the past and present. The past is "a stable image" that is continually shaped by new elements from present concerns and ideologies. But even these "continuity perspective" researchers emphasize that elements of the past that are most relevant or useful for current concerns will be the most strongly emphasized in collective memory. In other words, "Memory and history, far from being synonymous, are thus in many respects opposed."[12]

In a similar manner, Bible reception scholars trace the complex ways that the interests and needs of any period influence how the Bible is "received"—that is, understood, interpreted, utilized, and exploited. As James G. Crossley asks, "How do receptions and constructions of the Bible fit into what we now know of the past? Is it really much of a surprise that we find understandings of the Bible that fit into what we can now see as one dominant ideological pattern?"[13] In a study of the use of the Bible in English political discourse, Crossley explores conflicting threads of Bible reception history that shaped and reflected English politics of the twentieth century.[14] He develops a typology to compare and contrast the different "Bibles" that go along with political trends and shifting national identities.

For instance, the "Liberal Bible" emphasizes passages and themes from the Bible selected to support "freedom of conscience, rights, law, government and consensus." In contrast, an historically earlier "Absolute Monarchist Bible" conferred divine approval on the British monarch. The "Liberal Bible" has been utilized to "support the typical privatization of `religion' and assumptions regarding the separation of Church and State," and demote forms of political organization supposedly encouraged in the Qur'an.[15] "The Neoliberal Bible" took hold in the Thatcher era of Great Britain. This interpretation emphasized individualism, charity, patriotism, the free market, and the value of social order.[16] Crossley shows how, during the Thatcher era, the Bible was "repackaged" in a kind of "commodity fetishim" to be marketed to various targeted audiences (e.g., "The Holy Bible: Stock Car Racing Version," "The Bible for Teen Guys," and "The Queen James Bible," which edited out verses that might encourage homophobia).[17] Meanwhile, in the United States, this was the era of "The Soldiers Bible," published in 2004, featuring "military insignia, photographs of soldiers, a helicopter," and an American flag on the cover. This version also included quotes from General George S. Patton and President George W. Bush, and it engineered an overarching message to emphasize biblical support for US militarism and "men and women who serve the cause of freedom around the world."[18]

A final example from Crossley is "The Radical Bible," associated with socialism and revolutionary transformation in politics. This interpretation emphasizes themes such as "land and wealth redistribution, confronting power and wealth, communitarianism, egalitarianism, anti-clericalism, and direct access to God." Crossley claims that especially with the emergence of the Labour movement in the twentieth century, the Radical Bible assumed a more central role in leftist politics, such as in the Campaign for Nuclear Disarmament. Nevertheless, after 1968, the Radical Bible underwent a strong decline in dominant practices of British biblical reception. Increasingly, it was out of step with the ways and means of English political power and national identity, as the Neoliberal Bible took center stage, exploiting themes pertinent to a new political agenda.[19]

Overall, Crossley shows that the Bible has continued to be a powerful force in British collective memory and political/national identity since 1968. The Bible has continued to be a powerful force, though many English citizens have moved away from active membership in church institutions.[20] Additionally, one of Crossley's important insights regards seeing how dominant trends in biblical reception influence and underpin the rising and falling of political power linked with the morphing of collective identity. As he writes, "politicized biblical interpretation" continues to be "modified in light of major international political concerns, most notably the Cold War and the War on Terror."[21]

THE "US WAR-CULTURE BIBLE"

Biblical reception history such as that exemplified in Crossley's analysis provides a helpful framework to analyze how people receive and use the Bible (and to what ends) in a variety of contexts. Recently Crossley asked, "What should we do about the use of the Bible in contemporary American politics, a significant area of contemporary reception-historical research?"[22] He describes biblical scholars who explore various uses of the Bible in advertising, fashion, and popular culture, as well as the textual intersection with race, nationalism, and global capitalism. To this list, we should add the critical examination of how the Bible is used to shelter direct, structural, and cultural violence in US war-culture.

American readers of the Bible have interwoven biblical texts with military institutions and ways of war from the nation's very outset.[23] In the various books of the Bible, however, one finds diverse theologies of war and theologies of peace. But what in particular characterizes the "US War-Culture Bible" in the post-9/11 era? A blog for Memorial Day 2018, written by Russell Gehrlein of The Institute for Faith, Work and Economics, provides an apt example of the current ethos. The blog likens veterans, who "wrote a blank check made payable to the United States for an event up to and including their life," to 1 Jn 3:16: "This is how we know what love is. Jesus Christ laid down his life for us. And we ought to lay down our lives for our brothers and sisters."[24]

Though this example of biblical reception comes from an evangelical Christian think tank, I find very similar language and cognitive framing across Christian denominations, and more largely, in US civil religious practice apart from any specific religious affiliations. For example, Gehrlein's use of the biblical text parallels President Trump's reliance on Jn 15:13 to sway popular opinion following the death of Ryan Owens. But, as a candidate, Trump clearly communicated his lack of familiarity with Christianity during his visit to the evangelical stronghold, Liberty University. People in the audience tittered when he mangled the name of "Second Corinthians"—mistakenly referring to it as "Two Corinthians." Trump exemplifies how dominant and powerful forms of biblical reception impacting politics and culture do not necessarily correlate with religious commitment or with belonging to a religious institution/group.

Both examples above, however, illustrate that the dominant theme in the "US War-Culture Bible" is an emphasis on sacrifice.

SACRIFICE AND THE US WAR-CULTURE BIBLE

The "US War-Culture Bible" foregrounds sacrificial interpretations of biblical events, such as the death of Jesus on the cross in the New Testament. According to this kind of biblical reception, Jesus's "ultimate sacrifice" on the cross is a template that mirrors and undergirds the sacred ideology of the necessity of war-as-sacrifice. This biblical reception dominates popular understanding of the Bible in connection with US ways of war and strongly influences popular culture.

Take, for instance, the widely viewed "House of Cards" Netflix series about a fictional evil and power-hungry US president and First Lady. In one telling episode, the president attends a funeral at Arlington Cemetery for a service member who died as a result of his orders. The graveside homily reflects widespread practices of biblical reception in post-9/11 US war-culture. First, the Episcopal priest references Genesis 22, the story of Abraham's (near) sacrifice of Isaac. The passage is mobilized in the priest's homily as a sacrificial template to sacralize and simultaneously justify contemporary military losses, as visually, the camera moves between shots of the grieving widow at the graveside and the uneasy president a few feet away. The clergyperson proclaims that Abraham's (near) sacrifice has been overwhelmed by God's actual sacrifice, and provides Jn 3:16 as evidence: "For God so loved the world, that he gave his only Son, that whoever believes in him shall not perish, but have eternal life." The minister concludes, "Devotion. Sacrifice. Love. This is what the Lord teaches, and what these young men have exemplified. We will forever honor them, and in heaven they will have eternal life."[25] This homily comes across as utterly unremarkable because this cognitive framing and reception of the Bible are so deeply ingrained in American culture. The "U.S. War-Culture Bible" promotes a smooth and uncritical line of continuity from Abraham's (near) sacrifice to Jesus's "ultimate sacrifice," to using the language of the "ultimate sacrifice" to describe the meaning of military injury and death. All these events are on the same continuum; they are necessary sacrifices for the nation that are required by God, and also actions performed or lauded by God.

This sacrificial rhetoric almost equally pervades both major political parties of the United States. Compare George W. Bush's and Donald Trump's reliance on the sacrificial framework with similar examples found in speeches by Hillary Clinton and Barack Obama. Though leaders in the Democratic Party equally rely on sacred sacrificial framing to justify war and militarism, they connect it less frequently to biblical texts than their Republican counterparts. Even so, the "US War-Culture Bible" both impacts how certain biblical texts are interpreted and conflates a particular civil religious emphasis on nationalist identity as sacrifice with sacralizing war. This framing then shapes the experience of grief in the face of war's losses, determining what is "grievable" and what isn't.[26] For instance, at a key moment in the 2016 Democratic National Convention, Hillary Clinton consolidated her electability and commander-in-chief credentials through a glossy short film about the centrality of national sacrificial values.[27] The film emotionally portrayed the life and tragic death of Captain Humayn Kahn, who perished from wounds caused by an improvised explosive device in Iraq when he stepped forward to protect those in his command. As the lights came back up on the stage, the parents of the young man appeared at the podium. Their short speech spotlighted the centrality of their sacrifice, using it to burnish Clinton's sacrificial vision of American nationalism. Then they criticized Donald Trump. Standing together with Mrs. Kahn at the podium, Mr. Kahn compared his family's sacrifice for the country with the character of Donald Trump, who, as Mr. Kahn emphasized, "had sacrificed no one, and nothing." Convention footage focused on members of the audience visibly weeping and applauding. All relevant criticism of Trump aside, the spectacle had its intended impact: no one at the convention seemed to remember earlier questions about Clinton's own position on the Iraq War, not unlike the way protest was tamped down in the example of Trump earlier in this chapter. The sacrificial spectacle at the convention neatly thrust out of view Clinton's vote of approval for the war that resulted in Captain Kahn's death.

The sacrificial identity that Clinton's campaign exploited so easily and well reflects the national establishment of "Gold Star Mothers," who were recognized with a congressional resolution in 1936 for their "supreme sacrifice of motherhood."[28] A Pinterest "Gold Star Mothers" webpage portrays the sacrificial architecture dominating popular biblical reception in the post-9/11 era. Short and pithy quotes illustrate sacrificial exchange logic, such as "Paying the ultimate price for our freedom"; "America will never forget their sacrifices"; "Home of the Free—Because of the Brave." These are juxtaposed with direct references to Christianity and biblical texts, and here again, sacrificial exchange logic predominates: "Every time the blood of Jesus is applied, there is victory"; "I will restore to you" (Joel 2:25); "Keep calm; the Lord will fight for you"; "I am covered by the blood of Jesus"; and more. The commonly quoted "freedom is not free" sums up the logic at the heart of these messages. Only through the ideology of the necessity of war-as-sacrifice may freedom be obtained and protected. Here we find only that definition of freedom as requiring blood sacrifice, with no awareness of any conflict with the Declaration of Independence, wherein "life, liberty and the pursuit of happiness" are not described as commodities to be purchased through blood, but as the gift of a beneficent Creator.

Additionally, the "War-Culture Bible" intermixes with a type of biblical interpretation we might call the "free-market orthodoxy Bible." The evangelical think tank mentioned above, The Institute for Faith, Work and Economics, sponsored staff member Elise Amyx's 2014 speech, "Christianity and Libertarianism" at the International Students for Liberty Conference. In Amyx's speech, Crossley's "Neoliberal Bible" holds sway, emphasizing individualism and the evils of so-called big government and the welfare state. Amyx cites 1 Samuel 8 to provide "biblical evidence" for divinely approved "smaller government."[29] The climax of the speech focuses on "appropriate charity," based on John 18, as Amyx puts a specific spin on the gospel writer's message. She proclaims, "No one takes his life from him, but he offers it of his own accord." Here Amyx would appear to be drawing on certain verses from the biblical chapter. Jesus "knew all that was to befall him," as soldiers come to arrest him in the garden (Jn 18:4), and he rebuked Simon Peter, who drew his sword and cut off the ear of the high priest's slave in an attempt to protect him. Jesus responds, "Put your sword into its sheath; shall I not drink the cup which the Father has given me?" (Jn 18:11). As Amyx would have it, this "fully voluntary sacrifice" establishes "a bond . . . at the cross between Christ the ultimate giver and his people the ultimate receivers." She summarizes, only through individual, and thus "voluntary," acts of charity may Christians partake in this great gift. In contrast, she warns, government "redistribution. . . ruins this connection."[30] Beyond using the "necessity of war-as-sacrifice" framing and providing sacred cover for war through reference to Jesus's death, the use of John 18 makes it possible to use the Bible to marry the sacrificial canopy over US ways of war with a libertarian/neoliberal philosophy of small government.

THE US WAR-CULTURE BIBLE AND MILITARY MORAL INJURY

Finally, we arrive at two key questions: 1) What role does the "US War-Culture Bible" play in the lives of people who are struggling with military moral injury? and 2) How does this "Bible" shape the response of US society to the prevalence of moral injury among our fellow citizens sent to war zones on our behalf? Here I propose three areas for continued investigation regarding the "US War-Culture Bible" and moral injury research.

Honesty and Moral Injury

The "US War-Culture Bible" undermines honesty about the nature of US war-culture and the impact of its direct, structural, and cultural violence on people struggling with military moral injury. I appreciate the understanding of moral injury articulated by VA chaplain Chris Antal:

> The MIG (Moral Injury Group) model offers Veterans an alternative perspective on their moral pain. Veterans' moral pain and anguish (e.g., shame, guilt, sorrow, disgust, resentment) is evidence of an active conscience, an intact moral framework, moral sensitivity and seriousness, and is "the inevitable outcome of moral engagement with the harsh reality of war and killing."[31]

In contrast, the "U.S. War-Culture Bible" subverts deeper honesty about the moral devastation arising from "the harsh reality of war and killing" that is so deeply imbricated in the development of military moral injury. The sacrificial sacred canopy over war and militarism mystifies and falsely glorifies war and militarism, and distracts citizens from understanding and taking charge of their reality.

How does this same sacred canopy, aided and abetted by the "US War-Culture Bible," deform service members' and veterans' own understandings of what is happening in the longest wars of US history and what they should do about it? Does the "US War-Culture Bible" also deter both health care and religious professionals in their commitment from providing open, honest, and reflective resources of healing to those who are suffering? Moral injury research stresses that witnessing and participating in the suffering, harm, or death of others is a key causal factor in this wound, yet very little research examines the cultural violence of sacrificial frameworks that not only justify the destruction of some for the benefit of others, but mandate and sacralize it.[32] Frameworks such as those in the "War-Culture Bible" cannot help but exacerbate the sense of betrayal and crisis of identity that many service members experience. One veteran in Antal's moral injury group described his own reaction to what he had perpetrated in Iraq when he called for an air strike on a target that killed nineteen men, eight women, and nine children:

> I was defeated by my hypocrisy. The shame of my unholy perpetration. My targets were proud Iraqis in an occupied state, bakers and merchants, cousins and priests, mothers and fathers, big brothers and baby sisters. . . . To obscure this truth will only ensure it happens again. I confess to you this reality in hope of redemption, that we might all wince and marvel at the true cost of war.[33]

How should this veteran respond to dominant "avoidance strategies" in the wider public, such as thanking him or her for his "sacrifice?"[34] What must it be like for such an individual to attend Veterans Day or Memorial Day rituals that unabashedly compare the injuries or deaths of service members to what Jesus did on the cross? No biblical verses are referenced in such settings to acknowledge the unimaginable pain of people in those countries where the United States is applying lethal force. No, the "US War-Culture Bible" places strict limits on what is "grievable" and how losses may be framed and mourned. Does such containment exacerbate the suffering of moral injury, as it prevents a deeper and more honest reckoning from taking place about "the true cost of war?"

Credible Biblical Interpretation

The "US War-Culture Bible" fails to match up to the best of historical-critical biblical and theological scholarship. In the case of this "Bible," we can say that the "constructivist" view of biblical reception has taken hold, as the pressing urgency of immediate interests eradicates the integrity of biblical historical study. But religious professionals educated in historical biblical criticism may not ignore New Testament and contemporary theological research that unsettles such conflation; contemporary war-related notions of sacrifice do not unequivocally align with biblical and theological interpretation that investigates Jesus of Nazareth's life, passion, and death.

For instance, Christian theologian Delores Williams came to the realization that the Christian portrayal of Jesus as the surrogate/substitute who sacrifices himself for human sin encourages destructive cultural constraints in the lives of African American women in the United States.[35] For Black women, hearing sermons about mirroring their own lives on this "substitute" only leads to reification of socially required subjugation and sacrifice. Williams traces links between sacrificial theology and three dominant social roles imposed on Black women: "mammy," sacrificing care for her own children in order to provide domestic labor for white families; "sexual surrogate," being forced to sacrifice ownership of her own body and be preyed upon sexually by white men; and "field slave/sharecropper," forcibly giving physical labor demanded as a sacrifice/surrogate for male labor and expected to match that of any man's. This theologian concludes that to attach any spiritual value to Jesus's death on the cross as a sacrifice/surrogate to be emulated only encourages ingrained destructive religio-cultural assumptions that are deeply oppressive and unjust. The meaning of the life of Jesus of Nazareth, she emphasizes, was not to die, but to promote a vision of a different way of living free from dependence on any sacrificial grist. To ponder Jesus's execution by the Roman Empire is to look upon sin in its most degraded form. It is to visualize more clearly the consequences of war-culture: this is what happens when societies insist on maintaining themselves through practices of blood sacrifice, violence, and war.

Joanna Dewey also investigates the inequity in sacrificial logic placed on the backs of the least powerful, justified and sacralized through use of the Bible. For instance, "taking up one's cross" has become a cognitive metaphor in many cultures. It is shorthand for understanding suffering as an unchosen redemptive experience. Dewey turns to Mark 8:34 to investigate this cultural interpretation: "Then he called the crowd to him along with his disciples and said: 'Whoever wants to be my disciple must deny themselves and take up their cross and follow me.'" Verses like this are appropriated in the "War-Culture Bible" to sacralize military service, injury, and especially death, as sacrificial.[36] In contrast, Dewey shows that this interpretation is not consistent with biblical scholarship that explores "taking up one's cross" in its first-century context. Glorifying victimhood was exactly the opposite of what the gospel writer hoped to emphasize. "Taking up one's cross" signified remaining faithful and committed to the work of discipleship. According to Dewey, Jesus of Nazareth's vision of discipleship included insistence on naming and refusing the violence (not sacralizing it) and a nonviolent means of living and understanding ultimate reality. But this vision was in conflict with prevailing powers of Jesus's society. His teaching and actions drew inevitable opposition his way, and he was killed.

Finally, Elisabeth Schüssler-Fiorenza explores dissonance in conflicting messages from Christian texts of the first century regarding the nature of the vision of Jesus of Nazareth. There are traces of a distinct vision in these early texts that she describes as "the discipleship of equals." But this vision conflicts with other textual threads that emphasize the values of "kyriarchy," a view of reality based not on equality, but on hierarchized roles, use of coercive power, and control through violence. In other words, the dominant culture of the first-century Roman Empire was not all that different from our own in the twenty-first century. There, too, "necessity of sacrifice" prevailed as a cognitive framework, and especially was assigned to those most vulnerable, or to marginalized or threatening sectors of the population. Uncovering these conflicting signposts in early Christian texts, Schüssler-Fiorenza concludes that it is up to people in every age, through the moral energy we muster, to determine which ethical road and which vision we will follow.[37]

Roadblocks to Moral Healing

The "US War-Culture Bible" undermines the work of those who would alleviate the distress of military moral injury. I wonder about the double-bind this "Bible" places especially on chaplains of the armed forces, and on health care providers, because a common response is to shame anyone who dares to question the sacrificial frame dominating US ways of war. Does this shaming specter also heighten the burden carried by the morally injured, as those who struggle find it impermissible both to honor grief and also honestly question the sacrificial frame propping up war and militarism? The "War-Culture Bible" inhibits honest access to the moral realities of war. This "Bible" sacralizes cultural violence, forecloses the wider, deeply ambiguous experiences of our veterans and soldiers, delimits what is "grievable" to fit within the sacrificial narrative, and posits moral injury as inevitable, or worse, necessary.

As an Army chaplain, Antal dared to question the US sacrificial frameworks of war in a Veterans' Day sermon he preached on Kandahar Air Base in 2012. He invited those gathered "to reflect upon and lament the gap between our ideals and reality":

> We have made our veterans into false idols,
> blood sacrifice on the National Altar of War.
> Parades and medals perpetuate the hero myth,
> glorifying those who kill and die on our behalf.[38]

Such words drew censure from his commanding officer. He was reprimanded for his "politically inflammatory message," released for a time from active duty, and punished with a "do-not-promote" evaluation.[39] Challenging the frameworks of US war-culture, including its "Bible," is not easy or without risk.

But ultimately the "War-Culture Bible" undercuts the health of those who are struggling with moral injury. It derails honest social analysis the nation needs if it is to face its ways of war and sincerely address the urgent task of helping to lessen the burdens of war for those in military service. It contributes to deluded assessment of the moral costs of war and stymies thought about alternatives to dealing with the very real conflicts and dangers that face all human beings in the contemporary world. What will it take for religious professionals, health care givers, people of faith, and citizens at large to challenge the hold of this "Bible" on our imaginations? What holds us back?

NOTES

1. "Buttigieg Slams Republicans for Their Use of Religion," *CNN Politics* (June 28, 2019). https://www.cnn.com/videos/politics/2019/06/28/pete-buttigieg-religion-child-separation-democratic-debate-vpx.nbc-news.

2. Aaron Bandler, "11 Times the Anti-Bible Democrats Cited the Bible to Defend Their Big Government Programs," *The Daily Wire* (March 17, 2017). https://www.dailywire.com/news/14534/11-times-anti-bible-democrats-cited-bible-defend-aaron-bandler.

3. Dan Merica, "Navy SEAL's Widow Provides Emotional Highpoint in Trump Speech," *CNN* (March 1, 2017). https://journalstar.com/news/national/govt-and-politics/navy-seal-s-widow-provides-emotional-highpoint-in-trump-speech/article_944d6a29-609a-514e-aadb-af2927abc017.html.

4. "Gold Star Luminary Initiative: Mission and History," http://luminaryinitiative.com/mission.asp.

5. "Memorial Monuments," Hershel Woody Williams Medal of Honor Foundation, http://hwwmohf.org/monument-projects.html.

6. "Wounded Warriors Family Support High Five Tour," https://www.wwfs.org/.

7. Elsewhere I have written at length about the nature of US war-culture. See my *U.S. War-culture, Sacrifice and Salvation* (New York: Routledge, 2014).

8. National Priorities Project, "Discretionary Spending," https://www.nationalpriorities.org/budget-basics/federal-budget-101/spending/. See also Peter G. Peterson Foundation, "U.S. Defense Spending Compared to Key Allies," (May 3, 2019). https://www.pgpf.org/chart-archive/0184_ally_defense_spending.

9. Overseas Base Realignment and Closure Coalition, "U.S. Military Bases Overseas: The Facts," https://www.overseasbases.net/fact-sheet.html.

10. "United States Counter-Terror War Locations," 2015–October 2017, Watson Institute of International and Public Affairs, Brown University. https://watson.brown.edu/costsofwar/files/cow/imce/papers/Current%20US%20Counterterror%20War%20Locations_Costs%20of%20War%20Project%20Map.pdf.

11. Chris Keith, "Social Memory Theory and Gospels Research: The First Decade (Part One)," *Early Christianity* 6 (2015): 361. doi: 10.1628/186870315X14404160894938.

12. Chris Keith, "Social Memory Theory and Gospels Research," 366–69, 375.

13. James G. Crossley, "On Reception History, Audiences, and Disciplinary Receptions: A Response to Ibrahim Abraham," *Relegere: Studies in Bible and Reception*, 4 no. 2 (2015): 249.

14. James G. Crossley, *Harnessing Chaos: The Bible in English Political Discourse since 1968* (London: Bloomsbury, 2014).

15. James G. Crossley, *Harnessing Chaos*, 12, 15.

16. James G. Crossley, *Harnessing Chaos*, 16.

17. James G. Crossley, *Harnessing Chaos*, 14, 17.

18. James G. Crossley, *Harnessing Chaos*, 16–17.

19. James G. Crossley, *Harnessing Chaos*, 18–19.

20. James G. Crossley, *Harnessing Chaos*, 33.

21. James G. Crossley, *Harnessing Chaos*, 277.

22. James G. Crossley, "An Immodest Proposal for Biblical Studies," *Relegere: Studies in Religion and Reception* 2 no. 1 (2012): 162.

23. See the following: Susan Juster, *Sacred Violence in Early America*, repr. (Philadelphia: University of Pennsylvania Press, 2018); Phillip Jenkins, *The Great and Holy War: How WWI Became a Religious Crusade* (New York: HarperOne, 2014); Paul Boyer, *By the Bomb's Early Light: American Thought and Culture at the Dawn of the Atomic Age* (Chapel Hill: The University of North Carolina Press, 1994); Robert Meagher, *Killing from the Inside Out: Moral Injury and Just War* (Eugene, OR: Cascade, 2014); Kelly Denton-Borhaug, *U.S. War-culture, Sacrifice and Salvation* (New York: Routledge, 2014).

24. Russell Gehrlein, "Honoring the Sacrifice and Calling of Military Service," (May 28, 2018). Institute for Faith, Work and Economics. https://tifwe.org/honoring-the-sacrifice-and-calling-of-military-service/.

25. "Season Three: Chapter 30," *House of Cards* (February 1, 2013). Media Rights Capital and Panic Pictures, TV Series. See other publications from Denton-Borhaug in the bibliography for additional analysis of this and other popular culture references.

26. I borrow from Judith Butler's analysis of "grievability" that is impacted by the frames of war. See Judith Butler, *Frames of War: When Is Life Grievable?* repr. (New York: Verso, 2016).

27. "Hillary's America: Captain Kahn," Democratic National Convention, July 29, 2016. https://www.youtube.com/watch?v=JxyGEd6K7RU.

28. "JOINT RESOLUTION Designating the last Sunday in September as 'Gold Star Mother's Day,' and for Other Purposes," Resolution 123, 74th Congress, Approved June 23, 1936 (40 Stat 1895). http://legisworks.org/sal/49/stats/STATUTE-49-Pg1894a.pdf.

29. Tyler O'Neill, "Five Reasons Christianity and Libertarianism are Compatible, Young Evangelists Say," (February 18, 2015). https://www.christianpost.com/news/5-reasons-christianity-and-libertarianism-are-compatible-young-evangelicals-say-114724/.

30. O'Neill, "Five Reasons."

31. Chris J. Antal, Peter Yeomans et al., "Transforming Veteran Identity Through Community Engagement: A Chaplain–Psychologist Collaboration to Address Moral Injury," *Journal of Humanistic Psychology* (April 29, 2019): 1–26. https://doi.org/10.1177/0022167819844071.

32. See Brett T. Litz et al. "Moral Injury and Moral Repair in War Veterans: A Preliminary Model and Intervention Strategy," *Clinical Psychology Review* 29 (2009): 695–706.

33. Antal et al., "Transforming Veteran Identity," 15.

34. See Antal et al., "Transforming Veteran Identity," 5–6 regarding their analysis of the ways US citizens employ various "work avoidance strategies" to turn away from the deep pain of military moral injury.

35. Delores S. Williams, "Black Women's Surrogacy Experience," in *After Patriarchy: Feminist Transformations of the World Religions*, eds. Paula N. Cooey, William R. Eakin, Jay B. McDaniel (Ossining, NY: Orbis, 1991), 1–14. Williams writes, "Thus, to respond meaningfully to black women's historic experience of surrogacy-oppression, the theologian must show that redemption of humans can have nothing to do with any kind of surrogate role Jesus was reputed to have played in a bloody act that supposedly gained victory over sin and/or evil" (p. 11).

36. Joanna Dewey, "'Let Them Renounce Themselves and Take Up Their Cross': A Feminist Reading of Mark 8:34 in Mark's Social and Narrative World," in *A Feminist Companion to Mark*, ed. Amy-Jill Levine and M. Blickerstaff, Feminist Companion to the New Testament and Early Christian Writings (Sheffield: Sheffield Academic, 2001), 23–36.

37. Elisabeth Schüssler-Fiorenza, *In Memory of Her: A Feminist Reconstruction of Christian Origins*, 10th ed. (Chestnut Ridge, NY: Herder and Herder, 1994); see also Kelly Denton-Borhaug, "'Like Acid Seeping into Your Soul': Religio-cultural Violence in Moral Injury," in *Exploring Moral Injury in Sacred* Texts, ed. Joseph McDonald (Studies in Religion and Theology; London: Jessica Kingsley, 2017), 111–34, for further analysis and description of "kyriarchy."

38. Chris J. Antal, "Patient to Prophet: Building Adaptive Capacity in Veterans Who Suffer Military Moral Injury," (Ph.D. diss., Hartford Seminary, 2017), 127.

39. Antal, "Patient to Prophet," 25–28.

BIBLIOGRAPHY

Antal, Chris J. "Patient to Prophet: Building Adaptive Capacity in Veterans Who Suffer Military Moral Injury." Ph.D. diss. Hartford Seminary, 2017.

Antal, Chris J. et al. "Transforming Veteran Identity Through Community Engagement: A Chaplain–Psychologist Collaboration to Address Moral Injury." *Journal of Humanistic Psychology* (April 29, 2019): 1–26. https://doi.org/10.1177/0022167819844071.

Bandler, Aaron. "11 Times the Anti-Bible Democrats Cited the Bible to Defend Their Big Government Programs." *The Daily Wire* (March 17, 2017). https://www.dailywire.com/news/14534/11-times-anti-bible-democrats-cited-bible-defend-aaron-bandler.

Boyer, Paul. *By the Bomb's Early Light: American Thought and Culture at the Dawn of the Atomic Age*. Chapel Hill: The University of North Carolina Press, 1994.

Butler, Judith. *Frames of War: When Is Life Grievable?* Repr. New York: Verso, 2016.

"Buttigieg Slams Republicans for Their Use of Religion." *CNN Politics* (June 28, 2019). https://www.cnn.com/videos/politics/2019/06/28/pete-buttigieg-religion-child-separation-democratic-debate-vpx.nbc-news.

Crossley, James G. *Harnessing Chaos: The Bible in English Political Discourse since 1968*. London: Bloomsbury, 2014.

—. "An Immodest Proposal for Biblical Studies." *Relegere: Studies in Religion and Reception* 2 no. 1 (2012): 153–77.

—. "On Reception History, Audiences, and Disciplinary Receptions: A Response to Ibrahim Abraham." *Relegere: Studies in Bible and Reception* 4 no. 2 (2015): 241–58.

Denton-Borhaug, Kelly. "'Like Acid Seeping into Your Soul': Religio-cultural Violence in Moral Injury." Pages 111–34 in *Exploring Moral Injury in Sacred Texts.* Edited by Joseph McDonald. Studies in Religion and Theology. London: Jessica Kingsley, 2017.

—. "Political Theology in the Trump Era: Sacrificial Frameworks in the U.S. 'Neoliberal Disimagination Machine.'" Pages 179–96 in *Taking It to the Streets: Public Theologies of Activism and Resistance.* Edited by Jennifer Baldwin. New York: Lexington, 2019.

—. "Sacrificial U.S. War-culture: Cognitive Dissonance, and the Absence of Self-Awareness." *Journal of Religion and Violence* (April 28, 2017). doi:10.5840/jrv201742538.

—. *U.S. War-culture, Sacrifice and Salvation.* New York: Routledge, 2014.

Dewey, Joanna. "'Let Them Renounce Themselves and Take Up Their Cross': A Feminist Reading of Mark 8:34 in Mark's Social and Narrative World." Pages 23–36 in *A Feminist Companion to Mark.* Edited by Amy-Jill Levine and M. Blickenstaff. Feminist Companion to the New Testament and Early Christian Writings. Sheffield: Sheffield Academic, 2001.

Gehrlein, Russell. "Honoring the Sacrifice and Calling of Military Service." May 28, 2018. Institute for Faith, Work, and Economics. https://tifwe.org/honoring-the-sacrifice-and-calling-of-military-service/.

"Gold Star Luminary Initiative: Mission and History." http://luminaryinitiative.com/mission.asp.Gold.

"Hillary's America: Captain Kahn." Democratic National Convention, July 29, 2016. https://www.youtube.com/watch?v=JxyGEd6K7RU.

Jenkins, Phillip. *The Great and Holy War: How WWI Became a Religious Crusade.* New York: HarperOne, 2014.

"JOINT RESOLUTION Designating the Last Sunday in September as 'Gold Star Mother's Day,' and for Other Purposes." Resolution 123, 74th Congress. Approved June 23, 1936. http://legisworks.org/sal/49/stats/STATUTE-49-Pg1894a.pdf.

Juster, Susan. *Sacred Violence in Early America.* Repr. Philadelphia: University of Pennsylvania Press, 2018.

Keith, Chris. "Social Memory Theory and Gospels Research: The First Decade (Part One)." *Early Christianity* 6 (2015): 354–76. doi:10.1628/186870315X14404160894938.

Litz, Brett T. et al. "Moral Injury and Moral Repair in War Veterans: A Preliminary Model and Intervention Strategy." *Clinical Psychology Review* 29 (2009): 695–706.

Meagher, Robert. *Killing from the Inside Out: Moral Injury and Just War.* Eugene, OR: Cascade, 2014.

"Memorial Monuments." Hershel Woody Williams Medal of Honor Foundation. http://hwwmohf.org/monument-projects.html.

Merica, Dan. "Navy SEAL's Widow Provides Emotional Highpoint in Trump Speech." *CNN* (March 1, 2017). https://journalstar.com/news/national/govt-and-politics/navy-seal-s-widow-provides-emotional-highpoint-in-trump-speech/article_944d6a29-609a-514e-aadb-af2927abc017.html.

National Priorities Project. "Discretionary Spending." https://www.nationalpriorities.org/budget-basics/federal-budget-101/spending/.

O'Neill, Tyler. "Five Reasons Christianity and Libertarianism are Compatible, Young Evangelists Say." (February 18, 2015). https://www.christianpost.com/news/5-reasons-christianity-and-libertarianism-are-compatible-young-evangelicals-say-114724/.

Overseas Base Realignment and Closure Coalition. "U.S. Military Bases Overseas: The Facts." https://www.overseasbases.net/fact-sheet.html.

Peter G. Peterson Foundation. "U.S. Defense Spending Compared to Key Allies." (May 3, 2019). https://www.pgpf.org/chart-archive/0184_ally_defense_spending.

"Season Three: Chapter 30." *House of Cards.* Media Rights Capital and Panic Pictures (February 1, 2013).

Schüssler Fiorenza, Elisabeth. *In Memory of Her: A Feminist Theological Reconstruction of Christian Origins.* 10th ed. Chestnut Ridge, NY: Herder and Herder, 1994.

Watson Institute of International and Public Affairs, Brown University. "Current United States Counter Terror War Locations." https://watson.brown.edu/costsofwar/files/cow/imce/papers/Current%20US%20Counterterror%20War%20Locations_Costs%20of%20War%20Project%20Map.pdf.

Williams, Delores S. "Black Women's Surrogacy Experience." Pages 1–14 in After Patriarchy: Feminist Transformations of the World Religions. Edited by Paula N. Cooey, William R. Eakin, Jay B. McDaniel. Ossining, NY: Orbis, 1991.

Wounded Warriors Family Support. "Wounded Warriors Family Support High Five Tour." https://www.wwfs.org/.

Chapter Fifteen

Christian Theology and Moral Injury

Brian S. Powers

In contrast to an oft-perceived rift between science and religion to define the nature of human experience, in the case of moral injury, there is general agreement as to the importance of religious language in our moral perceptions. Science and religion have distinctive conceptual vocabularies: medicine (in this regard, primarily psychiatry and psychology) helpfully converses in terms of health, wellness, and functionality, while religion deals in language that speaks of moral concepts directly—of things good and evil and the complex ways humans move between the two. A critically important aspect of the language and practice of religion, then, is in dealing with moral and ethical questions. Accordingly, some work on moral injury has differentiated it from posttraumatic stress disorder (PTSD) and argued for the positive effect of a religious community in treating moral injury, noting in particular the importance of dialogue with both a real and imagined moral authority. As Brett Litz and colleagues write, "The hope is that faith, communion with, and empathy from others who share a faith, and messages based on 'good' theology—centered on love and forgiveness—will help heal moral injuries over time."[1]

While the aspects of love and forgiveness are certainly critical and indispensible aspects of theology—and are certainly primary tenets of most major world religions—Christian theology has a profound resonance with moral injury by its very nature. It provides a framework of meaning within which the deep concepts of guilt, shame, sin, and violence contrast with ideas of holiness, purity, peace, and justice and interact through avenues of mercy, salvation, atonement, penance, forgiveness, and sanctification. These concepts define a moral landscape—a trajectory in which we can understand both the weight of bad acts and the value of good ones—but also speak to a personal participation in both the sinfulness and brokenness of the world as well as communities of resurrection and hope. The powerful rituals of the Christian tradition that grow out of the soil of these concepts—confession, penance, baptism, and eucharist—represent the roots of the church in thinking about what it means to feel a deep sense of moral disquiet and the hope for forgiveness and renewal offered in the life, death, resurrection, and promised return of Jesus Christ.

In what follows, I will explore how several important aspects of Christian theology resonate deeply with the experience of moral injury. This is, of course, not a one-way street. As theology can provide a framework of meaning in which we can wrestle with our own experiences, so, too, do those experiences focus and shape how we view theology. Moral injury is no exception, and in many cases its complexity and the reality to which it testifies help to identify and prune away doctrinal formulations that have grown wild and have begun to choke the life out of their own capacity to speak authentically to the world. Religious language and symbols certainly have the ability both to encourage healing as well as give weight to horrific violence. A great deal of responsibility falls on the shoulders of religious leaders to examine the effects of their rhetoric and the theologies behind them, particularly when dealing with those who have encountered significant violence in the world. I will thus also describe how what we have come to know about moral injury challenges some time-honored doctrines and forces us to reexamine patterns of Christian thought in order to fashion some tools that might promote healing, wholeness, forgiveness, and resurrection rather than propagate cycles of violence, hatred, and death.

SIN

If Christian theology is to speak meaningful words to any moral situation, then a great deal hangs on the capacity of the term "sin" to describe how things have gone, and continue to go, wrong. As it is often used in modern culture, it is fair to argue that the term is sequestered in ways that cast doubt on its ability to speak to real evil. It is often mentioned as some trivial indulgence that might detract the pious from their Bible reading or to enforce cultural norms on sexuality and other ethical matters that those who have experienced the horrors of combat might find relatively insignificant. Additionally, in a modern world with so many scientific understandings of psychology, psychiatry, and the motivations that drive us as human beings, it might seem quaint even to attempt to use a term with such mythological connotations to illuminate the lived experience of combat and its myriad forms of death and suffering. Yet precisely because "sin" speaks to the connection between a sense of moral wrongness and ourselves it is valuable in shaping a nuanced moral universe that can account for the good intentions, betrayals, horrors, guilt, and profound consequences of combat actions.

While "sin" is often thought of as a single act, it is spoken of frequently in both the Old and New Testaments as a force that pervades and infects humanity, poisoning its moral capacities in insidious ways. Paul describes it in the book of Romans as a power that "exercises dominion" over human beings, one that enslaves and snares us—a force against which we seemingly have little internal capacity for resistance (see Rom 5:12, 21; 6:20). Conversing with Cain in Gen 4:7 (when he is struggling with jealousy before he kills Abel), God describes how "sin is lurking at the door," a malevolent impulse seeking to colonize and devour. We might say broadly that sin is a corrupting force that produces individual sins (sinful acts) in particular circumstances.

Augustine of Hippo, the fifth-century theologian widely regarded as one of, if not the most, influential philosophers in the Christian tradition, nuanced this distinction even further in a way that is particularly salient in exploring moral injury. Augustine contended that after Adam chose to turn his will from the pure goodness of God, human nature itself was damaged and that we each inherit congenitally a malformed version of the humanity that God intended. The damage occurs in the capacity of our will—the locus of our agency in the world. The will inclines toward that which it determines to be good, so that, broadly speaking, by nature we do try to "do the right thing." Disconnected from the pure good of God, however, we are bound in pursuit of lesser "goods," as our perception of what is good is influenced by near-subconscious forces that shape and form it.[2]

For Augustine, our willing is "bound" because our very sense of what is good and our desires to make choices that move us toward it are shaped by forces over which we do not have control. Unlike Pelagius, who argued that in any situation, we begin from a neutral point and have an equal ability to make a morally good or morally ill choice, Augustine contended that our situations exerted a great deal of influence on our capacity to make good choices, and that the purely good choice that was not conditioned by that situation was simply not available to us.[3] For him, our experiences, cultural histories and values, personal encounters, feuds, grudges, and beliefs about things—in addition to the circumstances of a situation—could compel our willing by influencing our sense of what is "good." We never come into any situation with a blank slate or from a neutral position. Yet the power of the force of sin leads us to pursue distorted and compromised "goods" that constrict our willing, "sequester" it into certain locales, and narrow our horizons of choice.[4]

Augustine contends, then, that our willing is constricted by these forces, yet, within these bounds, we do exercise agency and make personal choices. These constrictions condition, but do not remove, free will. For Augustine, this produces a complex moral psychology. Because of the choices we make—even within bounds that we cannot consciously alter or shake—we are responsible for our actions. Yet, Augustine also contended that we were not exhaustively responsible, as the larger forces that shaped our particular situation and bound us within certain psychological and cultural conditions were responsible as well. We could be responsible for our actions (as our willing was exercised) yet simultaneously bound by factors beyond our control that exerted considerable influence on our available choices and trajectories. As our wills naturally incline to what we think of as "good," humans may sin not only when we consciously make poor moral choices, but often when we righteously pursue what we think is "good."[5]

In my view, this Augustinian sense of moral order and the distorting power of sin is resonant with the experience of combatants who feel the guilt and shame of moral injury. Combatants do not encounter combat situations in a moral vacuum. Their values are formed within a cultural context—in the United States, a very particular one that extolls the virtues of the national enterprise through the valorization of its past and present military members at sporting events, in movies, and in contemporary political discourse. Combatants are instilled with a strong sense of allegiance to the national cause and toward the ultimate "good" of defeating the enemy and winning wars, and their training then conditions their decision-making in particular ways. Ground combatants are put through realistic training scenarios in which real bullets are fired at realistic-looking targets, and speed and efficiency in navigating these scenarios are rewarded. The result makes firing at an enemy an almost reflexive action, and certainly one that often bypasses the cognitive processing involved in most of our deliberative decision-making.[6]

Even so, US Army psychologist Dave Grossman records numerous accounts of combatants who willingly followed their training and committed their energies to the "good" of killing the enemy, only to experience an immediate sense of revulsion and guilt in the aftermath.[7] In other words, many combatants believe themselves to be acting in morally virtuous ways up until the moment they kill another, witness death on a large scale, or fail to prevent the deaths of others. Other veterans recount experiences of a sudden onset of intense feelings of guilt and shame years after they left the military. Still others, particularly veterans of the most recent conflicts, often experience a sense of moral ambivalence about their participation in the enterprise as a whole.

The Augustinian moral framework of sin as distortions of "good" may help contextualize these experiences. It has the benefit of providing an ethical framework that takes veteran guilt seriously, yet acknowledges that the actions which often haunt those combatants long afterward did not occur in a vacuum. They were the product of a myriad of conditioning factors from cultural ideas about violence to particular behaviors inculcated in military training to the local politics, rules of engagement, and mission parameters in a particular situation. This view of sin resists simple answers that tell a veteran, "it's not your fault" or "it's entirely your fault." Rather, this moral framework allows them to explore their own responsibility within the grip of other forces, perhaps finding a path to absolution by witnessing to the power of those conditioning forces and testifying to their ability to distort one's own sense of goodness toward destructive ends.

For theologians, the phenomenon of moral injury challenges us to confront the simplicities that often surround the language of sin. Notions of moral autonomy underlie many implicit theologies of sinfulness and are present in our legal systems and the implicit judgments found in much of our societal discourse (particularly on social media). The pheonomenon of moral injury testifies to the inadequacies of these perspectives to describe the complexity of our world, and musters evidence against notions of sin that focus on individuals and individual events. The situations of moral suffering that combatants face problematize a simple and individual morality—the idea that at any moment we can transcend our individual and collective social locations, institutional conditioning, and personal habituations, and reach for a morally pure choice. Instead, perhaps a view focused on the corruptive power of sin should force us to examine the ways in which our collective actions create morally injurious situations. The phenomenon of moral injury testifies to the complexities of our larger moral trajectories as societies and nations, and the ways in which individual service members bear the intense psychological burden of larger collective policies and decisions. This should encourage Christians to explore the complex formulations of their tradition that account for the communal effects of evil and brokenness in the world and force them to confront Christianity's complicity in comfortable ideas of nationalism and uncritical communal goodness.

IMAGO DEI (IMAGE OF GOD)

Another theological way of nuancing the critical issue of killing in combat and its attendant moral consequences is through the language of the "Image of God" (Latin, *Imago Dei*). The first creation narrative in Genesis presents God as creating humanity "in our image" (Gen 1:26), which has served as a particular marker for what sets humanity apart from other creatures. Some early Christian theologians viewed the Imago Dei as an aspect of the pristine state of humanity before the fall of Adam, lost thereafter and only restored through Christ.[8] John Calvin understood the Imago Dei to be marred and corrupted after the fall, and that "whatever remains is frightful deformity."[9] Other theologians have attempted to articulate of what exactly the image consists, whether it is analogous to the human soul, our intellect, and our sense of reason.[10] What seems to be critical about the doctrine as theologians wrestle with interpretations of it, however, is that there is something that we are endowed with at creation that reflects the divine life of God. Whether we determine it to be the soul, divine spark, intellect, or will, it connotes an essence of our humanity that we share in an intimate way with God.

The early Christian theologian Lactantius argued that being created in the image of God forms all of humanity into a unique fellowship, and this comes with certain moral obligations. One of the critical aspects of our human character that particularly reflects our existence in the Imago Dei for Lactantius is our capacity for kindness. As humanity enjoys the gift of its close ontological connection to God, Lactantius argues that "kindness is the greatest bond of human society," as "[hu]man[s] should protect, love, and cherish [hu]man[s], and both receive and afford assistance against all dangers."[11] He illuminates a negative side of this coin as well, noting, "We are plainly of one blood; and therefore it must be considered the greatest wickedness to hate a [hu]man, even though guilty."[12] To do violence to one's fellow human being was to violate this implicit bond, and to negate the divine image and return to something less—a lesser, more animalistic being which lacked the wisdom, kindness, and love that God shared from God's own being with humanity.

In this particular regard, the Imago Dei is a theological interpretation of the phenomenon that Grossman describes as an innate human resistance to killing other human beings. He argues that there is a strong psychological "resistance to killing one's fellow [hu]man," and that this injunction is so powerful that soldiers in combat will often refuse to fire on an enemy even though such refusal may cost them their lives.[13] As modern militaries have trained their recruits, they have focused implicitly and explicitly on dehumanizing their enemy in order that the soldiers will have an easier time pulling the trigger when the moment arises in combat. Yet when confronted with the actual humanity of their enemy, often after a combatant has killed them, psychological devastation can result. For Grossman, this kind of trauma is inversely proportional to distance from killing—the soldier who has to stab an enemy with a bayonet is forced to confront the humanity of the enemy in a way that a pilot, for example, dropping bombs from thirty thousand feet is not. Thus the pilot is less likely to suffer the traumatic realization of the enemy's humanity, while the knife-range soldier is more likely to be traumatized by the experience.[14]

This distinction is both affirmed and challenged by recent studies of the psychological suffering of military drone operators. It has been observed that American military drone operators experience psychological trauma at the same rates as combat pilots in theater, although their incidences of PTSD were significantly lower.[15] Drone operators experience none of the normal stresses (i.e., extreme fear and the concomitant endocrine response) experienced by their comrades deployed in Afghanistan and Iraq. If combatant PTSD is conditioned by repeat exposure to extreme stress in the life-or-death situations that soldiers experience repeatedly in combat, then certainly drone operators do not experience this kind of fear-based risk. Even so, many of their public testimonies describe that they experience the moral stress of killing their targets in fairly profound ways. Drone operators experience an intimate portrait of their victims, which breaks down the distance when it comes to denying the humanity of their enemy. Christian Enemark states that "the camera's very capacity to facilitate discriminate use of violence is also that which makes that individual's humanity starkly obvious to a drone operator. Such humanity—so familiar and so richly perceived—might then be harder to extinguish because it is harder to deny."[16] A drone operator might follow targets for days before being ordered to fire upon them, and might watch them pray, shop for groceries, eat, and play with their children. It is precisely this "beholding of a normal life" that is lived by their enemies that makes the act of killing them so deeply morally traumatic for the drone operator.[17] This again suggests that the drone operator experiences conflict and its trauma in a deeply ethical and personal, if not physical sense. As one operator put it when asked about PTSD, "My deal is more moral injury. . . . I did the job, I did it as best I could. . . and. . . I paid a spiritual and mental price for that. And I think that's something that people really discount, because I didn't take any physical injury through it."[18]

In terms of giving voice to moral pain, the profound benefit of the language of the Imago Dei is that it upholds a moral stance that killing another human being, even one that as Lactantius says, we might deem "guilty," feels shameful. It can feel like a rending of the human fabric in a very personal way, and, as Grossman notes, is something that many combatants feel after employing violence against others.[19] As might be deduced from Augustine's description of sin, there are a multitude of theological views on the justifications of armed conflict. In a world distorted by sin, we do not have access to morally pure choices: wars may be deemed "just" by politicians, philosophers, and even religious leaders in light of less desirable choices of inaction or acquiescence to an unjust status quo. Targets for drone missions might also be chosen based on criteria put in place to ensure the killings meet a particular legal standard for armed conflict. Yet to the operator who is traumatized by firing the missile and watching those targets die, the justifications often cannot assuage the moral trauma of the act of killing itself. The moral language expressed by the concept of the Imago Dei may provide a way to conceive of the pain of killing in a way that does not seek to argue with those justifications or legalities, but frames the trauma in a broader and more abstract—yet more experientially accessible—context. In focusing on the shared bond of humanity that is rent in warfare, it might hold the power to validate the feelings of loss and disconnection from human community experienced by combatants.

Theologically, the moral pain of those who kill might challenge theologies that argue that our sinfulness and guilt have utterly blotted out the image of God in us as humans. Grossman's argument about the human resistance to killing and the way that drone operators experience the anguish of killing someone after watching them participate in normal human activities seem to evince Lactantius's ancient argument that there is a kinship of those endowed with the divine image that we can perceive and feel intensely, even when ordered to kill those who have committed heinous killings themselves. Writing about the inborn resistance to killing others, Grossman argues that "it gives us cause to believe that there may just be hope for [hu]mankind after all."[20] Rather than focus on the ways in which sin blots out the divine character of human life, perhaps the trauma of those who are in the difficult position of killing should challenge Christian theologians to articulate the existence of the bond that we share as a marker of our common humanity and initial created goodness, glimpsed fully in the person of Jesus Christ, but still discernable in each of us—even those we understand as guilty and an enemy.

RESURRECTION AND ESCHATOLOGY

From this small shred of hope perhaps springs a greater question about God's ultimate position as moral authority and lawgiver. The morally injured seem to feel the sting of the world's injustice in a unique way—when they are valorized as heroes for the actions about which they feel guilt and shame, it can color their perception of the world as fundamentally unjust. So how does God ultimately put things to rights in the end? God's final actions and "last things" reveal a great deal about the moral character of God and God's perfect justice, often understood as foreshadowed in the resurrection of Jesus. Christian theologians have classically understood the resurrection as a validation of Jesus's life and teachings and the marker and promise of God's triumph over sin and death through Christ. Yet they have also understood it to foreshadow the general resurrection of all to face divine judgment and justice, primarily viewed through the vivid imagery of the book of Revelation. Those who have embraced Christ and his forgiveness then live with God in the holy city for eternity, while the nonbelievers are cast into hell for eternal punishment.[21]

In light of moral injury and the possibility of a theology focused on love and forgiveness, another articulation of God's promised future and the hope of resurrection is particularly salient. It comes from the German theologian Jürgen Moltmann, himself a veteran of World War II, who articulates in his autobiography a profound sense of guilt and shame about both his and his nation's conduct in the war.[22] Viewing sin as the corruption of our innate sense of goodness, the inborn and congenital defect that disfigures even our best intentions, he understands God's final eschatological act as a two-stage event. First, the final judgment, and then what he calls "the awakening to new life." Describing the interplay between these two, he writes,

> In that Judgment all sins, every wickedness and every act of violence, the whole injustice of this murderous and suffering world, will be condemned and annihilated, because God's verdict effects what it pronounces. In the divine Judgment all sinners, the wicked and the violent, the murderers and the children of Satan, the Devil and the fallen angels will be liberated and saved from their deadly perdition through transformation into their true, created being, because God remains true to himself, and does not give up what he has once created and affirmed, or allow it to be lost. . . . It is a source of endlessly consoling joy to know, not just that the murderers will finally fail to triumph over their victims, but that they cannot in eternity even remain the murderers of their victims. The eschatological doctrine about the restoration of all things has these two sides: God's judgment, which puts things to rights, and God's kingdom, which awakens to new life.[23]

Moltmann's view of God's ultimate justice is thus not simply the forgiveness of those who had participated in the sinfulness of the world, but the destruction and annihilation of the forces and actions which cause so much pain, misery, death, and anguish. It is the restoration and awakening of all those trapped in the suffocating forces that condition our lives and disfigure even our best intentions. Notable, of course, is the separation of those forces themselves from those infected by them—for Moltmann, for God to condemn those who had been infected by this contagion would mean that God would lose parts of God's beloved creation to the corruption of sin, and God, in his estimation, would be untrue to Godself if this were to occur.

Further, it is Moltmann's particular view of how this eschatology continually breaks open new possibilities in the present that may prove most intriguing in exploring the moral world of modern combat. For Moltmann, the resurrection of Christ marks the defeat of the forces of death and destruction that normally cause the end of lives, movements, civilizations, and groups of peoples. In this view of resurrection, Moltmann sees hope for many lives ended and brutally altered by war and violence. He writes that "the Spirit of eternal life is first of all a further space for living, in which life that has been cut short, or was impaired and destroyed will be able to develop freely."[24] In other words, history literally "breaks open" with new possibilities for flourishing, as all historical events—death, destruction, violence, and collapse—must be understood as "open and unfinished," rife with new potentiality in the future of God.[25]

Consistent with several of the experiences described earlier, researchers studying PTSD and moral injury have found that the act of killing itself is the most consistent predictor of combat trauma and its severest manifestations in veterans.[26] One might understand that the responsibility for the act is so devastating due to its acute finality—it definitively and completely ends a life, and there is no way to restore it or make it right after the fact. Consequently, the experience of combat guilt is the leading predictor of a veteran "re-experiencing" a traumatic combat event and is indicative of a high degree of psychological distress.[27] Combatants are on the front line of the most violent form of "law and order" we can mete out as a human civilization.

Yet Moltmann's vision of divine justice articulates two salient points that put the traumatic act of killing into a wider, if more imaginative, moral context. First, it sets our own imperfect justice into a particular temporal perspective: while we must indeed take justice seriously, particularly in matters that might end a life, the resurrection and God's restoration perhaps might allow those who kill to envision that they are not the ultimate arbiters of either life or death in the universe. For many veterans, one of the haunting aspects of killing is the seeming moral irrevocability of it. Yet perhaps God's action in the resurrection conveys the sense that we can neither foresee nor foreclose the future. The imaginative possibility might serve as an anchor to what resurrection hope is for those who have killed—the renewed possibility and potentiality of life for the many victims of war and violence. Second, and following from this first, the possibility of new life for the victims of wartime violence might offer peace and hope for the perpetrators of it as well. Against the closed system of killing and the crushing weight of impossible moral responsibility, God's justice is not retributive, punitive, nor even restorative, but envisions a future in which bad acts are simply annihilated so that killers and victims cannot remain so, and that the forces that seemingly cut off lives and decide who is allowed to flourish are finally rendered powerless. It is not simply forgiveness of the bad acts, but the annihilation of their source and the opening of a world in which it has no hold. This is undeniably an imaginative (and theologically controversial) envisioning of what God's justice might look like, but particularly as it comes from a theologian impacted by the violence, moral chaos, and human anguish of war, it is a powerful way to re-envision a future with infinite possibilities against the suffocating boundedness of ethical options that so many of the morally injured experience.

It is perhaps this experience of boundedness that pushes Christian theology to articulate and imagine the consequences of the resurrection in new ways. Those who are morally injured have often seen situations that simultaneously cry out for justice and that cause them to question moral certitude in any endeavor. The experience of moral injury often results in greater degrees of empathy and less tolerance for violence—even in punishment for the "guilty"—and thus demands a complex and nuanced articulation of God's ultimate judgment. A deity who seems to glory in the eternal torture of those who have sinned will likely seem petty and morally compromised to those who have seen torture, as will a god who cares little for the suffering of anyone—friend or enemy. The nuanced experience of moral injury challenges theology to articulate God's judgment as renewal, new life, and infinite possibility, and to discover roots in this area apart from its sometimes macabe focus on retribution and comeuppance for the guilty, even though this latter view may still serve those in situations of oppression and violence.

NOTES

1. Brett Litz et al., *Adaptive Disclosure: A New Treatment for Military Trauma, Loss, and Moral Injury* (New York: Guilford, 2016), 126.
2. See, for example, Augustine, *The City of God against the Pagans*, ed. R. W. Dyson (Cambridge: Cambridge University Press, 2007), XIV.xii–xiii.
3. Here, I am distilling a complex argument that Augustine makes most directly in "On the Spirit and the Letter," in Philip Schaff, ed., *Nicene and Post-Nicene Fathers: A Select Library of the Christian Church*. Vol. 5 (Peabody, MA: Hendrickson, 2004), IV–VI and again from LVIII–LX.
4. Alistair McFadyen provides a rich and meaningful vocabulary of concepts and terms like "sequestered" and "colonised" to describe the effects of sin that are deeply resonant with the experience of moral injury in *Bound to Sin: Abuse, Holocaust and the Christian Doctrine of Sin* (Cambridge: Cambridge University Press, 2000), 229. He also provides an excellent summation of Augustine's larger view of human willing on pp. 167–99.
5. For an extended discussion of these themes, see Brian S. Powers, *Full Darkness: Original Sin, Moral Injury, and Wartime Violence* (Grand Rapids, MI: Eerdmans, 2019) and Brian S. Powers, "The Applicability of an Augustinian Moral Psychology in Light of Moral Injury and Combat Trauma," *Theology Today* 77, no. 4 (January, 2017): 325–77.
6. See, for example, the account of Camelo Mejia, a veteran of the Iraq war, who was in an active combat situation on a rooftop with his weapon trained "on an adolescent young man who appeared to have a grenade in his hand." Meijia reports that "he still has no memory of shooting. All he remembers is the young man standing and then lying dead in a pool of blood in the dirt. He was appalled that his ability to decide what to do had been taken away by his training" (see quote in Rita Nakashima Brock and Gabriella Lettini, *Soul Repair: Recovering from Moral Injury After War* [Boston: Beacon, 2012], 34).
7. Dave Grossman, *On Killing: The Psychological Cost of Learning to Kill in War and Society* (New York: Back Bay, 1995), 88–93.
8. For example, see Irenaeus in "Against Heresies," in Alexander Roberts, James Donaldson, and A. Cleveland Coxe, eds., *The Ante-Nicene Fathers: Translations of the Writings of the Fathers Down to A.D. 325*. Vol 1. (Peabody, MA: Hendrickson, 2004), III.xxiii, 2–7 and V.vi.1.
9. John Calvin, *Institutes of the Christian Religion,* Vol. 1, ed. John Baillie et al. (Louisville, KY: Westminster John Knox, 1960), 189.
10. See Augustine, "On the Holy Trinity," in Philip Schaff and W. G. T. Shedd, eds., *Nicene and Post-Nicene Fathers: A Select Library of the Christian Church*. Vol. 3. (Peabody, MA: Hendrickson, 2004), X.xi.17–19, for example, for his famous exposition of the Imago Dei as "Memory, Understanding and Will," as reflective of the Trinity itself.
11. Lactantius, "The Divine Institutes," in Alexander Roberts, James Donaldson, and A. Cleveland Coxe, eds., *The Ante-Nicene Fathers: Translations of the Writings of the Fathers Down to A.D. 325*. Vol 7. (Peabody, MA: Hendrickson, 2004), 6.10.
12. Lactanius, "The Divine Institutes."
13. Grossman, *On Killing,* 39.
14. Grossman, *On Killing*, 98.
15. Christian Enemark, "Drones, Risk, and Moral Injury," *Critical Military Studies* 5 no. 2 (2017): 150–67, 154.
16. Enemark, "Drones, Risk, and Moral Injury," 161.

17. Enemark, "Drones, Risk, and Moral Injury,"
18. Enemark, "Drones, Risk, and Moral Injury," 155.
19. Grossman, *On Killing*, 88.
20. Grossman, *On Killing*, 39.
21. See Augustine's description of the ends of the two cities in *City of God* XXI and XXII.
22. Jürgen Moltmann, *A Broad Place: An Autobiography*, trans. Margaret Kohl (Minneapolis: Fortress, 2008).
23. Jürgen Moltmann, *The Coming of God: Christian Eschatology*, trans. Margaret Kohl (Minneapolis: Fortress, 2004), 255.
24. Moltmann, *The Coming of God*, 118.
25. Jürgen Moltmann, *Theology of Hope*, trans Margaret Kohl (Minneapolis: Fortress, 1993), 267–69.
26. Brett T. Litz et al., "Moral Injury and Moral Repair in War Veterans: A Preliminary Model and Intervention Strategy," *Clinical Psychology Review 29* (2009): 695–706.
27. Litz et al., "Moral Injury and Moral Repair in War Veterans," 697.

BIBLIOGRAPHY

Augustine. *The City of God against the Pagans*. Edited by R. W. Dyson. Cambridge: Cambridge University Press, 2007.

—. "On the Holy Trinity." Pages 1–228 in *Nicene and Post-Nicene Fathers: A Select Library of the Christian Church*. Vol. 3. Edited by Philip Schaff and W. G. T. Shedd. Peabody, MA: Hendrickson, 2004.

—. "On the Spirit and the Letter." Pages 83–115 in *Nicene and Post-Nicene Fathers: A Select Library of the Christian Church*. Vol. 5. Edited by Philip Schaff. Peabody, MA: Hendrickson, 2004.

Brock, Rita Nakashima and Gabriella Lettini. *Soul Repair: Recovering from Moral Injury After War*. Boston: Beacon, 2012.

Calvin, John. *Institutes of the Christian Religion*. Edited by John T. McNeill. Translated by Ford Lewis Battles. Louisville, KY: Westminster John Knox, 2006.

Enemark, Christian. "Drones, Risk, and Moral Injury." *Critical Military Studies* 5 no. 2 (May 2017): 150–67.

Grossman, Dave. *On Killing: The Psychological Cost of Learning to Kill in War and Society*. New York: Back Bay, 1995.

Irenaeus. "Against Heresies." Pages 309–567 in *The Ante-Nicene Fathers: Translations of the Writings of the Fathers Down to A.D. 325*. Vol 1. Edited and translated by Alexander Roberts, James Donaldson, and A. Cleveland Coxe. Peabody, MA: Hendrickson, 2004.

Lactantius. "The Divine Insititutes." Pages 9–328 in *The Ante-Nicene Fathers: Translations of the Writings of the Fathers Down to A.D. 325*. Vol 7. Edited by Alexander Roberts, James Donaldson and A. Cleveland Coxe. Peabody, MA: Hendrickson, 2004.

Litz, Brett T. et al. *Adaptive Disclosure: A New Treatment for Military Trauma, Loss, and Moral Injury*. New York: Guilford, 2016.

—. "Moral Injury and Moral Repair in War Veterans: A Preliminary Model and Intervention Strategy." *Clinical Psychology Review* 29 (2009): 695–706.

McFadyen, Alistair I. *Bound to Sin: Abuse, Holocaust, and the Christian Doctrine of Sin*. Cambridge: Cambridge University Press, 2000.

Moltmann, Jürgen. *A Broad Place: An Autobiography*. Translated by Margaret Kohl. Minneapolis: Fortress, 2008.

—. *The Coming of God: Christian Eschatology*. Translated by Margaret Kohl. Minneapolis: Fortress, 2004.

—. *Theology of Hope*. Translated by Margaret Kohl. Minneapolis: Fortress, 1993.

Powers, Brian S. "The Applicability of an Augustinian Moral Psychology in Light of Moral Injury and Combat Trauma." *Theology Today* 77, no. 4 (January, 2017): 325–77.

—. *Full Darkness: Original Sin, Moral Injury, and Wartime Violence*. Grand Rapids, MI: Eerdmans, 2019.

Chapter Sixteen

Approaching Moral Injury through the Lens of Social Ethics

Joseph Wiinikka-Lydon

What does social ethics have to say about moral injury and its repair? In the following, I look at moral injury and healing as a social ethicist, as someone who is concerned not only with individual morality but also with the moral life of individuals and communities as they are formed and affected by institutions, politics, and broader areas of social life. In particular, Christian social ethics aims toward social justice in the world and investigates the ways in which social justice is strengthened and impeded and how injustice is created corporately. Looking at moral injury and repair seen through this lens can help us see how shot through with politics morally injurious experiences and morally injured people can be. This approach can also show how moral injury can be the beginning of a critique of the ills of society, as such injury itself, I argue, is an embodiment of social ills enacted through the bodies of soldiers executing policy. Always looking for grace in social spaces and those situations where prophetic critique can be the basis for healing and repair, a social ethics of moral injury can illustrate how such injury may not be only a harm but for some it may become the basis of prophetic critique.

THE POLITICAL DIMENSION OF WARTIME EXPERIENCE

Moral injury is defined in various ways. What it aims to capture, generally speaking, is an experience of war that leaves one feeling they can no longer strive to be good, however that is defined, because of what they have seen, done, or failed to do. Jonathan Shay, who is usually seen as coining the term, calls such harms "moral" because they are a kind of harm to one's character, or at least, how one understands their character.[1] It is an injury to the way one evaluates oneself, the world, and one's place in that world. Such an injury is not easily or even possibly tracked onto changes in brain chemistry but, instead, as other authors such as theologians Rita Nakashima Brock and Gabriella Lettini have suggested, touches on that nebulous area of experience of the self poetically called the "soul."[2]

Indeed, "soul" might be more helpful in trying to describe moral injury than other vocabularies related to mind or the brain. "Soul" is a word that does a lot of work, and it is used not only in Christian theology but also more broadly in art, music, culture, and philosophy. Here, we might think of it as a word that aims to capture that part of the individual that strives toward goodness. Often spoken of in terms of "depth" and being at one's core, we can think of it as an aspect of the person that is largely felt (think about when someone describes something saying, "that was soulful"), though not unintellectual, and a space in one's self that yearns for those goods, objects, experiences, and ways of living called "spiritual." In this way, we can call a moral injury a harm to one's soul, as it seems to hit that part of us that most yearns to be good or virtuous.

And yet—soul language can mislead us. It can turn our gaze away from just how complex our experiences can be. When we invoke soul or souls when speaking of suffering, too often it directs our attention to the individual and the experiences of inner life at the expense of our communal, social, and even political nature. In particular, the "soul" is often seen as apolitical, as something untouched by the messiness and utility of political wrangling. This is a problem, however, because moral injury is inherently political, and one cannot truly understand at least some forms of moral harm without understanding the political context without which such suffering would not have arisen. We are not just talking about moral harm to individuals in general, after all. We are talking about people carrying out specific roles, even vocations, within a specific institution in specific situations where a great deal is on the line.

This institution, the military, understands itself as a school of virtue, an understanding that many in the United States as well as those within the military share. It is tasked with carrying out policies, to be sure, but also to spread broader social values in the world. This is reflected, for example, in the notion that US wars are just and good wars and that the US military presence around the globe spreads important values, as well as the freedoms that make such values possible. The soldier, then, is a member of such an institution, tasked with carrying out policies, as well as important values, and striving to embody them even under significant duress. Defining moral injury in terms of a harm to the soul, then, can be helpful in certain ways, as it describes how deep and profound moral injuries can be. Soul language by itself, however, can all too easily miss these political dimensions of war, which together create the very seat of moral injury.

I draw this idea of the political in moral injury from Shay, who was the first to use and think about such harms. From the start, Shay stressed an important political aspect, and even more, a political origin, to moral injury. He argued that moral injury arises when a soldier feels betrayed by someone in the military chain of command who has authority over them in a high-stakes, often life-and-death situation.[3] Shay understands the relationship between soldier and superior as one of power, certainly, but also centrally as one of trust. Shay developed his notion of moral injury while working with US veterans of the wars in Vietnam and Southeast Asia, where it was not uncommon for soldiers to feel that their superiors showed a disregard for their survival and their well-being. The narrative of betrayal—by officers, by generals, by politicians, and even by society—is a central one that came out of the US veteran experience of these wars and that continues to influence both policy and cultural expectations around the treatment of veterans. Understood this way, moral injury arose from a betrayal of one's trust in one's superiors—a trust that those superiors would ensure that one's sacrifice in war, however that was understood, was not in vain.

What Shay proposed, then, was in part a political understanding of moral injury. I say political because the injury arises from one's experience of and work in the military, an inherently political institution, where soldiers execute policies. This is, however, an understanding of moral injury that has been obscured by later writers, what I have called elsewhere the "second wave" of moral injury theories.[4] The seminal writings of this second wave looked at moral injury mainly as a soldier's betrayal of their own most cherished values, resulting in feelings of shame and guilt. This is in contrast to Shay's understanding, where moral injury arises from the betrayal by another within a relationship of trust (chain of command) that is itself located within a political and politicized institution (the military) in situations where life and soul are at risk (war). For this second wave, the context remains war, and by focusing on soldiers and veterans, the military chain of command is implied. The way that moral injury is defined, however, does not foreground these important factors, and instead focuses on the soldier as both the sufferer of such injury and as central to the cause. According to a seminal second-wave definition used widely in moral injury research, moral injury arises from a soldier "perpetrating, failing to prevent, or bearing witness to acts that transgress deeply held moral beliefs and expectations [and] may be deleterious in the long-term, emotionally, psychologically, behaviorally, spiritually, and socially."[5] The focus here is on the soldier and their actions, while Shay's formulation focused on the actions of military superiors and their effects on subordinates.

Over the last few years, as these various approaches have come into contact, definitions of moral injury have become more nuanced. Second-wave definitions now include betrayal not only by oneself but by others (or at least perceived betrayal by others), and Shay has acknowledged moral injury in terms of self-betrayal.[6] Even so, there remains little in the way of accounts of moral injury that look at the way in which politics and the political dimension of a soldier's life affect one's sense of their own character and moral ability. Even when understandings of moral injury account for the possibility of betrayal by another, this is often framed in terms of a "perceived" betrayal that refocuses the moral injury on the individual. It is a betrayal against the morally injured person without attending adequately to the broader political and institutional causes. Even Shay, who focuses on the military chain of command, does not fully expand his analysis to look at politics more broadly construed.

This is important. Soldiers are, after all, executors of militarized foreign policy.[7] Their job is to realize policies and orders on the ground. They are, then, part of governmental policymaking and implementation. This makes their work and the context in which they work inherently political and makes soldiering a deeply political activity. It is in this context of executing policy where moral injury occurs. Moral injury should be seen as a political injury, as clunky as that phrase may sound, as notions of individual morality and politics become entangled and problematic in the person and body of the soldier. It is not just the values of the individual soldier that are involved, nor is it only the soldier's relationship to superiors. The soldier is a central participant in a chain of policy making and creation—policies that themselves arise from a specific society.

In the following, then, I look at two main examples taken from veterans who have discussed their wartime experiences in terms of moral injury. They see the concept of moral injury as a means to analyze that experience and their role in war seen as a form of policy implementation. This is moral injury seen as a lens to engage critically the institutions, relationships, and structures that enabled the context in which such injury became possible. These veterans are already taking such an approach, viewing their injuries not just as a personal issue but symptomatic of broader social ills and injustices. Such veterans have used moral injury to become more politically active, even to become activists, using what is often seen as a vulnerability to empower themselves.[8] This does not remove the pain of these injuries. It does mean, however, that such injuries, which may make one feel vulnerable or morally compromised, do not have to be disabling but can be the means, even if such injuries were not sought out or welcome, to find a new way to be active in the world. This is, then, what we could call a critical, and even more, prophetic approach to moral injury, as it aims to use experience as a jumping off point to dig more deeply into the workings of one's soul, as well as one's society.

This may be a type of moral injury that not all share, although I argue that all moral injury, given the nature of the soldier and their role in the politics we call war, is a political injury to some extent. The veterans discussed, however, have gone further, engaging in politics and activism, turning their experience into a lived social ethics. The theologian Gary Dorrien has defined social ethics as embodying a "mission to transform structures of society in the direction of social justice," and the two veterans I quote in the following pages reconceived their postwar lives into a new social ethic, where they work to transform what they see as those injustices of their society that gave rise to what they consider an unjust war.[9] When speaking of this form of moral injury, forms of repair might require not just traditional therapy, though that remains important. Instead, repair might require one to refashion their lives and the way they evaluate themselves and others into a new social ethic where they attempt to repair their own injuries by contributing to social justice in their communities and broader culture.

TOWARD A POLITICAL MORAL INJURY: TWO CASES

The first example is from a US veteran, Ellen Barfield, who shared her story with me personally. Barfield was a sergeant in a maintenance unit stationed in South Korea in the early 1980s as part of the continued US military presence in that country. She was stationed there right after a military coup in that country. In 1980, there was a student uprising against the South Korean military, which retaliated, killing several hundred to several thousand people in what has been called the Kwang Ju Massacre or Uprising. During this time, Barfield's maintenance unit was put on high alert, given riot training, and was preparing to follow orders to deploy on the side of the South Korean military. As she relates,

> We higher-ranking women (I was a Sergeant by then) joined a unit conversation about whether the women would also draw their M-16 rifles and hit the streets to repress Korean civilians if so ordered. I agreed with all the other women that we were soldiers too and would join the men. Things quieted down and we were never deployed. I have since felt guilt to have potentially oppressed civilians.

In the end, Barfield and her unit were never ordered into combat. Nevertheless, she felt complicit in the oppression and domination of a population, in the way that philosopher Iris Marion Young phrases key aspects of injustice. She felt guilty even though she was never ordered finally to suppress the democracy protests.[10] The women in the group were put in a difficult position, for at that time women were not allowed to assume a combat role in the US military. Refusing to do so when asked, then, could appear as if they were not true soldiers after all, at least when compared to the men in combat. Such appearances could undermine the very argument for women in combat—

namely, that they could be relied upon just the same as men. It is, then, a complex example, one where dilemma, issues of gender and race, as well as geopolitics, saturated her experience.

What is interesting about Barfield's reflection of this time is that she does not just focus on her own actions and motivations. Instead, she takes the further step of connecting her experience and sense of guilt to the broader politics of her country. She relates, "Korea is as close as I ever got to combat. I never aimed a weapon at anyone. But I supported US domination with my body." Barfield ends her reflections by connecting her moral injury critically to the policies not only of the war but also of her society and of the work of her society in the world.

It is a move, however, that is not singular to Barfield. We can see this move, too, in another veteran, Tyler Boudreau, a former US Marines officer and writer on issues of moral injury, who came to see his time during the US occupation of Iraq in the early 2000s in a similar way to Barfield. Drawing from his own experience of the occupation, Boudreau defines moral injury in the following way:

> Moral injury is about the damage done to our moral fiber when transgressions occur by our hands, through our orders, or with our connivance. When we accept these transgressions, however pragmatically (for survival, for instance), we sacrifice a piece of our moral integrity. That's what moral injury is all about.[11]

What Boudreau is getting at in this definition is the way in which one's sense of responsibility in war occurs within a context of wider responsibility. The soldier is participating in the transgression, but he or she is acting within a larger framework of policy and even cultural will. For Boudreau, his moral injury involves participation in unjust wars, yet this need not mean the perpetration of atrocity. Boudreau first felt the beginnings of injury when he conducted a search of an Iraqi home. Although no shots were fired, and even though the family smiled and his soldiers played with the children, he realized that the profound asymmetry of power in that situation. He had the power to engage someone's child and enter their home when such people had done nothing wrong. For Boudreau, that was an injustice, perhaps an evil. For him, as for Barfield, it was enough just to agree to participate in occupations or police actions (as the conflict in South Korea is historically referred to in the United States) that oppressed individuals, families, and whole peoples for moral injury to arise.

My focus here is not just the political nature that both Barfield and Boudreau see in their moral injury. It is also the way in which those contentious, and in their minds, unjust politics are expressed through their bodies. Barfield's sense of wrong, for example, came not just from the realization that

US policy was on the side of dictatorship and what she saw as domination, but that she herself was prepared to implement such domination policy with her own body. Policy here is not an abstract notion but comes into the world through the actions of limbs and torsos. Boudreau, as well, writes that before he knew what to call it, he felt a pain when he left the Iraqi farmhouse. Even though it seemed as if the engagement went off perfectly, something made him "hurt."[12] A dis-ease. He later writes how he felt his very presence was an injustice. The radical asymmetry of power between a troop of armed US Marines and an Iraqi family seemed a great wrong to him, as soon did the larger occupation of Iraq. Instead of feeling ennobled and virtuous through his activity in the Marines, as he once did, he began to feel that such participation actually degraded him.

What we find in both accounts, then, is a bodily reaction to perceived injustice. Ethics, so often discussed in academic circles in term of reason and principle, is rarely spoken of in terms of a felt, bodily experience. There are certainly exceptions, and feminist and liberative ethicists, theologians, and philosophers have pressed on what is called the "embodiment" of the political and the ethical. With this understanding of moral injury, however, we see a more acute example of how what we call more dispassionately, "ethics," is a felt phenomenon, as well. Indeed, it is felt before it is even thought, reflected upon, or deliberated, as Boudreau's example shows, where he felt the injustice long before he knew what to name it or how to understand it. Likewise, Barfield felt such injustice physically, as an embodied person: "I supported US domination with my body." Both veterans held roles in the military to execute US foreign policy and make such policies come alive through their actions, their bodies. If we are to ask what policy looks like beyond its traces on ink and paper, it looks like bodies engaged in everyday life attempting to translate someone else's vision or imperative on communities such policy makers have most likely never experienced.

Moral injury, then, is political in this more literal sense in terms of policy. But it is also political in that the individual soldier, as well as others not mentioned here, must execute such policy physically. It is through their bodies that politics, and really geopolitics, are realized. It should, then, be no surprise that such grave matters may leave their mark in a way best referred to as an "injury." In the case of Barfield and Boudreau, their participation created tension, painful tension, between what they thought they were doing as US citizens and soldiers—that is, doing good—and their experience of US foreign policy in its actuality—which seemed unjust. The US support of an oppressive dictatorship in South Korea and the realities of the US occupation in Iraq seemed to each veteran to be at odds with the narrative of the United States as a bastion of freedom, and its military as a force for good out in the world. This did not just create cognitive dissonance. First and foremost, it seems, it created a dis-ease, a felt, bodily, phenomenological dissonance that can make one question their values, how they see their country and the world, and their identity. Boudreau, who took a noble view of his identity through his participation in the Marines, began to question such an institution, which was prompting him to execute injustice. This was the same for Barfield. For both, this created a cascade of reflections, which brought into doubt the very fundamentals of their moral universe. This dis-ease with who they were and the world from which they drew their identity and sense of right and wrong created a feeling of injury—not just of guilt, shame, and betrayal but also a loss of identity and an entire moral world. It struck at their core, possibly at their soul, and their assumptions of good and evil, justice and injustice.

Moral injury of this sort, then, is the bodily experience not just of policy but of policy as injustice. The experience arises from this injustice as something that should be foreign, but instead is now not only intimate but formative of who one is. Caught at the interchange of broader politics and more intimate ethics, it can feel that the body and one's sense of self are torn. Such injury is also a change to the very possibility of what type of moral person one can be. It can be very difficult to feel one can be good or strive to be good when it feels like one's hands and feet have so wronged others. One can feel that not only the soil but their own flesh cries out at the injustice.

REPAIR THROUGH SOCIAL ETHICS AND APPLIED CRITIQUE

Given the explicitly political nature of such moral injuries, then, what are the possible means of repair? Both Boudreau and Barfield have become activists and writers, trying to work against militarism, in the case of Barfield, and to raise awareness in the United States about the costs of the war, in the case of Boudreau. For Barfield, this has been a lifetime of working against what she sees as US militarism, including serving as an active member and vice president of an organization called Veterans for Peace, which campaigns against United States wars and also organizes veterans to help rebuild countries in which the United States has fought. Boudreau has written critically about his experience, traveled across the United States to educate communities about the war, and even participated in charitable work for Iraq.

In other words, given the political nature of their experience of war, they have responded by trying to shape discussion of US involvement in the world. They do this through the lens of their experience and that of other veterans, as well as, importantly, persons who have been on the receiving end of their country's militarized foreign policy. They have also taken what were difficult, morally injurious experiences and tried to reshape their lives by embodying a social ethic continuously developed through their wartime experience and collective political engagement. This need not be the answer for every veteran. For those whose injury is defined by political critique, such an approach may help create stronger agency and empowerment, revealing their perceived vulnerability to be a basis—though painful and unasked for—from which they build a new life and create new understandings of themselves and the world.

I do not judge whether such perspectives are accurate, though to be honest, I see much in current US wars to be deeply unjust. The point, however, is that these veterans have been so shaped and affected by their injurious experience and their understanding of the war that it has transformed how they engage with their society. They have, in a real way, embodied policy, using their bodies to implement a militarized foreign policy in another land, experiencing how some of these policies actually feel. On this level, policy is no longer to be understood mainly in terms of debates, directives, or programs. Instead, it is the transformation of relationships and of individual souls and virtues carried out in and through bodies—both those bodies who execute policy and those, particularly in war, who have policy done to them.

Policy and war, then, can now be seen as the mortar and pestle of a powerful moral alchemy. For some soldiers, the alchemy of wartime experience can be felt as ennobling. In the case of veterans like Barfield and Boudreau, however, this transformation morally injured them. They became in their own eyes participants in injustice. They came to see that their role in militarized US foreign policy violated their vision of how a just person should act, as well as how the military should act as a just institution. These evaluations cast a poor light on their participation, on the military, on the politics of their country—perhaps even their culture. In the case of Boudreau, his bodily hurt was the first whisper of a critique and reaction against this transformation. It was a bodily manifestation revealing how far from his ideals he felt he and his country had fallen. This was also the case for Barfield, who felt what she called the domination of her country over others through the workings of her flesh. This is critique understood as something embodied and enfleshed, something that not so much finds its way into one's anatomy but begins there.[13]

CONTRASTING APPROACHES

To summarize thus far, moral injury as a political harm can be seen as an injury to one's whole being. Cast as a psychological form of harm, clinicians present it as a mental health issue, which it certainly is. It is, however, also a harm of the person taken as a whole, and as such, one might need, beyond traditional therapy, to shape one's life to reflect the way they have changed and how they see and feel about themselves, others, their culture, and the world. If one feels that they are harmed through participation in injustice that comes from the broader institution or culture, then in addition to traditional therapy, there may be a need to respond to that injustice explicitly in order to experience repair. It may become necessary to help repair one's society in order to repair oneself.

This understanding of repair contrasts, however, with second-wave moral injury writings, which focus on the individual. Self-forgiveness is emphasized in the important work on moral injury by Brett Litz and his coauthors, an emphasis that has been taken up by moral injury writings in general. This approach may be important for many soldiers and many forms of moral injury. It is not clear, however, if self-forgiveness, focusing as it does on the veteran as patient, is sufficient for forms of moral injury where the veteran sees their moral injury arising from broader injustices. Self-forgiveness implies that the soldier or veteran has done something wrong, is the main source of the injury, and needs to place their actions in a context that allows them to move on. Litz and his coauthors have argued that, when it comes to moral injury repair,

> the idea is not to try and fix the past, but rather to draw a firm line around the past and its related associations, so that the mistakes of the past do not define the present and the future and so that a pre-occupation with the past does not prevent possible future good. Making reparations can help morally injured service members or veterans begin to reconnect with their values, as well as allow them to feel like a contributing member of society.[14]

The idea seems to be to find a way for veterans to put the past behind them by making reparations to those they have wronged, or, at least, in a way that gestures toward that wrongdoing.

What, however, if the wrong is not so much an explicit action of the soldier but instead participation in a larger wrong that did not originate with the soldier but, instead, to quote Boudreau, was realized through the soldier, "by our hands, through our orders, or with our connivance?"[15]

If the goal is to reenter and contribute to society, what if society is already understood to be central to the problem? The experience of veterans like Boudreau and Barfield reveal that it may be necessary to critique those former values, and perhaps not to become a "contributing member of society" but rather contribute to a prophetic critique that calls on society to change.

Going even further, philosopher Nancy Sherman argues against forgiveness as letting oneself "off the hook" for being responsible for moral injury. Instead, she sees moral injury arising when veterans think they have more power over situations than they actually do. Moral injury here is a result of veterans feeling more responsible for what has occurred in the warzone than they actually are. Instead of forgiveness, she argues for "self-empathy," where one still acknowledges their actions but also acknowledges that they only have limited power over events, particularly as a soldier in the complex environment of war.[16]

Sherman's perspective is important for those veterans whose sense of responsibility exceeds their power to affect change. The way that she frames forgiveness and self-empthay, however, is too individualistic to respond to the kind of injury described in this article. Sherman's approach overly emphasizes the individual as the key source of their own moral injury. It is one's betrayal of their own values or that of another individual close to them, an inability to deal with moral stress, or their own sense of agency that is the issue. There is little to no mention of how the perception of unjust policies, and one's participation in them, can be a powerful source for moral harm. What Barfield and Boudreau demonstrate is that the origins of moral injury are much broader than that of the individual. This also makes notions of repair based on a too individualistic approach inadequate to respond to the concerns of a more political injury.

A soldier allowing oneself some forgiveness for what they have or have not done does not touch on the feeling that the larger war was unjust, and that this injustice is something for which one's society, or at least parts of it, is responsible. Even speaking in the register of "injustice," or more specifically, social injustice, makes talk of individual forgiveness, even an emphasis on self-empathy, inadequate. Injustice on the level of war requires more than an inward change of affect. It requires outward gestures, at the very least, and more likely practices and changes of policy. Here, the discourse of repair, reparation, social change, and justice creation, or other forms of systemic atonement, are more appropriate and speak to the social, collective level, where prophetic voices coming from hard-earned experience can shed light on the social injustices and ills facing their communities.

CONCLUSION

Moral injury is not just a mental harm but can also be an embodied critique. It is a form of knowledge, or at least its beginnings, which is eventually understood, at least for some, as a reaction to one's participation in a chain of unjust policy creation and execution. It is not just something that happens to a veteran and soldier as a result of their values, their inability to incorporate their experience into their life, or even a feeling of over-responsibility. It may include such aspects, but it is also importantly, even centrally, a moral crisis where 1) one is not who they thought they were, 2) the institution, such as the military, in which they have been formed as moral persons, is not the school of virtue they thought it was (or not always), and 3) their culture is not what they thought it was. One can feel lost, as the world no longer makes sense.

One feels they have not been striving toward goodness but, in fact, have been working within a structure striving toward something unjust. The good news is that such an experience can form the basis, even if painful and unasked for, of insight, and even a new prophetic voice, to help others see such injustice. A response to such a moral, political injury may need to include the development of a lived social ethic arising from the experience, a new way of life for the individual that, in concert with others, can help one heal while helping one's larger community move away from the social injustice in its own corporate body.

NOTES

1. Jonathan, Shay, *Achilles in Vietnam: Combat Trauma and the Undoing of Character* (New York: Simon and Schuster, 1995), 14.
2. Rita Nakashima Brock and Gabriella Lettini, *Soul Repair: Recovering from Moral Injury after War* (Boston: Beacon Press, 2012).
3. Jonathan Shay, "Moral Injury," *Psychoanalytic Psychology* 31 no. 2 (2014): 182.
4. Joseph Wiinikka-Lydon, "Mapping Moral Injury: Comparing Discourses of Moral Harm," *The Journal of Medicine and Philosophy: A Forum for Bioethics and Philosophy of Medicine* 44 no. 2 (2019): 175–91.
5. Brett T. Litz et al., "Moral Injury and Moral Repair in War Veterans: A Preliminary Model and Intervention Strategy," *Clinical Psychology Review* 29 no. 8 (2009): 695.
6. Nathan R. Stein et al., "A Scheme for Categorizing Traumatic Military Events," *Behavior Modification* 36 no. 6 (2012): 787, 802; Shay, "Moral Injury," 184.
7. I am excluding here times and political systems where the military also executes, and even creates, domestic policy.
8. Joseph Wiinikka-Lydon, "Moral Injury as Inherent Political Critique: The Prophetic Possibilities of a New Term," *Political Theology* 18 no. 3 (2016): 219–32.
9. Gary Dorrien, *Social Ethics in the Making: Interpreting an American Tradition* (Malden, MA: Wiley-Blackwell, 2010), 1.
10. Iris Marion Young, *Justice and the Politics of Difference* (Princeton, NJ: Princeton University Press, 2011), 37–38.
11. Tyler Boudreau, "The Morally Injured," *The Massachusetts Review* 52 (2011): 749.
12. Boudreau, "The Morally Injured," 749.
13. For more on the ways that politics can enter into the body and cause illness or physical symptoms, see Arthur Kleinman, "'Everything That Really Matters:' Social Suffering, Subjectivity, and the Remaking of Human Experience in a Disordering World," *The Harvard Theological Review* 90 (1997): 315–35.
14. Litz et al., "Moral injury and Moral Repair in War Veterans," 704.
15. Boudreau, "The Morally Injured," 749.
16. Nancy Sherman, *Afterwar: Healing the Moral Wounds of Our Soldiers* (New York: Oxford University Press, 2015), 77–104.

BIBLIOGRAPHY

Boudreau, Tyler. "The Morally Injured." *The Massachusetts Review* 52 (2011): 746–54.

Brock, Rita Nakashima and Gabriella Lettini. *Soul Repair: Recovering from Moral Injury after War*. Boston: Beacon, 2012.

Dorrien, Gary. *Social Ethics in the Making: Interpreting an American Tradition*. Malden, MA: Wiley-Blackwell, 2010.

Kleinman, Arthur. "'Everything That Really Matters:' Social Suffering, Subjectivity, and the Remaking of Human Experience in a Disordering World." *The Harvard Theological Review* 90 no. 3 (1997): 315–35.

Litz, Brett T., Nathan Stein, Eileen Delaney, Leslie Lebowitz, William P. Nash, Carolina Silva, and Shira Maguen. "Moral Injury and Moral Repair in War Veterans: A Preliminary Model and Intervention Strategy." *Clinical Psychology Review* 29 (2009): 695–706.

Shay, Jonathan. *Achilles in Vietnam: Combat Trauma and the Undoing of Character*. New York: Simon and Schuster, 1995.

—. "Moral Injury." *Psychoanalytic Psychology* 31 no. 2 (2014): 182–91.

Sherman, Nancy. *Afterwar: Healing the Moral Wounds of Our Soldiers*. New York: Oxford University Press, 2015.

Stein, Nathan R., Mary Alice Mills, Kimberly Arditte, Crystal Mendoza, Adam M. Borah, Patricia A. Resick, and Brett T. Litz. "A Scheme for Categorizing Traumatic Military Events." *Behavior Modification* 36 (2012): 787–807.

Wiinikka-Lydon, Joseph. "Moral Injury as Inherent Political Critique: The Prophetic Possibilities of a New Term." *Political Theology* 18 no. 3 (2016): 219–32.

—. Joseph. "Mapping Moral Injury: Comparing Discourses of Moral Harm." *The Journal of Medicine and Philosophy: A Forum for Bioethics and Philosophy of Medicine* 44 no. 2 (2019): 175–91.

Young, Iris Marion. *Justice and the Politics of Difference*. Princeton, NJ: Princeton University Press, 2011.

Index

About the Contributors

Tyler Boudreau served twelve years of active service in the US Marine Corps and was deployed to Iraq in 2004 as an infantry captain with 2d Battalion, 2d Marines. After resigning his commission, Boudreau earned a doctorate in Communication at the University of Massachusetts, and is now a professor at the Smith College School of Social Work where he teaches MSW candidates about combat stress, moral injury, collective trauma, post-traumatic stress, military sexual trauma, and other issues related to armed conflict, recovery, and resiliency.

Nancy R. Bowen is professor of Old Testament at Earlham School of Religion in Richmond, Indiana. In addition to engaging feminist hermeneutics in all her work, she is most interested in engaging the text in dialogue with other disciplines in ways that intersect with contemporary issues, such as moral injury. Her commentary, *Ezekiel* (Abingdon Old Testament Series), reads the book of Ezekiel through the lens of trauma and posttraumatic stress disorder. She is the lead author of a forthcoming commentary, *Wisdom of Solomon.*

Jessica Carney began her work on moral injury as a research technician at the VA Boston Healthcare System under the mentorship of Dr. Brett Litz. She graduated from the University of Colorado at Boulder with a BA in psychology in 2010. Jessica is currently working toward a doctoral degree in clinical psychology the University of Notre Dame under the direction of Dr. Laura Miller-Graff. Her research examines power dynamics and betrayal in relationships and the effects of violence exposure on women and children's psycho-socio-spiritual well-being.

Warren Carter is Meinders Professor of New Testament at Phillips Theological Seminary, Tulsa Oklahoma. He has taught previously at Brite Divinity School at TCU in Fort Worth, TX. His publications include commentaries on the Gospels of Mark and Matthew (*Matthew and the Margins*), as well as introductions to the Gospels (*Telling Tales About Jesus*) and to the New Testament (with A-J Levine). He has published several studies on the ways in which the early Jesus movement negotiated Roman power including *Matthew and Empire* , *The Roman Empire and the New Testament*, *John and Empire: Initial Explorations*, *What Does Revelation Reveal?*, and *Seven Events That Shaped the New Testament World*. He is a regular speaker at ecclesial conferences and Sunday school classes.

Alanna Coady conducts research on trauma, posttraumatic stress disorder, and moral injury in military and health contexts. She received her master of divinity degree from Harvard University and is a doctoral student in clinical psychology at the University of British Columbia.

Amy C. Cottrill is the Denson N. Franklin Associate Professor of Religion at Birmingham-Southern College in Birmingham, Alabama. Her area of specialization is the Hebrew Bible, particularly the lament psalms, though her work extends to the general representation of suffering and the encounter with violence and its aftermath in the biblical text. She is the author of *Language, Power, and Identity in the Lament Psalms of the Individual*, co-chair of the Bible and Emotion section of the Society of Biblical Literature, and researches, publishes, and teaches in the areas of violence, trauma, moral injury, affect studies, and gender.

Joseph M. Currier, PhD, is a licensed psychologist who serves as associate professor and the director of clinical training for the Clinical and Counseling Psychology doctoral program at the University of South Alabama. Joe's research primarily focuses on testing and validating core dimensions of the emerging construct of moral injury, illuminating ways in which spirituality can help and hinder recovery from mental health conditions, and identifying culturally sensitive strategies for addressing health-related needs of military veterans, first responders, and other trauma-exposed groups. He has published more than one hundred peer-reviewed articles and invited papers on trauma, moral injury, and the interplay between spirituality and mental health. He coauthored the book *Trauma, Meaning, and Spirituality: Translating Research into Clinical Practice* with the American Psychological Association, and has recently served as lead editor on *Addressing Moral Injury in Clinical Practice*. He also serves as the interim clinical director for Veterans Recovery Resources, an interdisciplinary and community-based organization in Mobile, Alabama, serving veterans and first responders suffering from substance abuse, PTSD, and other health-related issues.

Kelly Denton-Borhaug is professor of Global Religions and Peace and Justice Studies at Moravian College in Bethlehem, Pennsylvania. She has been studying and writing about the nexus of Christian soteriology and US war-culture since not long after 9/11. Her first book was *U.S. War-culture, Sacrifice and Salvation*, and currently she is writing *Moral Injury and the Triangle of Violence: Seeing War Through a Different Lens,* in addition to publishing many articles and book chapters. She is the executive director of "InFocus," a college initiative that focuses each year on one of four challenge areas to involve students, faculty, and staff in research, learning, and activism addressing the urgent issues facing human beings: War, Peacebuilding and the Just Society, Health, Sustainability, and Poverty and Inequality. She is ordained in the Evangelical Lutheran Church in America.

Sheila Frankfurt, PhD, LP, is an investigator with the VA VISN 17 Center of Excellence for Research on Returning War Veterans, located at the Waco VA Medical Center, Waco, Texas. Dr. Frankfurt completed her PhD in counseling psychology at the University of Minnesota, Twin Cities, and completed her postdoctoral fellowship at the VISN 17 Center of Excellence. Her research and clinical work focuses on developing assessment tools and treatments for combat trauma and moral injury.

Brad E. Kelle, PhD, is professor of Old Testament and Hebrew at Point Loma Nazarene University in San Diego, California. He holds a PhD in Old Testament from Emory University, a masters in Theological Studies from the Candler School of Theology (at Emory University), and a BA in Religion from Trevecca Nazarene University. He has authored or edited more than a dozen books and numerous scholarly articles, with a particular focus on Israelite history and the Old Testament prophets, and a special interest in warfare, trauma, and moral injury. Recently, he has published *The Bible and Moral Injury: Reading Scripture Alongside War's Unseen Wounds* , *Telling the Old Testament Story: God's Mission and God's People*, and served as co-editor for the *Oxford Handbook on the Historical Books of the Hebrew Bible.* Among other earlier works, he has written *Biblical History and Israel's Past: The Changing Study of the Bible and History* (coauthored with Megan Bishop Moore; and is currently writing the commentary on the book of Hosea in the Old Testament Library series. Kelle also serves as the regional coordinator for the Society of Biblical Literature Pacific Coast Region and the Old Testament editor for the journal, *Currents in Biblical Research.* He is an ordained minister in the Church of the Nazarene.

Duane H. Larson., PhD, is an ordained Lutheran pastor since 1979, and has served as a professor of systematic theology since 1993, including a decade as a seminary president. His writing has focused on theology and natural science, ecclesiology, and ethics. Recent publications include articles on Luther's influence on natural science, public theology and the current rise of fascism, and (with Jeff Zust) the book, *Caring for the Sorrowing Soul: Healing Moral Injuries from Military Service and Implications for the Rest of Us*. He currently serves as senior pastor of Christ the King Lutheran Church in Houston, Texas, and teaches in religious studies at the University of Houston.

Gabriella Lettini, PhD, is dean, chief academic officer, and AH Reinhardt Professor of Theological Ethics at Starr King School for the Ministry, a member of the Graduate Theological Union in Berkeley, California. A native of Torino, Italy, Lettini is an ordained minister of the Waldensian Church. She studied theology at the Facoltà Valdese di Teologia in Rome and received her PhD at Union Theological Seminary in New York. She is a past president of the American Waldensian Society. Lettini coauthored *Soul Repair: Recovering from Moral Injury After War* with Rita Nakashima Brock. She is also the author of *Omosessualita*, and an editor of the Italian version of the *Dictionary of Feminist Theologies*, as well as of book chapters and articles on feminist theologies, women's issues, spirituality and justice, and movies and religion. Lettini is a member of INTERFILM, and as such was on the Ecumenical Jury at the Cannes, Locarno, Berlin, and Montreal film festivals.

Brett T. Litz, PhD, is a professor in the departments of Psychiatry and Psychology at Boston University, the director of the Mental Health Core of the Massachusetts Veterans Epidemiological Research and Information Center, and the Assessment Core director of STRONG STAR and the Consortium to Alleviate PTSD. His research focuses on evaluating the mental and behavioral health outcomes associated with military deployments as well as developing and testing treatments for operational trauma, loss, and moral injury. Dr. Litz has 350 publications and has authored 3 books.

Wesley H. McCormick, PhD, MDiv, is a postdoctoral Psychology Fellow at the Bay Pines VA Healthcare System. He completed his doctorate in combined-integrated clinical and counseling psychology at the University of South Alabama and a masters of divinity at Asbury Theological Seminary. His research examines veteran mental health, trauma, and religious/spiritual struggles.

Joseph McDonald teaches languages and biblical studies at Brite Divinity School and Texas Christian University. He became involved with moral injury studies through the Soul Repair Center at Brite, and is the editor of *Exploring Moral Injury in Sacred Texts*, a collection that highlights the conversations between work on moral injury and the scriptures of Judaism, Christianity, Islam, Buddhism, and US civil religion.

Zachary Moon, PhD, is associate professor of practical theology at the Chicago Theological Seminary. He has published widely, including the books: *Coming Home: Ministry That Matters with Veterans and Military Families* and *Warriors between Worlds: Moral Injury and Identities in Crisis*. He is an ordained minister and has served as a chaplain in multiple contexts, including: the United States Navy Reserve (2011–2019); the Pathway Home, a residential treatment program for combat veterans diagnosed with posttraumatic stress disorder; and as a chaplain resident in the VA hospital system.

Brian S. Powers is the inaugural William Bernard Vann Fellow at Durham University, a former Special Operations Weather Team officer in the US Air Force, and a veteran of the conflicts in Iraq and Afghanistan. He holds a PhD in theological studies from Emory University. A systematic and constructive theologian, he is interested in the ways that Christian theology shapes our thinking about contemporary moral, ecclesial, and political issues—most notably, those involving the experiences of violence, moral injury, identity, and justice. Powers's recent monograph is a constructive work entitled *Full Darkness: Original Sin, Moral Injury, and Wartime Violence*. The book contends that a modified Augustinian conception of original sin holds deep explanatory power to illuminate the nature of wartime violence, particularly through the lens of veteran trauma. He is an ordained Minister of Word and Sacrament in the Presbyterian Church (USA).

Nancy J. Ramsay is director of the Soul Repair Center and is emerita professor of pastoral theology and pastoral care at Brite Divinity School in Fort Worth, Texas where she served on the faculty until June 2019. She also served as executive vice president and dean at Brite Divinity School from May 2005-May 2012. Prior to her service at Brite, Nancy was a member of the faculty at Louisville Presbyterian Theological Seminary where she served as the Harrison Ray Anderson Professor of Pastoral Theology. She is a clinical member of the American Association of Marriage and Family Therapists. She is an ordained minister in the Presbyterian Church USA. She is the author or editor of five books including most recently, *Military Moral Injury and Spiritual Care: A Resource for Religious Leaders and Professional Caregivers* (co-edited with Carrie Doehring).

Joe Wiinikka-Lydon is currently a researcher at the European-Union funded Center for Ethics at the University of Pardubice, outside of Prague. Previously, he held teaching positions at Denison University and Birmingham-Southern College. His research looks at the ways politics, war, and religion affect moral selves and communities and how such transformation affects our ability to imagine peaceful futures. He recently authored *Moral injury and the Promise of Virtue*, which examines moral injury among the civilian population during the Bosnian War in the 1990s through the moral philosophy of Iris Murdoch.

Michael Yandell is a PhD candidate in theological studies at Emory University, with concentrations in Religion, Conflict, and peacebuilding. A US Army veteran, Yandell served as an enlisted explosive ordnance disposal specialist from 2002–2006. Yandell completed the master of divinity at Brite Divinity School and is an ordained minister in the Christian Church (Disciples of Christ).